SKILLS AND VALUES:
CRIMINAL LAW

LexisNexis Law School Publishing
Advisory Board

SKILLS AND VALUES: CRIMINAL LAW

Andrew E. Taslitz
Director, Criminal Justice Practice and Policy Institute
Washington College of Law
American University

Lenese C. Herbert
Professor of Law
Howard University School of Law

Eda Katharine Tinto
Benjamin N. Cardozo School of Law

ISBN: 9781422484753
ebook ISBN: 9780327179689

Library of Congress Cataloging-in-Publication Data
Taslitz, Andrew E., 1956- author.
   Skills and values. Criminal law / Andrew E. Taslitz, Director, Criminal Justice Practice and Policy Institute, Washington College of Law, American University; Lenese C. Herbert, Howard University School of Law; Katie Tinto, Assistant Clinical Professor of Law, Benjamin N. Cardozo School of Law.
   pages cm
   ISBN 978-1-4224-8475-3
   1. Criminal law--United States--Problems, exercises, etc. I. Herbert, Lenese C., author. II. Tinto, Eda Katharine (Katie), author. III. Title. IV. Title: Criminal law.
   KF9219.T37 2014
   345.73--dc23
                                                                                                    2014002288

NOTE TO USERS
To ensure that you are using the latest materials available in this area, please be sure to periodically check the LexisNexis Law School web site for downloadable updates and supplements at www.lexisnexis.com/lawschool.

Editorial Offices
121 Chanlon Rd., New Providence, NJ 07974 (908) 464-6800
201 Mission St., San Francisco, CA 94105-1831 (415) 908-3200
www.lexisnexis.com

MATTHEW◆BENDER

Dedication

As this volume went to press, our wonderful co-author, Andrew Eric "Taz" Taslitz, lost his valiant fight with cancer. Although this loss has created an enormous void for those who respected his work, enjoyed his collegiality, and flourished under his mentorship, we are comforted by the knowledge that he completely contributed to this volume and cheered it to its conclusion. Accordingly, we dedicate this volume to Taz: our co-author, colleague, mentor, teacher, and friend.

PREFACE

All law students must take Criminal Law. Traditionally, Criminal Law is taught during the first year of law school via "case method" instruction. The case method requires students to study appellate decisions to uncover legal principles, classify and organize these principles, and then apply the doctrines to a more general set of facts in order to reach a solution to legal questions.

In recent years, reports such as the Carnegie Foundation's Carnegie Report,[1] *Best Practices for Legal Education*,[2] and the MacCrate Report,[3] stand for the idea that legal education needs to change. Unanimously, these reports suggest that, in order to better prepare students for the practice of law, legal education must bridge the disconnect between law school and lawyering by introducing lawyering skills and values to the law school curriculum. For example, the MacCrate Report identified problem solving as one of the ten most important skills for attorneys. Yet traditionally, students in Criminal Law do not work through legal problems with professors or classmates in order to learn from their application of facts to law (rather than only applying law to a given set of facts). In other words, Criminal Law rarely focuses on how to develop facts to which the law can be applied or on how facts and substantive law interact. Yet gathering and interpreting evidence in light of case theories and the substantive law is at the heart of much criminal lawyering. *Skills and Values: Criminal Law* fuses fact-creation and interpretation with traditional substantive law-application in the same manner that practicing lawyers do.

Skills and Values: Criminal Law provides students an overview of key criminal substantive law and a series of exercises (comprised of tasks) that includes complex fact patterns, relevant state or federal law (case and codified), and skills guides. This material enables students to explore actual legal issues and develop problem-solving skills in ways that arise in a criminal law practice, from both a defense and prosecution point of view. This approach is not typically found in a first year Criminal Law class. The combined use of common law, Model Penal Code, jury instructions, and "real" state and federal statutes is also a virtue. Real-world statutes add realism and frequently come with legislative history and applicable caselaw, enabling students to practice statutory interpretation with challenging novel issues as well as more mundane ones.

Criminal Law professors will find that they may use *Skills and Values: Criminal Law* as a primary teaching text. This is so partly because of the discussion of substantive law and the extensive links to case law and other materials in the on-line component (OLC). The OLC also includes sample documents, videos related to the requisite skills, and other ways of modeling tasks for students. In addition, there is self-assessment for each skills task. The self-assessment portion of the OLC provides an outline of what a good response should contain or an excerpt from a model response so that students cannot "cheat" by just looking

---

[1] William Sullivan et al., Educating Lawyers: Preparation for the Profession of Law (2007).

[2] Roy Stuckey et al., Best Practices for Legal Education (2007).

[3] American Bar Association, Legal Education and Professional Development — An Educational Continuum Report of the Task Force on Law Schools and the Profession: Narrowing the Gap (1992).

up the answer. At the same time, the exercise material is rich enough that even with on-line feedback, there remains much fodder for classroom discussion. The exercises also permit ample discussion of underlying policy issues and potential legal reforms. These policy discussions often appear in a practical setting so that lobbying or other means of achieving legal change can also be discussed.

Alternatively or additionally, the text can serve as a supplemental source of rich factual problems for classroom discussion of law application and the development of lawyering skills. Instructors can choose from a wide array of skills, from client interviewing and counseling, to conducting direct examinations, drafting motions, and crafting jury instructions. Already time-pressed instructors may wonder how they can "add" these skills and values to doctrinal instruction. The exercises are structured to permit many options. The tasks range in complexity and provide suggested times to allot for each task. Some exercises can be assigned instead of, or in addition to, reading the traditional case law text. The exercise itself can be used in class as the way to teach the substantive law. If cases are assigned, students can be drilled in case analogy. Sometimes it is helpful to break students up into "law firms," having them spend 15 minutes of class time brainstorming before one student is chosen, for example, to do a sentencing argument or oral motion. As still a third option, many tasks can be completed at home (e.g., a written motion to dismiss), using class time only to review and debrief the exercise. A teacher interested in using these materials must be willing to depart at least occasionally from her comfort zone to experiment with new methods, though the degree of experimentation is in the instructor's hands. The self-assessment materials are sufficiently detailed, as are the skills guides and the teacher's manual, that instructors who have long been away from legal practice should feel no intimidation in using these materials. Bold instructors with a supportive faculty might even seek an extra credit for a "skills lab," this text being used as the material for the lab, the remaining course hours taught in a mostly more traditional fashion. At the other extreme, the text might simply be recommended as a way for students to review basic criminal law doctrines.

Although each chapter may stand on its own, students may be best served by taking these chapters largely in order, as Criminal Law instruction necessarily builds upon requisite fundamental knowledge. Accordingly, we have largely structured this volume much in the same way that traditional Criminal Law course books are structured and crimes are defined in American jurisdictions: we begin with the basics of a crime and build upon that knowledge. We also cross-reference chapters and skill guides to facilitate the most beneficial use of the materials presented. This provides students and professors an optimal opportunity to address and assess where competency or challenges exist.

We thus offer *Skills and Values: Criminal Law* as a tool to enable law students to bridge the gap between law school and law practice as early as their first year of legal education. *Skills and Values: Criminal Law* exposes students to many of the essential tasks inherent in the practice of criminal law via an integrated approach, blending both traditional instruction with "Best Practices" reform, so that students may enjoy an interactive, skills-based, 21st century approach to the study of Criminal Law.

Organization of the Book

Each chapter contains: 1) an overview of the chapter's substantive criminal law topic; this information summarizes the key legal doctrines and concepts; 2) a minimum of two tasks,

PREFACE

i.e., assignments, in which the student can practice lawyering skills in the context of the applicable legal doctrine; 3) the relevant law (e.g. caselaw, statutes, or jury instructions); 4) a guide for how to engage in each assigned skill, e.g., how to draft a jury instruction, negotiate a plea, or interpret a statute; and 5) a self-assessment section that the student may use independently of, before, or after s/he has completed the assignment. In addition, all chapters contain supplemental materials related to the required tasks. Supplemental materials may include: 1) sample documents or models from which to begin to prepare the tasks or links to those documents; 2) short video clips ("SVCs"); and 3) optional further reading, including practitioners' texts and law review articles. These materials do not all appear in the hard copy text. Some of the materials appear in that text, but much of the material appears in the OLC for each chapter.

A Plea to Users

We are well aware that there are ample alternative ways to teach these materials and to improve the product. We encourage users to offer any suggestions to us using the contact information in the Acknowledgements section, and we cheerfully thank you in advance for this feedback. We hope you enjoy using this text as much as we have enjoyed putting it together.

September 3, 2013

ACKNOWLEDGMENTS

Endless appreciation to my wife, Patricia V. Sun, for putting up with my scholarly and teaching obsessions; to my sister, Ellen Duncan, for teaching me to read and write, thus releasing my words on an unsuspecting world; and to the Washington College of Law, American University, for its support of this project. A special thanks, however, to my co-authors, the ever-talented Lenese Herbert, now of Howard University School of Law, and rising young star Katie Tinto, now of Cardozo School of Law. Lenese and Katie bring brilliance and joy to every project they touch, and I am blessed to be able to work with them. Finally, my deepest appreciation to my friends and family and my dogs, B'lanna and Odo, for seeing me through some tough times, and to my students to whom these materials are directed and who give such meaning to my professional life.

Andrew E. Taslitz
Director, Criminal Justice Practice and Policy Institute
Washington College of Law
American University
4801 Massachusetts Avenue, NW
Washington, DC 20016
202-274-4058
ataslitz@wcl.american.edu

I would like to express gratitude to and appreciation of my co-authors, Andrew Taslitz, Director, Criminal Justice Practice and Policy Institute, Washington College of Law, American University, and Katie Tinto, Assistant Clinical Professor of Law, Benjamin N. Cardozo School of Law. Additionally, I would like to thank Lexis/Nexis Publications, especially Elisabeth Ebben, with whom working was a pleasure.

Lenese C. Herbert
Howard University School of Law
2900 Van Ness St NW
Washington, DC 20008
(202) 806-8000
lherbert@law.howard.edu

Thank you to my family, the Lawyering Program of NYU School of Law, Christine Yurechko for excellent research assistance, and my first-year NYU Law students for their advice, edits, and perspectives. In addition, I would like to thank Cardozo School of Law for its strong support and my wonderful co-authors, Andrew Taslitz and Lenese Herbert, for the opportunity to be a part of this fantastic project.

Katie Tinto
Benjamin N. Cardozo School of Law
55 Fifth Avenue, Room 1108
New York, NY 10003
(212) 790-0433
tinto@yu.edu

TABLE OF CONTENTS

Table of Contents

Table of Contents

Chapter 1

CHARGING AND SENTENCING

OVERVIEW

I. WHY SENTENCING PLANNING COMES FIRST

Sentencing is the last act to occur at the trial level in a criminal case. Yet understanding the purposes of sentencing and sentencing procedures is essential at the start of a case. The same purposes that guide sentencing are also what justify the existence of the criminal law and the substantive content of any specific crime in the first place. Prosecutors have great discretion at the charging phase of a criminal case, and the purposes of sentencing, and thus of the criminal law, may play an important role in what charges a prosecutor chooses to bring. Moreover, oftentimes the state's case against a defendant is a strong one. In such a case, the defense has a strong incentive to seek a guilty plea. But negotiating with the prosecutor requires the defense to be intimately familiar with the law of sentencing. To plead a defendant guilty to a charge — even the lowest possible charge among those alleged — without knowing the likely resulting sentence for the defendant would be malpractice. It is the sentence that most defendants care most about.

Even where a defendant insists on his innocence of some or all of the charges made, the defendant must know what penalty he will face should the jury disagree. A defense attorney must always plan for how to obtain the best sentence should a conviction result. Sentencing planning thus must start as early as case investigation. Prosecutors also often offer a discount in a guilty plea agreement for a plea entered early in a case, as that saves the state much time and money.

II. OVERVIEW OF THE CRIMINAL PROCESS AND SENTENCING PLANNING'S ROLE IN THAT PROCESS

A case usually begins with an arrest, followed by a complaint. A complaint is the initial charging document. At the preliminary arraignment, the defendant is presented with the complaint, assigned bail, and assigned counsel if he cannot afford to hire counsel on his own. In most jurisdictions, for felonies, the next stage of the proceedings is an adversarial preliminary hearing at which the hearing judge decides whether there is probable cause (or, in some jurisdictions, a prima facie case) justifying proceeding to trial on several or all of the charges. If the court finds such cause, it holds the case "for court" or "binds over" a defendant for trial. At that time, a prosecutor-

1

drafted document called an *information* replaces the complaint.

In other jurisdictions, instead of a preliminary hearing before a judge, there will be a grand jury hearing. In most jurisdictions, a grand jury hearing is attended only by the prosecutor, the grand jurors, a court reporter, and one witness at a time. The proceedings are also secret. If the grand jury finds probable cause or a prima facie case (again, the standard varies with the jurisdiction), the grand jury issues a prosecutor-drafted document called an *indictment*. The indictment also replaces the complaint as the charging document. A grand jury can issue a subpoena — a court order to produce documents or to testify. If the state lacks probable cause to arrest, it may turn to the grand jury first, using the subpoena power to uncover probable cause. In that instance, the indictment comes before the arrest. States relying primarily on preliminary hearings may convene investigating grand juries to seek to establish probable cause in difficult cases.

The next stage is usually the arraignment. At the arraignment, a defendant pleads guilty or not guilty, and the court schedules arguments and briefs on any pretrial motions. Such motions can seek to dismiss a case entirely, for example, because it was filed too late, contravening statutory or constitutional speedy trial rules; to dismiss certain charges as unsupported by any evidence available in the case; or to suppress certain evidence from the jury's hearing at trial, perhaps because the evidence was unconstitutionally seized or violated local evidence codes. The arraignment judge will also often try to resolve any discovery disputes. After motions hearings, the case proceeds to trial, either before a judge (a bench trial) or a jury. If the factfinder convicts, it renders a guilty verdict. A defendant is also usually free at any point in the criminal process to switch his plea to guilty or nolo contendere (no contest), generally doing so only if a plea agreement is reached with the prosecutor. After a guilty verdict, a defendant can choose to file pretrial motions, either for a new trial based on evidentiary errors or other mistakes at trial or for arrest of judgment, essentially a finding that no reasonable jury could have found guilt beyond a reasonable doubt. Alternatively, a pleading defendant might try to withdraw his plea as involuntarily made or otherwise flawed. If these motions are denied, the case proceeds to sentencing.

At every stage of this process, defense counsel will be preparing for the possibility of the eventual sentencing hearing. Defense counsel will be reviewing relevant sentencing statutes, guidelines, and rules; hiring investigators to check for positive things in the defendant's background; and getting the defendant into drug rehabilitation, job training, educational, and other programs to demonstrate to the sentencing judge that the defendant has changed his ways and has plans for a legitimate future. The prosecutor, of course, will be preparing to respond to likely defense arguments and also to raise the prosecutor's own arguments. Moreover, while the defense attorney must competently or zealously (again, the test varies with the jurisdiction) represent his client, the prosecutor is obligated to "do justice." Justice does not necessarily always require the prosecutor to seek the harshest penalty possible.

III.   SENTENCING PURPOSES

There are five common sentencing purposes. They are general deterrence, specific deterrence, education, isolation, and retribution.

General deterrence seeks to discourage persons other than the offender from committing future crimes. For example, in theory, observers seeing a drug dealer sentenced to 10 years in prison will choose not to deal drugs themselves in order to avoid his fate. Specific deterrence aims at discouraging the current offender — in this case, the drug dealer — from committing future crimes to avoid another 10 years' incarceration.

Education aims at enlightening the public about what society considers its highest moral values. Education is different from deterrence, not turning on fear of punishment. Rather, the thought is that sentencing the drug dealer sends the emphatic message that drug dealing is a great social evil. Observers, seeing that society condemns such dealing in deed, not merely in words, will themselves incorporate or reinforce a drug-dealing prohibition into their own moral code. They will refrain from dealing drugs not because they fear punishment but because they firmly believe that it is morally important to do so.

Isolation prevents harm simply by incarcerating or otherwise isolating the defendant. He cannot commit crimes against the general public if he is behind bars.

Retribution is often said to be backward-looking. It is concerned with giving the offender what he deserves, regardless of whether that helps to reduce crime or educate the public about selected moral norms embodied in the criminal code. Retribution is a cousin to the emotion of revenge. But while revenge is imposed by an individual for harm to her, retribution is imposed by the state for a perceived harm to the entire society. Moreover, individuals are often thought to seek excessive revenge. Retribution is limited by the principle that the punishment must be proportionate to the crime. A first-time pickpocket might deserve probation, while a brutally cold-blooded murderer might deserve the death penalty.

There are many theories that try to justify retribution and to define and limit it more specifically than just stated above. Two of the best known of these theories are retribution as repaying a debt to society and retribution as a communicative act.

The first theory turns on the idea of the social contract. Each member of society agrees to comply with the criminal law. That imposes a cost on each of us. For example, we cannot just wreak individual revenge on a person whom we perceive as wronging us. Instead, we must turn to the police, then to juries, accepting the latter's verdict and the judge's or jury's subsequent choice of punishment should the accused be found guilty. That denies each of us the personal satisfaction of assaulting the wrongdoer. But should an individual assault us for whatever reason (revenge, race hatred, extortion), he gets the benefit that we forego for the good of society. By getting a benefit denied to each of the rest of us and thus to society as a whole, he owes a debt to right that imbalance. Beating him up in return or torturing him is considered an unacceptable means for his settling that debt. Imprisonment settles it by denying him a different benefit than the one he took from his victim, but one thought to be of equal worth to society.

The second retributive theory turns on the idea that all crimes communicate the message that the victim is of less worth than the offender. If an offender robs another man, the offender says the message, "Your needs for money and safety are worth less than mine because you are worth less than me. Consequently, I can take what I want from you and do so by the means I choose, even by violence." This message violates our society's commitment to the equal worth of all persons. Criminal punishment lowers the criminal from his lofty perch, insulting him with equal force to the insult he gave his victim. That restores the message of society's valuing both victim and offender alike as equally worthy.

IV. THE PRACTICAL RELEVANCE OF SENTENCING PURPOSES

There are two broad types of sentencing schemes: indeterminate and determinate. A purely indeterminate scheme would allow a judge to impose any punishment he chooses, without limits. A purely determinate scheme would impose a single precise punishment for each crime, say, 10 years for a robbery. In the real world, systems fall between these two imagined poles of punishment. Thus, indeterminate schemes usually involve a statute specifying a minimum and maximum punishment, perhaps one to 10 years for robbery, leaving the judge free to choose a punishment between or including those extremes. The judge is supposed to be guided, however, in her decision by the purposes of sentencing and must state her reasons on the record or via a written opinion.

The most common determinate scheme involves sentencing guidelines. Guidelines jurisdictions rely on a chart or grid. One axis of the grid specifies a numerical score reflecting the severity of the crime. The other grid axis specifies a numerical score reflecting the quantity and severity of the accused's prior convictions. Various complex formulas might then raise or lower the initial scores based upon the presence of certain facts respectively favoring enhancing or mitigating punishment. The scores intersect in a box that specifies a sentence expressed in a fairly narrow range of months. The judge is supposed to use the purposes of sentencing to determine where within that range to sentence the offender.

Guidelines jurisdictions can also be of two types: mandatory and advisory. In a mandatory jurisdiction, the judge must follow the guidelines range. A jury must determine the facts that determine that range, except that the judge may determine the offender's prior record. The judge's only role thereafter is to choose where in the resulting grid to sentence the offender. But in an advisory jurisdiction, the jury need not find facts (the judge may do so), and the judge is free to depart from the guidelines if she gives a good enough reason. Those reasons stem from the purposes of sentencing.

Because prosecutors are always looking past the possibility of conviction to the possible sentence, prosecutors will also consult the purposes of sentencing to guide the prosecutor's choices about what to charge and whether to accept a guilty plea. The prosecutor's duty is to the People or to the system — the duty to "do justice." Too soft a sentence for a terrible crime by a repeat offender would not suit retributive or deterrent needs. Too harsh a sentence for a minor, non-violent crime by a first offender would also violate principles of proportionate retributive punishment and of deterrence. California, for example, labels some crimes "wobblers:" they may be charged either as misdemeanors or as felonies. The severity of the crime and of the accused's criminal record will guide the prosecutor in choosing whether to wobble up to a felony or down to a misdemeanor. Once charges are filed, these same concerns about crime severity and prior record, as well as other needs, such as to make the victim whole for her injury, will inform the prosecutor's decision to accept or reject a defense plea offer. Defense counsel, correspondingly, will use the purposes of sentencing to try to convince a prosecutor to accept a plea offer. All these charging and plea negotiation decisions are guided by codes of ethics as well as by the prosecutor's conscience and her office's policies.

V. SENTENCING PROCEDURES

After conviction, a date is usually set for a sentencing hearing. Usually, the probation department of the relevant jurisdiction will prepare a presentence report. This report will summarize the incident and offer background about the defendant, focusing on his character, upbringing, wrongs, and achievements. In a guidelines jurisdiction, the report will also contain the probation officer's calculation of the likely guidelines sentence. The report will also discuss any harm done to the victim and what is needed to provide the victim with adequate restitution. The report, or a companion mental health report by a psychologist or psychiatrist, will further discuss the defendant's mental capacities and incapacities, including reading and writing levels, math skills, personality disorders, and any mental illnesses. The report will also recount drug or alcohol addictions, indeed, anything relevant to the purposes of sentencing or to guidelines calculations. Hearsay is admissible at the sentencing hearing, and few, if any, rules of evidence apply.

Defense counsel, the prosecutor, or both may challenge the calculations, recommendations, and factual assertions in the probation officer's report. Those challenges might be made informally, perhaps by a letter copied to all relevant persons, protesting inaccuracies and laying out the case for corrections. The probation officer may or may not revise her report based on the lawyer's input. If the report is not fully revised to everyone's satisfaction, the challenges may again be made at the sentencing hearing. One side or the other, or both, might call witnesses to challenge the disputed portions of the report. Each side might also examine the probation officer or call additional witnesses, for example, perhaps defense witnesses testifying to the offender's usually good character or prosecution witnesses about the harm done the victim. The offender has the right to allocution, that is, to make any relevant statement he wishes to the court to support mitigation.

EXERCISE

Overview

The New York City Police Department and the Federal Bureau of Investigation jointly investigated the "Clinton Place Crew," an organization formed for the distribution of heroin and cocaine in the Bedford-Stuyvesant neighborhood of Brooklyn, NY ("Bed-Stuy"). The investigation covered the calendar years 2007 through 2011. The crew sold its wares primarily in the Louis Armstrong Houses, colloquially referred to as a "housing project" of 16 buildings bounded by Clifton Place and Herbert Von King Park to the North, Tompkins Avenue to the East, Gates Avenue to the South, and Bedford Avenue to the West. The project is managed by the New York City Housing Authority.

The crew membership varied from five to ten co-conspirators during this period. The crew sold drugs in the project daily, though there is no evidence that the crew sold to children. Members of the crew routinely carried guns or knives. Police surveillance, search warrants, and videotaping of gun and drug purchases resulted in police obtaining the following evidence: (1) 100 kilograms of crack cocaine ("cocaine base") and 100 kilograms of heroin seized from the person or homes of several of the crew members; (2) 14 guns, ammunition, a machete, a police radio scanner, $15,000 in cash and 15 "G-packs" of heroin (packs of about 75 grams each packaged for retail sale worth about $1,000 each) from several of the crew residences in Brooklyn; and (3) videotapes of 75 separate sales of drugs and guns.

One alleged member of the crew is Damien Bannister. Damien was a street-level dealer who sold crack and cocaine to confidential informants on three dates in July 2011. On August 9, 2011, a confidential informant observed Darrell Bannister, Damien's older brother, hand various bags to Damien, which Damien put into a backpack. Damien sold a small quantity of crack cocaine to a confidential informant on that same date. Shortly thereafter, police who had observed that sale arrested Damien. They searched his backpack and found several bags of crack and 90 glassine packets of heroin inside it. The total quantity of drugs found physically to be in Damien's possession on that date and on the three dates in July was 19 grams of heroin and 1.5 grams of crack cocaine. Damien was never observed by the police or any confidential informant to be in possession of weapons.

Audio recordings of Darrell Bannister's conversation with several confidential informants reveal Darrell bragging about being a member of the crew since its inception. In one such recording, Darrell also boasted about what a good street dealer his brother Damien had become since Damien joined the crew in August 2009.

New York has agreed to let the federal authorities prosecute the case against Damien under federal law.

REQUIRED TASKS

Task One: Drafting Indictments

Review the indictment prepared against Damien (provided below), the brief guide to indictment drafting, and the statutes and ethical rules that appear and are linked in the online component. Meet with another class member. The two of you are the prosecution team assigned to this case. During your meeting, critique the indictment. If your professor so requests, reduce your critique to writing, listing bullet points summarizing each individual aspect of the critique discussed.

Your critique should address technical matters but also strategic and ethical matters — for example, concerning whether to charge amounts based on "relevant conduct" (defined below) or to seek a mandatory minimum sentence (assume for this exercise that you cannot seek such a sentence unless you charge it in the complaint). You need not consult the federal sentencing guidelines but should simply assume that, if you charge only the amounts proven sold by (or possessed with the intention of being sold by) him personally, the guidelines numbers will be these: an offense level of 16 and a criminal history category of I (one criminal history point from one prior conviction), yielding a guidelines sentence between 21 and 27 months and a guidelines fine range of $5,000 to $50,000. (For purposes of this task, assume that juvenile convictions, though relevant to sentencing, do not affect his criminal history points or category). No mandatory minimum sentence will be required. If you charge all provable relevant conduct, on the other hand, the mandatory minimum statute requiring a minimum sentence of 10 years in prison will apply; that is, Damien will be held responsible for selling or possessing with intent to sell an additional 100 kilograms of heroin and 100 kilograms of crack cocaine. The guidelines numbers will then be as follows: offense level of 38, prior record score of 1, changing the guidelines sentencing range to 235-293 months.

Also consider the availability of one method for a defendant to avoid a mandatory minimum sentence, even if the noted relevant conduct is attributed to him: the "substantial assistance" or 5K1.1 motion made by a prosecutor. Such a motion would declare that the defendant has "provided substantial assistance in the investigation or prosecution of another person who has committed an offense. . . ." § 5K1.1 The size of the departure may result from considering many factors, including the usefulness of the assistance; its truthfulness, completeness, and the reliability of the information or testimony the offender gives; the nature and extent of his assistance; its timeliness; and any injury suffered or danger he risked by cooperating. § 5K1.1(a). Substantial assistance may thus be used both to circumvent mandatory minimums and, in addition, to obtain a downward departure. You must consider whether to approach the defendant or his counsel in advance of drafting the indictment to reach an agreement for substantial assistance or whether you can and should use the indictment as a way to gain such assistance.

In preparing for this task, you also should consult the following items to be found in the online component for this task:

- Sample Simple Indictment A: Hate Crimes: Dharun Ravi

- Sample Complex Indictment B: John Edwards
- SVC #1: The Process of Federal Indictment
- Relevant provisions of the United States Attorney's Manual (which guides the internal procedural and ethical conduct of prosecutors)

In addition, use an online database to read the following article: Hans P. Sinha, *Prosecutorial Ethics: The Charging Decision*, 41 PROSECUTOR 32 (Sept./Oct. 2007).

Relevant Conduct Explained: The Guidelines operate under a "real" conduct philosophy of sentencing offenders for all culpable "relevant conduct," not merely the conduct involved in the offense of conviction. U.S.S.G. Ch. 1, Pt. A, subpt. 1(4)(a). Relevant conduct includes "all acts and omissions committed, aided, abetted, counseled, commanded, induced, procured, or willfully caused by the defendant" if they "occurred during the commission of the offense of conviction, in preparation for that offense, or in the course of attempting to avoid detection or responsibility for that offense, ..." U.S.S.G. § 1B1.3(a)(1)(A). For example, drug type and quantity determines the base offense level for drug offenses. If a defendant was convicted of selling a specified quantity of a drug, thus suggesting a matching base offense level, but he counseled someone else to sell more of that drug, and did so in the course of committing the offense of conviction, the amount sold by that other person will be added to the amount for which the offender was convicted. The effect will be to raise the base offense level above where it would be if we relied solely on the amount for which the offender was convicted of distributing.

ESTIMATED TIME FOR COMPLETION: 90 minutes.

LEVEL OF DIFFICULTY (1 TO 5):

Task Two: Sentencing

Outline a list of the defense arguments to be made for deviating from, and the prosecution arguments for staying within, the guidelines range if the defendant is assumed to have pled guilty to charges putting him in the guidelines range of 46 to 47 months, specifically, to conspiring with Darrell and with other members of the crew to distribute and possess with intent to distribute cocaine base in the amounts noted above (assume the defendant is not being charged with possessing with intent to sell the amounts considered "relevant conduct"). Rely on the purposes of sentencing for making your arguments. Using those same purposes, also be ready to justify a particular sentence if the judge agrees to depart downward from the recommended guidelines range. Use the Presentencing Report excerpts in the online component and the relevant rule of criminal procedure (excerpted in the online component) to craft your arguments.

ESTIMATED TIME FOR COMPLETION: 90 minutes.

LEVEL OF DIFFICULTY (1 TO 5):

Task Three: Oral Argument; Sentencing

Prepare an oral argument on each of the points developed in Task Two to someone playing the role of judge (either imaginary or as someone in-role, in class). You will not be calling any witnesses. In preparation for this exercise, read the skills guide below on oral argument in the sentencing context and review the video clips found in the online component.

ESTIMATED PREPARATION TIME: 60 minutes.

ESTIMATED OPTIONAL IN-CLASS TIME: 20-30 minutes.

LEVEL OF DIFFICULTY (1 TO 5):

PRACTICE SKILLS USED:

Skill 1: Drafting Indictments

Skill 2: Editing Indictments

Skill 3: Planning and Brainstorming

Skill 4: Tactical Thinking

Skill 5: Oral Argument; Sentencing

SKILLS GUIDES

SKILLS GUIDE #1: Drafting Indictments

Criminal cases most often begin with an arrest. An arrest requires probable cause, but no warrant is required if the arrest is done in a public place. The first formal charging document in most jurisdictions is a criminal complaint. The complaint usually lays out in summary fashion the factual bases for the charges and the charges themselves. If an arrest is done with a warrant, the complaint will be filed at the time that the arrest warrant is issued by a magistrate or a judge. For a warrantless arrest, the complaint is filed after the arrest and is presented to the defendant at the initial or preliminary arraignment, where he is advised of the charges against him, conditions of release (if the defendant will not be held in custody pending trial) are set, and, if he is indigent, counsel is appointed.

Another way to begin a criminal case, however, is by the process of indictment. An indictment is issued by a grand jury. It, too, must generally find probable cause to proceed on the charges alleged, though in some jurisdictions the grand jury must find a "prima facie case" — a purportedly higher standard than probable cause. A prima facie case is enough for a reasonable jury to find the charges proven beyond a reasonable doubt. The indictment can thus be the first charging document, though it may be followed by a criminal complaint. In some jurisdictions, even if a case is started by a criminal complaint, the charges will be dismissed if a grand jury does not return a "true bill;" that is, issue an indictment based upon a finding of probable cause, within a specified period.

Perhaps in most jurisdictions today, indictments are rarely used, being replaced by an "information." An information is a charging document that replaces a previously filed criminal complaint. After preliminary arraignment, in felony cases, a "preliminary hearing" is held in which a judge decides whether there is probable cause to proceed on all charges recited in the complaint, only some of those charges, or none of them. The difference between a complaint and an information is that the complaint is based primarily on police reports, while the information occurs after (in many jurisdictions) at least some live witness testimony has been taken, though much more hearsay is allowed than would be at a trial. Similarly, indictments issue after a grand jury has heard at least some live testimony. Even in jurisdictions relying primarily on informations, however, a prosecutor can seek to call an "investigating grand jury" to return an indictment. A prosecutor will do so where he does not initially have probable cause to charge someone with a crime. The investigating grand jury can, however, subpoena witnesses; that is, issue court orders requiring witnesses to testify and documents to be produced before the grand jury. That investigating power can be used to develop probable cause, thus resulting in an indictment. In the federal system, indictments are generally required — unless waived by the defendant — in all serious cases.

Most indictments are short, simple, clear documents. They allege the minimum number of facts necessary. The allegations must, however, be sufficient so that, if they are assumed to be true, they at least establish probable cause for each of the charges made. Indictments must also cite to the specific statutes that the state alleges the defendant has violated. Every major factual allegation is usually made in its own separate numbered paragraph. Where different statutes have allegedly been violated, the indictment will usually contain separate "counts" (headings reciting the number of the count, accompanied by the factual allegations supporting that count) for each statute or collection of related statutes. If some facts from one count are relevant to another count, the later count will often simply "incorporate by reference" the relevant numbered paragraphs from the earlier count.

An indictment must also contain facts establishing the court's jurisdiction — its power to hear the case — and venue, that is, the proper location for the case. For example, crimes that occur on federally owned or operated property generally fall within the power of the federal courts to hear. Jurisdiction is not always exclusive. Thus, sometimes both a state and federal criminal statute are violated by an act on federally operated property within a state, potentially allowing either jurisdiction to mount a prosecution. In such instances, federal and local authorities might negotiate over which jurisdiction will prosecute, when, and for what charges.

Although the grand jury decides whether the particular indictment is in all respects supported by probable cause, grand jurors are ordinary citizens, not lawyers. Consequently, prosecutors usually draft indictments for the jury foreperson's signature, just as prosecutors often draft criminal complaints. The drafting principles for criminal complaints and indictments are similar.

Sometimes, however, a prosecutor will choose to draft an indictment that contains more factual detail than is necessary to establish probable cause. Prosecutors may do so for several reasons. First, some cases are so complex that the major allegations cannot be understood by a reader without more detail. Second, a prosecutor might believe that the case is one in which putting his cards on the table, rather than hiding the details of his case, might convince a defendant to plead guilty, or at least to enter into plea negotiations with the prosecutor. Third, if the case is of media interest, detail might help to convey to the public more effectively the nature of the charges and the work being done by law enforcement. On the other hand, too much detail phrased in too vivid a fashion might taint the potential jury pool — namely, all members of the local public. Prejudicing potential jurors against keeping an open mind raises serious ethical issues for a prosecutor, whose duty is to "do justice" rather than solely to obtain convictions.

SKILLS GUIDE #2: Editing Indictments

Editing indictments drafted by others requires looking for compliance with the technical requirements for indictment drafting, considering the wisdom of the initial drafter's tactical decisions, approving the drafter's ethical judgments, and ensuring that the document is clear and accurate. As to technical matters, a federal indictment must comply with Federal Rule of Criminal Procedure 7, largely limit each factual allegation to one numbered paragraph, appropriately separate out different categories of allegations into different counts, include facts establishing jurisdiction and venue, identify the specific statutes by citation number purportedly violated, and allege sufficient facts to establish probable cause to believe that all the elements of the charged offenses have been established. An indictment also should give adequate notice to a reader of any special remedies to be sought by the prosecution, for example, mandatory minimum sentences or the death penalty.

Tactical decisions to review are: the appropriate degree of detail to include, what charges to allege among those theoretically available and what to leave out, and whether further investigation should be done to determine the availability of still more charges or to build a case on which the prosecutor is likely to succeed at trial (rather than one supported by mere probable cause) before indicting. The likelihood and ability to obtain a guilty plea should be among the considerations affecting these tactical judgments. Making that evaluation in turn requires making early, perhaps tentative, judgments about what sentence or sentencing range the prosecutor deems appropriate.

Ethical judgments to consider are whether the indictment risks tainting the jury pool; whether it seeks remedies that "do justice" in light of the severity of the crime, the character and circumstances of the offender, and the risks posed to the public; and whether it overcharges ("overcharging" means including some charges that are either more serious than those the prosecutor believes he can successfully prove or call for harsher punishment than the prosecutor in fact plans to seek; the attack on overcharging is that it is done to coerce guilty pleas unfairly or wastes valuable defense time in seeking to dismiss baseless charges; some prosecutors may see certain charges as simply tough bargaining or protecting themselves should later investigation reveal more evidence, while many defense attorneys see the practice as an abuse).

Accuracy judgments require reviewing any relevant documents or testimony to ensure that there is evidence supporting each allegation precisely as it is phrased. Review for clarity means ensuring that the writing uses mostly brief sentences, varies sentence length, appropriately uses linking phrases and sentences to build logical connections, and complies in all respects with the rules of grammar, punctuation, and good writing style. A good indictment, especially the longer stylistic choice, should also tell a good story. Indeed, good storytelling is central to almost every litigator's task.

SKILLS GUIDE #3: Planning and Brainstorming

Planning is simply the activity of making informed, deliberative judgments about each lawyering task in advance of undertaking it. Planning in the litigation context requires knowledge of the law, the facts (more precisely, the evidence supporting the facts alleged), and the likely responses of opponents and judges to any action taken. Planning can be aided by visual tools, such as outlining elements and the evidence offered to support them or drawing charts and diagrams to aid in critical thinking. Although much planning takes place in isolation, two heads are indeed better than one; meaning, here, that brainstorming is advisable whenever time allows.

Brainstorming involves presenting the options occurring to the lawyer to one or more fellow lawyers and asking them for feedback. But this should not be a one-way process. Instead, that feedback should start a conversation in which all parties involved are encouraged to be creative, to throw out ideas freely, and to be critical of arguments made by others but in a friendly fashion. In short, brainstorming refers to the free flow of ideas about a problem among those trying to solve that problem.

There are many ways to brainstorm. One helpful way is to use a white board or post, e.g., against a wall or on a chalkboard, a large blank sheet of paper (or several such sheets). One person can serve as the facilitator, writing out the question(s) to be answered. The facilitator can then call on each person in the room to offer ideas on how the problem is to be solved. Broader conversation might begin among the group, prompted by the first called-upon speaker. But it is important for the facilitator to call on each person for a contribution because some people will not otherwise speak. Alternatively, if efforts are not made to hear from everyone, a single gregarious member of the group might dominate the conversation. That might stifle ideas. The facilitator or a note-taker can then put each idea on the board or blank paper, encapsulated in a word or a phrase. Everyone should be able to see each idea written down. Once all the ideas are exhausted, the facilitator can guide the group in looking for commonalities among ideas (grouping some of them together into one big idea) as well as in evaluating which ideas make sense and which do not.

Brainstorming can help with drafting documents, preparing witnesses for trial, investigating facts, interviewing witnesses — in short, in doing any lawyering task. For example, brainstorming can support ideas concerning how to interpret a statute. With oral argument, brainstorming can serve as the jumping-off point for the oralist to outline just what she wants to say and how. In the "real world," however, once an oral argument is planned, a different sort of brainstorming must occur. The oralist must engage in practice or mock oral arguments before other people, especially those familiar with the case. The observers should then each offer individual feedback but, ideally, there would be further group brainstorming about how to improve the oral argument. Brainstorming can also be helpful in coming up with tactical or strategic plans on how to handle a case.

SKILLS GUIDE #4: Tactical Thinking

"Strategy" refers to a case's overall game plan. We use the phrase "game plan" because the role of strategic judgment is to decide what you would like the ultimate case result to be and how best to get there. Strategic planning requires anticipating your opponent's likely actions and how you can counter them. You also must decide how to persuade your opponent to come closer to your view of the case. Strategy may include motions planning. For example, the defense might believe it can win a motion to suppress a confession. Even if there is ample additional evidence of the defendant's guilt, loss of the confession still makes the prosecution's task harder and gives the prosecution an incentive to settle. Thus, a defense strategic vision for a case might include filing such a motion. But it also might include getting the defendant into drug treatment and job training so that he can offer evidence of rehabilitation that might soften a prosecutor's or judge's heart away from the harshest sentence. Strategy might additionally involve finding the leading expert on eyewitness identifications to support a claim that the eyewitness's identification of this defendant was questionable. The combination of a multi-pronged defense approach that confronts the prosecution with no confession, a difficult opposing expert, and evidence of the defendant's reduced likelihood of recidivism builds a strong case for a defense-favorable guilty plea.

Tactics address each individual prong of the strategic plan. Thus, if filing a motion to suppress is one part of the strategic plan, tactics include the best way to win the motion to suppress. If the case for probable cause justifying a search is ambiguous, the prosecution might instead make its primary argument that the defendant consented to the search. That argument seems more likely to win. But tactics must also serve the strategic goal. If the prosecutor believes that the defendant can be rehabilitated and that the need for retribution is small, the prosecutor might use winning the suppression motion combined with offering generous settlement terms as ways to induce a plea. Even document drafting involves tactical judgments. Saying more than the minimum needed to win a motion or resisting a motion to dismiss a case might tip the prosecutor's strategic hand. But more detail in a motion or document might frighten the defendant with the apparent strength of the prosecutor's case. A prosecutor must thus decide what to put in a motion to win it or what to put in an indictment to avoid dismissal but must temper that initial judgment with serving the overall strategic goal: trial, plea, or something else entirely? Ethics codes must also temper the prosecutor's choices.

SKILLS GUIDE# 5: Oral Argument; Sentencing

Oral argument is, of course, one central focus of the first-year legal writing and reasoning course. Oral argument in the ordinary sentencing hearing, however, differs in important respects from an appellate argument or many trial-level motion arguments. A sentencing hearing may be based entirely on documents, such as the presentence report, or may involve taking additional testimony. Thus, a defendant might want to call witnesses to testify to his good character, his efforts to reform (perhaps shown by his completing a drug treatment program while on bail, finishing a job training program, or continuing his formal education), and his ability to pay restitution to a victim. Correspondingly, the prosecutor might call the victim to testify to the emotional and economic losses she has suffered and to express her own views about the appropriate sentence. Once testimony, if any, is completed, oral argument begins. Generally, the prosecutor goes first; the defendant's attorney follows or goes second. In each case, the argument begins by each lawyer asking for a particular sentence. Then the argument of each lawyer consists of justifying that sentence. That justification usually turns on summarizing for the court the relevant facts and explaining how and why the lawyer supports a particular sentence. Case law, and even statutory law, thus play little, if any, role in a routine sentencing argument. Notice the emphasis on the word "routine." Sometimes sentencing does turn on complex legal issues that are informed by case law. But that is not so in most instances. The relative dearth of discussion about legal precedent thus marks the typical sentencing proceeding as quite different from the typical appellate argument.

That does not mean, however, that law plays no role. The law determines the maximum and minimum sentences for the charge of conviction. Where sentencing guidelines apply, they outline the presumptive sentencing range. In an advisory guidelines system like the federal system, sentencing arguments may thus focus on arguments for departing from the guidelines range (downward requests made by the defense, upward requests by the prosecution) or on where within the guidelines range a judge should sentence a defendant.

There are federal statutes that lay out in precise statutory language the sorts of considerations a judge should take into account at sentencing. But, though in somewhat different language, the statutes boil down to urging judges to consider the standard purposes of sentencing as applied to the facts of the individual case. Thus, one way to structure an oral argument about sentencing is to arrange the argument by the relevant purposes of sentencing: deterrence (general and specific), retribution, education of the public, rehabilitation, and isolation. Not all these purposes are necessarily relevant in every case, but they all should be considered. By way of illustration, under the rubric of "retribution," a prosecutor might focus on specific case facts and evidence showing the defendant's evil intent, his corrupt motivations, his indifference to the harm he risked or caused to others, and the publicly shared moral principles he violated. The defense, by contrast, under the same heading might argue for motivations meriting some compassion (e.g., alleviating poverty, protecting the defendant's family), the relative mildness of the harms risked or done (compared to other more serious offenses), and the offender's demonstrated regret. Similarly, the prosecutor would argue for the unlikelihood that the defendant can be rehabilitated, either at all or without the stern message sent by a harsh punishment, while the defense would argue just the opposite. Support for each side's arguments should be drawn with specificity from the trial evidence, the presentence report, and the testimony of any witnesses at the sentencing hearing. Public policy arguments can be made as well, for example, whether racial and class inequality contributed to the defendant's criminality (without his denying responsibility for the crime and for doing better in the future).

ADDITIONAL MATERIALS FOR THE EXERCISE
THE ORIGINAL INDICTMENT:
UNITED STATES DISTRICT COURT

EASTERN DISTRICT OF NEW YORK
. . . .   } X
UNITED STATES OF AMERICA

INDICTMENT

Cr. No. . . . .

— against —

DAMIEN BANNISTER,

Defendant } X

. . . .

THE GRAND JURY CHARGES:

COUNT ONE

1. On or about February 9, 2011, within the Eastern District of New York and elsewhere, the defendant, Damien Bannister, sold or possessed with intent to sell substances containing at least 19 grams of heroin and 1.5 grams of crack cocaine, in violation of Title 21, United States Code, Section 841.

COUNT TWO

2. Between approximately January 1, 2007 and February 9, 2011, within the Eastern District of New York and elsewhere, the defendant, Damien Bannister, conspired with members of the Clinton Place Crew to distribute for profit heroin and cocaine in the Bedford-Stuyvesant neighborhood, especially in the Louis Armstrong Houses.

A TRUE BILL

FOREPERSON

_____
MORRIS JOHNSON
UNITED STATES ATTORNEY
EASTERN DISTRICT OF NEW YORK

DATE: . . . .

Chapter 2

STATUTORY INTERPRETATION

OVERVIEW

All modern criminal law in the United States is statutory. That does not mean that case law plays no role. It does. But the cases consistently address interpreting statutes. Moreover, many cases of statutory interpretation are questions of first impression, limiting the usefulness of analogous case law alone. Laypeople may have the impression that statutes are sets of simple, clear rules. All a lawyer need do is find the right rule and mechanically apply it to a particular set of facts. That understanding of statutes is wrong. Statutes are necessarily general because the legislature cannot foresee every set of circumstances that may implicate the statute's purpose. But broad, general language can, of course, often hold multiple, reasonable meanings. Even more specific language can be subject to debate. Indeed, looking up words in any English dictionary reveals multiple possible meanings for a single word. Add the reality that statutes are the result of political compromise, sometimes intentionally containing language of debatable meaning (so that the competing sides can continue their battle over meaning in the courts), and it becomes clear that giving meaning to statutes is no mechanical exercise. Additionally, even when the meaning of a word or phrase is clear, the application of that word or phrase to a particular case may not be quite as clear. Statutes are, therefore, necessarily ambiguous. The process of giving such ambiguity meaning is called "statutory interpretation."

I. THE PURPOSE OF, AND APPROACHES TO, STATUTORY INTERPRETATION

Academics debate the proper approach to statutory interpretation, as do many judges. Nevertheless, the dominant approach purports to give to statutes the meaning intended by the legislature. This can be a difficult task. First, each legislator may have a different understanding of a particular statute's meaning. Second, the legislature may never actually have thought about how the statute would apply to a host of possible scenarios. Third, the evidence of the legislature's intentions can itself be conflicting and ambiguous or incomplete. Nevertheless, analysis tends to proceed as a debate either over what the legislature actually intended or what it would have intended had it thought about the particular issue before the court. The legislature, as an entity, is assumed to have a single joint intention, much like a basketball team can be said, as revealed by its actions, to have a team intention or goal. That group intention is attributed to the team by observers, even though individual team members may vary in their understandings of the group goal or their individual motivations for sharing it.

The truth is that it is often hard to say with any confidence that a legislature had, or would have had, a single clear legislative intention concerning a particular statute. Nevertheless, advocates will argue that there is such a singular intention, and courts will often divine one.

Another problem in determining a legislature's intention is that it can be stated at differing levels of generality. A legislature might have had a very specific expectation that a bicycle would *not* constitute a "vehicle" for purposes of a statute barring vehicles from a park. But the legislature might have the more general intention of keeping out as "vehicles" only devices creating danger to human life akin to that created by cars or trucks. Bicycles might not have created such a danger at the time that the statute was passed in 1901. But larger, faster bicycles today might arguably now create such a danger. Which intention should control: the specific expectation to exclude bicycles from the definition of "vehicles" or the broader intention (often called the statutory "purpose") to exclude devices creating a serious danger to human health and safety? Where the text of the statute does not clearly answer this question, lawyers and judges will differ. Some will argue that the legislature is like a commander, giving instructions to the future, brooking no deviation, and interpreting courts must follow the specific intention. But others will argue that the commander expects his instructions to allow field officers to have some discretion to further the very goals the commander (the legislature) sought to attain. Favoring broader statutory purpose better achieves the legislature's goals and prevents statutes from becoming quickly outmoded, an especially undesirable outcome, given the political difficulty of passing new legislation promptly or repealing old statutes.

The primary pieces of evidence as to legislative intent are these: (1) statutory text, (2) legislative and committee debates, (3) broader history, (4) administrative agency interpretations, and (5) the "rules" or "canons," which are in fact more like guidelines, of statutory interpretation. The "plain meaning" rule declares that the plain meaning of a statute's text ordinarily controls. But advocates will debate whether the meaning is plain in the first place. Text is always a starting point, but it is never the end point where the statute is ambiguous. Moreover, many courts reject plain meaning if it would lead to an absurd result. What is an absurd result? Courts rarely define the term, but it seems to mean a result that would seriously undermine the policy goals of the legislature. In such a circumstance, many courts assume that the legislature simply could not have intended a meaning contrary to the goals it sought to attain. Accordingly, these courts override plain meaning to replace it with a more practical or useful meaning. Dictionaries can be a helpful starting place to delineate the possible meanings of a word or phrase. But where the legislature intended a more technical (but not statutorily defined) meaning, more technical texts containing definitions (perhaps an engineering text if a mechanical engineer's terminology is used in the statute) will be consulted. Other sections of the same statute may help in giving a word meaning, as may the definitions in analogous statutes addressing similar subjects and using similar language.

II. LEGISLATIVE HISTORY, BROADER SOCIAL HISTORY, AND ADMINISTRATIVE REGULATIONS

Legislation usually begins in legislative committees. Those committees issue reports and hold hearings on the record (i.e., a court reporter records every word that is said). Subcommittees may also issue reports and hold hearings. Legislation eventually makes it to the full house of a legislature, there then being on the record debates among all the present legislators of that house. The other house of the legislature will next consider the same or a similar bill through a similar process. If the two houses pass slightly different bills, a conference committee will seek to reconcile them, issuing its own report explaining the compromise language. Both houses then vote to approve the compromise. All these reports, hearings, and debates are part of the history that can enlighten interpreters as to the legislature's intentions or purposes. Of course, these sources themselves often conflict with one another, or there may be conflicts within a single source. Two legislators in debate may express very different views of a statute's meaning. House reports and Senate reports may differ concerning the legislation's goals. Where this is so, each advocate must craft arguments that the pieces of evidence supporting their interpretations are deserving of greater weight than the pieces of evidence supporting their opponent's interpretation. Such arguments might be that one interpretation is, e.g., more consistent with committee reports, that the words of the original sponsor of the legislation matter more than those of an opponent, that changes made during political compromise are more consistent with one intended meaning than another, or that one set of views better responds to the underlying social problem than does another.

Indeed, examining what social problem prompted the legislation can be important too. If a particular criminal statute was designed to address a problem of fraud rather than of violence, that might affect the meaning given certain terms in the statute.

A statute might charge an administrative agency with passing regulations to implement a statute. Those regulations might clarify or enhance the meaning of certain statutory language. Sometimes courts defer to administrative agency understandings on grounds of their expertise in such matters, at least where the agency's choices do not clearly contradict statutory text or legislative history. Other times, an agency interpretation may have stood for years without the legislature seeking to change it, arguably raising an inference that the legislature therefore implicitly approved of the agency's interpretation.

III. CANONS OF INTERPRETATION

The canons of interpretation, also called the canons of construction, are presumptive rules about what legislatures intended. They are presumptive only, that is, absent countervailing evidence. One such rule is *"ejusdem generis:"* where general statutory language follows a series of specific statutory terms, the general language is assumed to be limited to the same class of items as are embodied in the more specific terms. For example, if a statute read, "No cars, trucks, mopeds, or other vehicles are allowed in this park," the general term "other vehicles" might reach anything that helps people move around more easily. That interpretation would include bicycles. But the three more specific terms preceding the general one all involve *motorized* vehicles (cars, trucks, and mopeds). *Ejusdem generis* requires limiting the general term "vehicles" to the same class, namely, to motorized vehicles, unless text or legislative history clearly suggests another meaning.

Another common canon is *"expressio unius est exclusio alterius,"* which means "the expression of one thing is the exclusion of another." For example, a statute prohibiting the transportation of illegal drugs from "noncustoms territory" to customs territory would not, under this maxim, prohibit the reverse flow of the drugs. The argument would be that the legislature obviously knew that drugs could flow both ways yet mentioned only one direction of flow, so its silence as to the other direction must have been intended to exclude from the statute's coverage that alternative direction. Again, however, other clear legislative history might trump this maxim.

A maxim or canon specific to the criminal law area is the "rule of lenity." This rule says that an ambiguous criminal statute (one with two or more potential meanings) should be given the meaning that most benefits the defendant. The theory behind the rule is that where human freedom is at stake, and where defendants accordingly deserve the clearest possible guidance about how to preserve their freedom, they deserve the benefit of the doubt when statutes are unclear. Of course, if this rule were mechanically applied to all ambiguous criminal statutes, defendants would automatically win every case where a statute is ambiguous. That does not occur. The rule is thus better understood as a default principle where all other sources of statutory interpretation fail to bring clarity. If examining text, legislative debates and reports, broader history, and other canons of interpretation do not readily resolve a dispute over meaning, the defendant should win that dispute.

Another canon is the "no surplusage" rule. That rule declares that the legislature is assumed not to intend that any language in a statute be "mere surplusage." In other words, whenever different language is used in different parts of a statute, readers should assume that the legislature intended the different words to mean different things. Moreover, every clause and word of a statute should be given effect, no word to be understood as merely repeating a concept already recited in another word.

One further relevant canon should be mentioned, namely that, wherever possible, statutes should be interpreted in ways that keep them consistent with constitutional demands. The theory here is that the legislature could not have intended a useless act, namely, the enactment of an unconstitutional statute. The constitution trumps statutes. One relevant constitutional principle often arising in criminal cases is the Due Process clauses' prohibitions on unduly vague statutes. Most statutes suffer from some ambiguity. But statutes that are so vague that they do not give fair notice to potential offenders about what conduct is prohibited or that do not adequately limit law enforcement discretion fail the due process test of fundamental fairness. Case law interpretations clarifying a statute help to avoid undue vagueness challenges. Indeed, few vagueness challenges are successful.

Related canons address broadly understood principles underlying our constitutional system. For example, a common canon is that a federal statute should not be interpreted to upset the traditional state-federal distribution of power concerning prosecuting crimes. The canon is rooted in ideas of federalism — that the states and the federal government each have distinct, though sometimes overlapping, roles to play in our constitutional system. Of course, the canon might also be rooted in specific constitutional provisions, but exploring that argument is unnecessary here. Thus, prosecutions for simple murder of persons not employed by the federal government is traditionally viewed as a matter reserved to the states. On the other hand, a murder of persons not employed by the federal government but committed by international terrorists aiming to overthrow the government of the United States would not likely infringe on traditional state prerogatives.

Two other pieces of background information specific to criminal statutes must be noted. First, with rare exceptions, almost all serious criminal statutes — those imposing potentially severe punishments — contain a *mens rea* or mental state requirement. Mental state is thus one element of a crime. Other potential elements are an act (a required voluntary bodily movement), a result (a fact, other than mental state or an act, that the defendant must cause to come about, such as death in murder), and an attendant circumstance (a fact, other than mental state or an act, that must exist to hold the defendant criminally liable but that he need not have caused to come about; for example, a burglary at old common law can only occur at "night," but the defendant does not cause night to fall). The severity of a crime is partly thought to be reflected in the seriousness of the mental state. Thus an intentional or purposeful killing (one done with the goal of killing the victim) is viewed as more serious or "culpable" than a knowing killing (one done with awareness of a practical certainty that the result will be the victim's death, even if the assailant had no desire to kill the victim). Likewise, a knowing killing is viewed as more culpable than a reckless killing (one done with the offender's conscious awareness that he would cause the victim's death), which is in turn more culpable than a merely negligent killing (one where the offender was not even aware of a risk of causing a death but should have been so aware). Because of this mental state/punishment proportionality concern, courts generally disfavor strict liability (no mental state required) under statutes silent about mental state where harsh punishments are imposed. Likewise, the courts tend to read ambiguous statutes as imposing higher mental states (and thus ones more difficult to prove), given higher punishments. Second, the state must prove every element of a crime beyond a reasonable doubt.

EXERCISE

Overview

Last March, around 4:00 a.m., five men met at an Arlington County, Virginia, cemetery to discuss robbing a nearby federally insured bank in Arlington, Virginia. These five men were Christopher Ash, Jonathan Paige, Randy Newman, Harold Gamble, and Tom Arnold. The men were each dressed in black, each wearing black gloves, and each carrying a black mask to use in the robbery. One of the men, Christopher Ash, had stolen a car that the entire group had used the day before to surveil the bank. The group planned to use the car as a means of getaway from the upcoming robbery. The group met in the car in the cemetery to finalize plans for the robbery, which was to occur as soon as the bank opened that morning, and to build up their courage for the robbery by drinking alcohol and using drugs. Each of the men held an unlicensed gun at his waistband. Jonathan Paige had a handwritten map of the bank in his back pocket. Although all the men were using drugs and drinking alcohol while listening to loud music on the car radio, Tom Arnold briefly left the group in the car to use cocaine, as he did not want to share it with his compatriots.

Shortly after Arnold left the car, Arlington County Officer David Corner drove his police car directly behind the stolen car, shining a spotlight on the men. Corner was patrolling the cemetery because he knew it to be a high-crime area for drug use and selling stolen vehicles. He exited the police car, with his gun drawn, walked up to the driver's window, shined a flashlight on the four men, and asked them what they were doing. The driver's seat passenger, Harold Gamble, offered an excuse for their presence. Corner backed up, heading toward his police car, saying that he wanted to check whether any of the men were wanted on warrants. The men, however, assumed that, upon seeing their clothing, Officer Corner caught them in the act of attempted robbery and was going to call for backup. As Officer Corner backed up, Arnold came up behind him and grabbed Corner's gun. Officer Corner looked at Arnold's face and immediately recognized him as someone whom the officer had arrested for robbery as a juvenile, a crime for which Arnold served time in a juvenile facility. The officer said, "Tom, you don't have to do this." Gamble got out of the car then, along with the other men, and Gamble said, "Ah, man, he knows who you are. Now we can't walk away from this thing." Paige said, "Give me the gun and I'll kill the copper; we got no choice now." Newman yelled, "I ain't going to jail; shoot him!" Arnold said, "You're right; we can't do more time." Arnold ordered the officer to his knees, and the officer complied. Arnold then shot the officer once in the back of his head, killing him instantly.

At first, investigators had no idea who had killed Officer Corner. They found his body in the cemetery, but no evidence linking anyone to the crime. When Gamble was later arrested on another murder charge, however, he confessed to all the above facts and offered to testify against Arnold in exchange for a recommendation of leniency from the prosecutor on both murder charges (the one on which Gamble had been arrested and the one involving Officer Corner).

The federal prosecutor, rather than any state or local prosecutor, filed charges against Arnold. A grand jury returned a "true bill" on a federal indictment against Arnold, containing two counts. Count One charged Arnold with murdering Officer

Corner with the intent of preventing him from communicating to a law enforcement officer information concerning the possible commission of federal offenses, thereby violating 18 U.S.C. §§ 1512(a)(1)(C) and (a)(3)(A), 1111, and 2. The relevant federal offenses were identified as conspiracy to rob a bank under 18 U.S.C. §§ 2113 and 371; possession of a firearm by a convicted felon under 18 U.S.C. § 922(g); and possession of cocaine and marijuana in violation of 21 U.S.C. § 844(a). Count Two charged Arnold with murdering Officer Corner in the course of using and carrying a firearm during and in relation to crimes of violence, thus violating 18 U.S.C. §§ 924(c)(1)(A) and (j)(1), 1111(a), and 2.

If Gamble's testimony is believed, there can be no serious doubt that Arnold intended to kill Officer Corner to prevent the officer from reporting the crimes to other law enforcement officers or to prosecutors (with the ultimate goal of filing criminal charges). However, the defense disputes whether there is adequate proof of all the *federal* offenses charged, particularly all the elements of 18 U.S.C. § 1512. The defense also plans to challenge Gamble's credibility at trial.

REQUIRED TASKS

Task One: Draft Jury Instructions

Assume that this case has gone to trial and both sides have rested. The only evidence offered at trial is that summarized in the above statement of facts. Before closing arguments, the judge asks to see both sides' attorneys in chambers to hear any motions for proposed jury instructions. Draft proposed instructions for the defense, then draft proposed instructions for the prosecution, concerning the meaning of Title 18, U.S.C. § 1512(a)(1)(C), reproduced below, and of any related sections. More specifically, the instructions should focus on what mental state must be proven beyond a reasonable doubt under this section to hold a defendant liable. Be ready to discuss in class the differences between the two instructions and the legal and strategic reasons for those differences.

In preparing for this task, review the supplemental material provided in the online component (pertinent statutes, legislative history, and optional caselaw). In addition, watch the suggested video clip, "Statutory Interpretation." Remember that this task, like all the others in this chapter, first requires you to craft arguments as to the statute's meaning, because that will control what the jury instructions must recite.

ESTIMATED TIME FOR COMPLETION: 60 minutes.

LEVEL OF DIFFICULTY (1 TO 5):

Task Two: Appellate Oral Argument; Jury Instructions

Now assume that the trial court denied the defense motion to use the defense version of the instructions in Task One, above. Instead, the trial court granted the prosecution's motion to use the prosecution's version of the instructions. The defendant was convicted of all charges and appeals his conviction under § 1512(a)(1)(C) on the grounds that the instruction given erroneously explained the statute's meaning. Be ready to engage in oral argument before the appellate court on this question. Your instructor will assign you to argue for the prosecution or for the defense. If you have not already reviewed the supplemental materials in the online component for Task One, do so now.

ESTIMATED TIME FOR COMPLETION: 90 minutes.

LEVEL OF DIFFICULTY (1 TO 5):

Task Three: Drafting Legislation

Next assume that you are on a Senate committee charged with redrafting § 1512(a)(1)(C) to clarify its meaning concerning the accused's mental state under circumstances like those raised in this problem. You will be assigned to small groups to serve as the staff to a Senator. The Senator wants the language to establish strict liability — no mental state whatsoever — as to whether the defendant was or should have been aware that the information to be reported would have specifically been reported to federal (rather than state, local, or other) authorities. Your group should debate the underlying issues and draft a clarified statute. Where there are group member disagreements on language, the will of the majority should control. Select from each group one member to serve as chief of staff to report to the Senator in class. Each chief of staff should be ready to respond to questions from the Senator or from other chiefs of staff about minority versus majority views and the reasons that certain language was ultimately chosen.

ESTIMATED TIME FOR COMPLETION: 60 minutes.

LEVEL OF DIFFICULTY (1 TO 5):

Task 4: Discovery Planning

Prepare a discovery plan focusing on challenging Gamble's credibility. Read the corresponding skills guide (Discovery Planning) before beginning this task.

ESTIMATED TIME FOR COMPLETION: 45 minutes.

LEVEL OF DIFFICULTY (1 TO 5):

PRACTICE SKILLS USED:

Skill 1: Drafting Jury Instructions

Skill 2: Appellate Oral Argument

Skill 3: Planning and Brainstorming

Skill 4: Drafting Legislation

Skill 5: Statutory Interpretation

Skill 6: Discovery Planning

SKILLS GUIDES

SKILLS GUIDE #1: Drafting Jury Instructions

The purpose of a jury instruction is to explain to the jury what is the law governing each aspect of the case before them. A tension is present in every jury instruction between accurately stating the law and doing so in a simple, clear way understandable to laypeople. The goal in drafting an instruction is to reconcile this tension: to prepare a legally correct instruction in laypersons' language, or at least one that, after reciting the legalese text, translates that text into understandable lay English.

Usually, not every portion of the law relevant to a case requires drafting new instructions from scratch. Jurisdictions commonly have court-approved "standard jury instructions." These instructions cover a wide array of common matters, such as the meaning of the "beyond a reasonable doubt" standard or the fact that the state, not the defense, has the burden of proving every element of a crime. But some legal issues are unique to an individual case, thus requiring drafting new jury instructions. Other times, an existing standard jury instruction must be molded to reflect unique or unusual circumstances present in a case. Alternatively, one side may view a standard instruction as legally incorrect, challenging its accuracy and arguing for an alternative. Furthermore, each side in a case may have a different view of what the new instruction should say. That possibility arises when the governing law, generally a statute, is ambiguous. Because the law is ambiguous, it must be interpreted and each side must raise arguments as to what the statute means. Each side submits its version of the proposed jury instruction to the trial judge. The trial judge might request memoranda from each side advocating its proposed instruction and explaining why the opponent's proposed instruction is unwise. The trial judge will usually hear oral argument, at least briefly, perhaps somewhat informally, in the judge's chambers, before ruling. The judge, based upon her own interpretation of the statute, will then either adopt one side's instruction, modify one side's instruction, combine aspects of each side's proposed instruction, or draft an entirely new instruction. The result will be the instruction read to the jury.

Some courts require each side to submit complete sets of instructions — every instruction required in a case. Again, this will usually result in most of the instructions being standard ones, but some instructions will be modified and new ones will be added for the reasons noted above.

One helpful way to begin drafting a new instruction is to find at least an analogous one to use as a model, sample, or starting point. But do not simply reproduce a model. First, the model probably does not address precisely the issue that you may want to raise. Second, many older models were drafted before the rise of the "plain language movement" and may not be understandable by laypersons. Third, models may be incomplete, too short to be helpful, or so long as to be confusing. Fourth, because new instructions are usually required for novel issues, the instructions must result from a serious effort at statutory interpretation that favors your client. In the current exercise, you are asked to draft a single, narrow instruction, but you cannot do so without first interpreting the statute.

It is important to remember the consequences that poorly drafted instructions can have for the finality of criminal litigation. If the defendant is acquitted because of an incorrect or confusing instruction and the defendant would in fact have been found guilty had a proper instruction been given, an injustice has occurred. Nevertheless, the double jeopardy clause of the U.S. Constitution prohibits retrying an acquitted criminal defendant. The conviction stands, and the prosecution may not appeal. But if the defendant is convicted, claiming that he would have been acquitted had a more accurate, complete, or clear jury instruction been used, he will file a motion for a new trial on that ground. Should the judge grant the motion, a new trial is precisely what will occur. That is an enormous unnecessary expense. Moreover, fading witness memories, witness deaths or unavailability, and related aggravated-by-the-passage-of-time issues may render the second trial's result untrustworthy or even make it impossible to retry the defendant at all. Even if the trial judge denies the motion for a new trial, an appellate court may disagree, remanding for that second trial. Many cases in basic criminal law courses turn precisely on such flaws in jury instructions. Compare that situation to one in which no flawed jury instruction or other flawed procedure occurred at trial. Instead, the defendant files a motion to overturn the conviction entirely based upon the insufficiency of the evidence, that is, based upon the argument that the prosecution's evidence was so weak or incomplete that no reasonable jury should have been able to convict him of the crime alleged beyond a reasonable doubt. If the judge agrees with that judgment, then the case is dismissed, and the defendant may not be retried.

SKILLS GUIDE #2: Appellate Oral Argument

There is an old aphorism that "you can't win your case in oral argument, but you can lose it." What does that mean? Oral argument is the last meaningful opportunity for the parties in a case to address the court. It is also breathtakingly short, measured in minutes (versus the days, weeks, months, and even years of the trial matters that preceded it). The parties have little time to do anything more than emphasize their most important points and answer any questions the appellate court may have. Appellate judges report that on occasion, oral argument has changed their minds about an appeal or, at least, altered the grounds upon which they decided. In addition, some lawyers are better at presenting their cases orally than in writing, and some appellate judges learn better by listening than reading. What may have seemed like a winning case on paper may look and sound quite different in the well of the appellate courtroom and while the arguments are underway.

Before one stands before an appellate bench to field the judges' questions, it is important to study the trial record. This includes all pleading and evidence or exhibits, as well as all briefs, cited authorities, legislative history, and any scholarly commentary. This time-consuming review should provide you with an opportunity to begin identifying and selecting the important issues that need to be mentioned at oral argument. This initial review of the record should also allow you to begin becoming familiar enough with the case on appeal to answer any question that the appellate panel may have.

After this thorough review (which will likely occur more than once before your appellate argument), become more focused on the key issues that must be raised during questioning. In selecting these issues, resist the temptation to simply follow the Roman numerals, captions, and section headings of your appellate brief filed with the court. Though your brief is your starting point and, at a minimum, you should be prepared for any questions on any of the issues raised in your (and your opponent's) brief, that structure is for the *written* word, not those that will be spoken orally. Besides, the structure of the brief is almost never going to predict or mirror the organization (as it were) of your oral argument. In fact, after further review of the record and case law, it often becomes apparent that the more favorable issues and arguments for your oral presentation are not the lead arguments in the brief, but minor ones or even ones that you may have missed at the time you wrote the brief.

Prepare a flexible presentation to the court next. The easiest questions that you should expect and prepare for begin with these: (1) What is the case about? (2) What relief do you seek? (3) Is there a rule you want the court to adopt to justify the court's holding? (4) Is there any other rule that would satisfy you? (5) How will the holding you want work? (6) What are the practical consequences of the holding/rule you want? (7) Would it change current practices? (8) How? (9) Can the court do what you ask? (10) How far does your rule go? (11) Why should the court do what you ask? (12) Why should the court do what your opponent asks? This is your attempt at anticipating the types of questions that the bench may ask. Anticipating the judges' questions will help lay the intellectual groundwork for weaving together planned remarks and responses to questions. This will also help you avoid awkward moments during oral argument, when you may, for example, lose your place or train of thought after a barrage of questioning.

After you have spent time anticipating the questions the bench may ask, it is time to prepare a flexible outline. The outline should begin with concise statements covering the following areas: (1) the appellate posture of the case, (2) all of the issues raised, and (3) the pertinent facts. Next, it should highlight the main issues that the attorney has selected after his or her thorough review of the appeal. The outline should contain points or some other form of concise statement that must be mentioned at oral argument. Rehearse the argument to improve its clarity and impact. A rehearsal will allow you to cut wishy-washy positions, long-winded explanations, lengthy quotations, detailed case discussion, and distracting verbal or other tics. Rehearsing will also allow you to make necessary points. Most will realize, after rehearing the argument two or three times, that it must be trimmed down.

Additionally, rehearsal will allow you to discover your strong and weak points before your oral argument. You may learn these by engaging in at least one moot court argument before the actual appearance before the appellate court. It is quite helpful to have moot courts with people who have not been involved in the case, and who are brought in with the express purpose to be skeptical, critical, and perhaps even hostile toward your position. It is easy for you to work on a case not thinking about what the weak points are in your argument. It is also easy for your to spend so much time strengthening your arguments, that you forget that there is another advocate on the other side who is preparing just as hard to win and who may have as good an argument — or better — than yours.

Participating in a moot court, then, will be tremendously helpful. Many attorneys argue to a moot court panel several times. The moot court should occur at least several days before the argument, to give you time to digest the suggestions of the moot court panel and to refine any arguments for the outline. First, the panel should hear the complete argument to assess its strength and clarity. Moot court members will see problems, including gestures or fidgeting, of which you may not be aware. Then, rehearse the argument, with the moot court panel present, without time limitations so that you can respond to all questions that emerge and develop affirmative points during those responses.

Finally, practice the argument within the time constraints of the actual argument. After the moot court session, you may want to refine and condense the oral argument outline. If there is time, try to listen to others' oral arguments if you can. Many courts (including the U.S. Supreme Court) now either live-stream or record (via audio or video) appellate arguments that you may study at your leisure from the comfort of your computer. This not only helps you with becoming familiar with judges' questioning styles, but also some of the more mundane, yet unnerving, matters (e.g., Where do you stand? Is there a place to put your notes?).

After all of the preparation comes the argument. Before you are calendared to argue, undoubtedly your appellate court will have made you aware of your argument's time and location, as well as other standard details relevant to your case. For example, the typical format of an appellate oral argument allots a certain amount of time (e.g., as few as 15 minutes; likely closer to 20 or 30) for each side to argue its side of the case. The party appealing the lower court's ruling, usually called the appellant or the petitioner, proceeds first.

In the argument, be prepared to answer questions. Appellate judges' biggest gripe is that lawyers dodge their questions. When judges ask questions, it does not necessarily indicate disagreement with your argument. Moreover, if you have prepared properly, you should not be surprised by any of the questions, and if the questions are off-base, then you have the opportunity to explain why they are off-base. It helps to really know the court you are arguing before, as you have to figure out why it is that a particular judge asked a particular question. Is it because they do not understand the case, or are they being an advocate? You have to be very adaptable to the circumstances.

Do not tell the court you will get to the answer later in your argument. This is the opportunity you have been waiting for, to engage in a dialogue with the appellate judges who will decide your appeal upon the issues that they think are important. Of course, if you don't know the facts of your case and the main cases on your legal points, you should not bother with oral argument. But if you are really caught off-guard by a question, you can request the opportunity to provide the court with the answer in a letter brief.

Do not give a speech or memorize your entire argument. You have already made your points in the brief. You should not have held anything back. The judges have read all the briefs. They do not want you to recite your brief to them. Instead, know the record. Know it cold. Never be forced to say, "I don't know. I was not the trial attorney" or "I am new to the office and was just assigned this case." Additionally, do not treat this argument like you are making a closing argument to the jury. Emotion plays a factor in deciding appeals, but the court must follow the rules of appellate review. The appellate court cannot reweigh the evidence on disputed factual issues. The court will reverse a judgment only if it is convinced that there was prejudicial legal error. Argument should focus on convincing the court of such error.

Remember that, although this is called an argument and an oral one at that, do not argue; instead, you should persuade. Remember that the bench is the decisionmaker. Getting into an argument with the bench, then, is not necessarily the best idea. Certainly, you may be passionate in an attempt to persuade; however, what you are actually doing is explaining to the bench what your position is and why it should prevail. That said, be realistic in your expectations of what you can achieve during an argument. You cannot persuade everybody. Accordingly, think more about what you hope to accomplish in an oral argument. You are there to talk about what the judges want to talk about, not what you think is important. It is important to know when to concede a weak point in your case and move on to the stronger ones. As the ultimate goal is to have the court rule in favor of your client or position, you may feel as if you must win on every point. That would be nice. However, the law and cases that are calendared for appellate argument usually are not that cut-and-dried. Slam dunks are the exception. Be candid; candor is critical with a court. Where accurate and relevant, acknowledge that your position can have adverse consequences and be candid about that, and express why the court should rule in your favor nonetheless. Being straightforward is always best. Front-load, i.e., beginning your answer to each question with a "yes, your Honor" or a "No, Judge," and then explain after that. Give the judges your bottom line answer first. This lets the court know you are not going to dodge the question. Even when that is not the most helpful answer, you go on to explain why it is not fatal to your case. If the judge asks if there are any other cases that support your position, if the answer is no, say so. Say: "No, this would be the first case to support the position I'm arguing. Nonetheless, I think it is correct, and here is why the court should decide this way in this instance."

In being candid and responsive, try not to become pushy. Do not interrupt. The temptation to jump in can be almost overwhelming, but let the appellate judge finish his or her question or comment, and let opposing counsel finish his or her entire argument. Oral argument is for answering the questions of the court, not forcing the court to listen to your argument that they already drafted, copied, triple-spaced, and color-coded. Submit or perish, as being in control — versus trying to control the argument — is a mistake. The goal is a conversation with the judges. You are trying to generate a high-level dinner table conversation with bright, quick, and interested attendees in an intimate, yet public, space. There will be interesting points, informative comments, and even humor at times. Draw them out and make them happy to hear from you. One sure way to do this is to get to the heart of the matter. Before the hearing, the appellate judges usually have read the briefs and a bench memo prepared by experienced staff attorneys addressing the facts and issues. Repeating the procedural history and background of the case is generally a waste of your very limited time.

An overwhelmingly important but often ignored point for appellate argument is also a simple one: listen. A lot of people prepare for oral arguments constantly worried about what judges may ask. It may feel too stressful at the time (which is why mooting your argument multiple times is important), but you should welcome questions from the bench. The questions are your greatest insight into the judges' minds. Approach arguments eager to see the way the judges are thinking. The brief writing is your time; however, the oral argument is the judges' time. Let the judges lead. Be in conversation where you talk about what the judges want to talk about. As soon as you perceive that a judge wants to ask a question, stop talking, set aside whatever point you were trying to make, and answer the question.

When the bench is cold, sit down. If that is the case, then oral argument is unlikely to be very important. Proceed to make the essential points and if there are no further questions, sit down. Do not overstay your welcome. If the court says it understands your points and would prefer to hear from the other side, this is almost always a good omen. Thank the court and save your time for rebuttal.

If you must refer to the court below, do not use the trial judge's name. Instead, refer to "the trial court." Remember that you are appealing from a judgment, not a judge. The appellate judges do not need to be told that judge so-and-so "embarrassed the bench" or "made a mockery of the legal process." Calm down. Do not make it personal. Similarly, try not to mention opposing counsel. Appellate judges are uninterested in personal animosity between lawyers.

The appellant/petitioner may reserve, if s/he wishes, a few minutes of his/her time to rebut the opponent's argument. After the appellant/petitioner's opening argument, the party who is not appealing the lower court's ruling, usually called the appellee or the respondent, delivers his/her argument. After the appellee/respondent's argument concludes, the appellant/petitioner delivers his/her rebuttal argument. After the rebuttal, the oral argument is over.

There are optional videos in the online component for this Skills Guide on oral argument at the appellate level.

SKILLS GUIDE #3: Planning and Brainstorming

Please refer to Chapter 1, Skills Guide #3.

SKILLS GUIDE #4: Drafting Legislation

Drafting legislation is not entirely unlike drafting jury instructions. The legislative drafter must know what goals he wants to achieve, then express them in language. Those goals require understanding what policies the legislator submitting the proposed legislation wants to achieve and any legal limitations on what policies the law can pursue and by what permissible means. The process thus requires first studying any relevant law while, simultaneously, studying any underlying factual or value disputes. Brainstorming (discussed briefly below) is usually helpful both in crafting the message you want the statute to convey and the precise language to convey it. Once draft language is prepared, further brainstorming in a group can spot missing items, ambiguous or confusing words, unnecessary words, needed definitions, unintended policy consequences, and imprecision. Brainstorming about hypotheticals and how they might be resolved under the draft statute can often reveal problems with the draft.

As with jury instructions, modern legislative drafting should aim to use clear, simple language that is easily understandable. Nevertheless, technical concepts, concepts deeply embedded in the law, and the sheer complexity of issues may lead to tolerating language that is somewhat less accessible to the layperson than is true of jury instructions. Jurors are, in a sense, part of the audience for a statute because they must eventually apply a law to a case's specific facts. But judges and lawyers stand ready to draft instructions to interpret the law in understandable ways for the jury. The law often engages in a fiction that statutes are available and can be read and understood by anyone. It is important to understand that, although this is a lofty and desirable goal, it is indeed a fiction. The usual people reading statutes will be lawyers. That is not license to draft ambiguous or confusing statutory language. But it alerts you that most readers will bring a set of assumptions to reading statutes, at least the knowledge commonly shared by all lawyers. Moreover, lawyers stand ready to pounce on incompleteness, technical inconsistencies, and ambiguities. A drafter should anticipate the kinds of problems a statute might raise for practicing lawyers to minimize, to the extent possible, "creative lawyering" that might undermine the purpose of the statute or lead to its invalidation as, for example, unduly vague under the Due Process Clauses of the Fifth and Fourteenth Amendments of the United States Constitution.

Also, as with jury instructions, legislative drafting might begin with a model. But the same sorts of cautions against undue reliance on a model that apply to drafting jury instructions should apply to drafting statutes. The model is a starting point, not an endpoint.

In this case, the ambiguity in the statute that has led to oral argument over how to interpret the law and how to draft an appropriate jury instruction must be resolved. The drafter's goal is to decide the underlying policy issue and draft a statutory provision that takes a stand on the issue, drafting language to avoid future ambiguities.

SKILLS GUIDE #5: Statutory Interpretation

The introduction to this chapter is itself a guide to statutory interpretation. Little more need be said here. One point must be stressed, however: interpreting statutes is like riding a bicycle: you improve only with practice. You must get in the habit of identifying the interpretive issue; reading statutory text closely; reading legislative and committee debates, hearings, and reports closely; and paying attention to underlying policy arguments and how they can advance or retard an interpretive argument in your client's favor.

SKILLS GUIDE #6: Discovery Planning

The details of how to conduct criminal discovery are covered in advanced criminal procedure courses or in clinics. Nevertheless, thinking about discovery is important early in a law student's career because finding evidence is critical to proving facts, and proving favorable facts is critical to winning in the application of the law. Interrogatories and requests for admission, used in civil cases, are unavailable in criminal cases because of the constitutional privilege against self-incrimination, which protects a criminal defendant from being compelled to give the equivalent of testimony against himself. For reasons of reciprocity, such discovery tools are also unavailable to the defense using them against the prosecution. Depositions of persons other than the criminal defendant himself are not routine in most jurisdictions, generally requiring the court's permission for them to occur. But, if needed, such permission can and should be sought. A few jurisdictions permit depositions as a matter of course in every case. Whether or not depositions are allowed, both sides are free to interview witnesses other than the criminal defendant, but it is up to each witness whether to cooperate. If any witness is represented by counsel, each side should ethically communicate only with counsel. A lawyer usually should not interview a witness alone but in the company of someone else who can testify about what was said at trial, if the need arises. A lawyer cannot generally be a witness in the same case in which he represents a client. Police also prepare reports, including summaries of witness interviews and photographs or diagrams of physical evidence. Forensic laboratories might prepare reports as well, for example, mentioning DNA or fingerprint comparison results. Usually, each jurisdiction has formal procedures available allowing defense attorneys to request and then receive copies (or at least examine the originals) of at least many of the police and laboratory reports. Subpoenas can also be used to order third parties to produce documents that might have useful information. Sometimes there are legal grounds for opposing subpoenas, but those grounds would take us beyond our goals here.

Discovery rules also address certain specific situations, such as getting reports of planned experts to be offered at trial or notifying an opponent of the names, addresses, and substance of planned alibi witnesses' testimony. These rules again are often reciprocal, meaning that if one side asks for the information, the other side can make a similar request. Some prosecutors' offices follow an "open file" policy in which they simply routinely hand over to the defense all, or most, documents in the prosecution's possession, though sometimes conditioning that policy on the defense providing certain information in its control to the prosecution. Other prosecutors resist such open file policies, fearing that they will lead to threats against witnesses, efforts to bribe them, or aid in the defendant's (now alerted to what prosecution witnesses will say) crafting convincing lies. Other prosecutors see such concerns as limited to special cases and view open file policies as simple fairness more likely to promote accuracy, justice, and even guilty pleas when defendants are confronted with a strong prosecution case.

The bottom line here is to use brainstorming to come up with a simple list of formal and informal discovery methods to be used, what information they will seek, from whom, and why. The list should make clear which witnesses (even if a name is not yet known or even whether the witness exists) you will wish to call to the stand as a result of your discovery efforts. The list should identify what evidence you hope to uncover from each of your efforts.

Chapter 3

ACTUS REUS

OVERVIEW

Actus reus is the Latin term for "guilty act." In criminal law, it is the conduct that must take place before an individual is subjected to criminal punishment. There must be an act — or a failure to act where there is a legal duty to act — before the government can properly charge a defendant with a crime. Our criminal justice system requires human conduct that is codified as wrong and leads to harm; we do not criminally punish for mere thoughts. One must do (or fail to do what is required) before we are comfortable with charging that person with a crime. The *actus reus* represents the important point at which the government can distinguish mere thoughts of criminal conduct from criminal conduct.

The *actus reus* is not just any act. The *actus reus* is defined by a jurisdiction's legislature as part of/an element of a prohibited course of conduct defined as a crime. Identifying the accused's act — or failure to act when legally required to do so — is often the first step in identifying a criminal defendant's crime.

Proving *actus reus*, then, is one of the predicate steps before imposing criminal culpability. Before we assign criminal culpability to one or more individuals, the criminal law requires that prosecutors identify the actor(s) who engaged in conduct that legislators have defined under the jurisdiction's laws as a crime.

I. VOLUNTARY ACTS

Voluntariness is an important factor in determining whether there is an *actus reus*. Before an accused can properly be said to have committed the *actus reus* of a crime, s/he must have acted voluntarily.

Our criminal justice system does not seek to punish involuntary bodily movements (e.g., seizures, convulsions, automatism, and reflexes) that lead to harm. Even when involuntary acts cause harm, the criminal law does not treat that actor as one who deserves criminal punishment. Punishing for acts that are involuntary is unfair. More practically, punishing involuntary acts would not deter the offender or others who commit similar involuntary acts. There is no criminal liability for involuntary acts because they are not the product of the actor's free will. In fact, under the criminal law, the defendant did not "act" at all.

Voluntary acts manifest the defendant's free will. Free will is critical in the criminal justice system's requirements.

So, where a criminal defendant shoots and kills a victim, the voluntary act — the defendant's *actus reus* in a charge of criminal homicide — would be the willed movements leading to the trigger being pulled so that the bullet is propelled into the victim's body, causing death.

Some acts may seem more voluntary than others. Additionally, there may also seem to be degrees of voluntariness in an actor's conduct. This can pose a dilemma, as criminal laws (federal and state) do not currently recognize what may be a gray area between voluntary and involuntary acts.[1] For example, although the Model Penal Code defines "act" and proclaims that a person is not guilty of a crime unless culpability "is based on conduct which includes a voluntary act," the Model Penal Code does not define "voluntary."[2] Instead, it lists involuntary acts: reflexes/convulsion, movements during unconsciousness, conduct during or via hypnotic suggestion, and conduct not a product of will or effort.[3] There is no "middle road."

Because classifying "quasi-involuntary" or "quasi-voluntary" acts as involuntary would lead to no criminal liability, courts maintain the either/or divide, often to preserve public safety. Courts do this by identifying a point in time — one that occurs before the harm-producing involuntary act — where the actor's voluntary act led to or spawned the involuntary one(s). So, for example, if a criminal defendant knows he sleepwalks when he takes certain medication with alcohol and, irrespective of the knowledge, ingests the combination, sleepwalks, and causes a hapless driver to swerve, strike and kill a bystander after the defendant unconsciously wanders into a busy intersection, courts will generally find voluntariness not in unconscious sleepwalking, but in the ingestion of the sleepwalk-causing combination, which triggered conduct that led to a social harm, e.g., the bystander's death.

II.   OMISSIONS

If, in the face of a legally imposed (not merely moral) duty the accused fails to do what the law requires, the *actus reus* is satisfied. When the accused chooses not to act when the law requires that s/he act, the failure is defined as an omission. When the law criminalizes a failure to act, the law has created a duty to act.[4] Doing nothing is enough to merit criminal charges and prosecution because the law required you to do something. In this case, omission *is* commission.

Our criminal justice system criminalizes omissions less than voluntary acts. Although punishing omissions is regarded as appropriate, legislators and judges are

---

[1] For example, those who are addicted to alcohol or other intoxicants are, increasingly, seen as having little to no free will regarding the ingestion of the addicting substance by, e.g., neuroscientists. Additionally, certain mental illnesses may affect a criminal defendant's neural transmitters and, accordingly, his/her free will and/or an ability to exercise it.

[2] Model Penal Code § 2.01(1).

[3] Model Penal Code § 2.01(2).

[4] For example, Model Penal Code Section 2.01(3) states that criminal culpability "may not be based on an omission" unless "the omission is expressly made sufficient by the law defining the offense."

more reluctant to punish those who choose not to act (and a harm occurs) than those who do act (and a harm occurs).[5]

Omissions are defined by statutes and are not identical across states or between the federal and state laws. The law may create a duty to act when there is a special relationship between individuals and organizations. Such special relationships include, but are not limited to, parent/child, spouse/spouse, contractual relationships (where the contract creates a duty to act), employer/employee, situations when the accused placed the victim in danger or harm's way, when the accused has isolated the victim (which prevents others from attending to him/her). Additionally, some modern statutes (e.g., the Model Penal Code) do not impose a legal duty to act if the accused is physically incapable of acting.[6] Locating the duty within one or more of the jurisdiction's statutes is key to identifying the basis upon which *actus reus* via omission can arise and be proven.

III. CAUSATION: THE LINK TO PROHIBITED SOCIAL HARM

For criminal punishment to be appropriate, the *actus reus* must also cause a prohibited social harm. Causation regards the relationship between the defendant's conduct and the harmful effect. It is the explanation of why, under the criminal law, a social harm occurred. Given our generally retributive criminal justice system, if we can trace the "why" back to one or more persons, we identify one or more individuals the government is willing to accuse as responsible and, eventually, prosecute as criminally culpable.

The law defines the social harm in a variety of ways; legislators codify criminal laws to protect and maintain social order. Violations of those criminal laws are regarded as social (versus personal) harm. This is true even when the harm involves only the accused and there is no injury or loss to persons, property, or interests (e.g., speeding). Social harm may be statutorily defined as a prohibited result (e.g., the social harm of murder is death of a human being), "antisocial" conduct (e.g., driving without a seat belt or texting while driving: though both can be done without physical harm, they are often defined by legislatures as social harms because they threaten and endanger our desire to live without such risky behavior), and attendant circumstances (e.g., common law burglary — the breaking and entering the dwelling house of another at nighttime to commit a felony therein — defines the attendant circumstance — dwelling house of another — the breaking and entering of which constitutes social harm).

A criminal defendant's *actus reus* can be said to cause a prohibited social harm when one of two tests is applied. The first test is the "but for" test. It is satisfied when the social harm would not have occurred but for the accused's voluntary act or omission. The second test is the substantial factor test. This test is not used as much, because it

---

[5] A most common example of a legal duty to act is speeding. Posted speed limits create a duty to act (do not exceed, e.g., 55 m.p.h.). Failure to act as the law requires (driving at, e.g., 65 m.p.h.) is criminally punishable. *See, e.g.*, Model Penal Code § 2.01(1).

[6] *See* Model Penal Code § 2.01(1).

requires two (or more) actors, independently engaging in simultaneous conduct sufficient to bring about the harmful result alone, that operate together to cause the social harm. Under these rare circumstances, causation is satisfied if the accused's conduct is a substantial factor in bringing about the social harm.

Determining that the defendant is an actual cause of a prohibited social harm is the start of finding criminal culpability; however, it is not the end. The prosecution must also prove that the defendant was the legal cause of the prohibited social harm. This is done by proving that the defendant was either the direct or proximate cause of the prohibited social harm.

Direct causation is determined when there are no intervening factors or actors between the defendant's conduct and the prohibited social harm. Proximate causation is determined when the prohibited social harm is caused by an intervening factor or actor. Specifically, where the prohibited social harm is produced by an intervening force (factor or actor), the criminal culpability of the one who put an antecedent force in motion will depend on whether the intervening force was a sufficiently independent or supervening cause. Courts distinguish cases in which the intervening act was a coincidence from those in which it was a response (to the defendant's antecedent force). An intervening act is a coincidence when the defendant's act merely put a victim at a certain place at a certain time and — given that the victim was located in that particular place — it was possible to be acted upon by the intervening cause. By contrast, an intervening act may be said to be a response to the prior actions of the defendant when it involves a reaction to the conditions created by the defendant. In jurisdictions that assess proximate causation, a coincidence will break the chain of legal cause unless it was foreseeable. A response will break the chain of legal cause only if it is abnormal.[7]

Not all jurisdictions assess the causal relationship between the *actus reus* and the prohibited social harm via a common law proximate causation analysis. The Model Penal Code and a number of states speak in terms of criminal culpability via factors such as remoteness, independent forces, foreseeability, and the relationship (or remoteness) between conduct and result.[8]

IV. FAILURE OF PROOF DEFENSE TO *ACTUS REUS*

It is a long-standing principle of American law that in order to convict an individual of a crime, the government must prove every element of the crime beyond a reasonable doubt. The principle that a defendant cannot be convicted of an offense in the absence of proof of every element of the definition of the charged crime(s) is referred to as a "failure of proof" defense. A failure of proof defense is, generally, a criminal defendant's refutation of guilt based on the government's inadequate evidence. Failure

---

[7] *See* Kibbe v. Henderson, 534 F.2d 493, 499 n.1 (2d Cir. 1976).

[8] For example, Model Penal Code Section 2.03(1) states that conduct is the cause of a result when it is the antecedent but for which the result in question would not have occurred and the relationship between the conduct and result satisfies any additional causal requirements imposed. When the actual result differs from the contemplated or risked result, causation may still be found based upon and in accordance with the statutorily identified mental state of culpability. See Chapter 4, *Mens Rea Basics* for details.

of proof defenses involve the defendant's contention that the prosecution has not satisfied its burden and that the government failed to provide evidence of one or more required elements of the charged crime.[9]

Under a typical *actus reus* failure of proof defense, for example, the defendant highlights the weaknesses, inconsistencies, or gaps in the government's evidence. In doing so, the defendant creates a reasonable doubt in the factfinder's mind (one or more jurors in a jury trial, the judge in a bench trial). So, when the defendant attacks the prosecution's *actus reus* evidence via a failure of proof defense, the defendant challenges the sufficiency and quality of the prosecution's evidence that the defendant voluntarily acted or failed to act when s/he was legally required to act. In doing so, the defendant can highlight evidence of involuntariness to show s/he lacked the *actus reus*. In the case of an omission, the defendant can highlight evidence that s/he had no legal duty to act to show that s/he lacked the *actus reus*. (For more on failure of proof defenses, quickly review Chapter Five, Mens Rea Complications and Failure of Proof Defenses.)

---

[9] *See, e.g.*, Model Penal Code § 1.2(1) (requiring all elements of an offense be proved beyond a reasonable doubt for a person to be held criminally responsible).

EXERCISE

Overview

Stanley, while driving down a residential street, observed Browne driving toward him in an unsafe manner. Hoping to avoid an accident, Stanley pulled his car over to the curb and came to a complete stop. However, as Browne began to pass, he hit Stanley's car, clipped a tree, and crashed into a ditch.

Five minutes later, when police arrived at the scene, they performed field sobriety tests on Browne. Browne failed the tests and confessed to the police that he had been drinking. Subsequently, the police took Browne to the local hospital where a nurse drew blood and discovered that his blood-alcohol content measured .09. Browne was placed in custody and charged with Driving While Intoxicated ("DWI").

At trial, the government introduced into evidence Stanley's eyewitness testimony, police officer testimony of what he observed post-accident at the scene, emergency responder and hospital medical personnel testimony, and the blood-alcohol test results in their case-in-chief against Browne.

Browne, after consulting with his defense attorney, decided to take the witness stand and testified on his own behalf. On the stand, Browne testified that he had consumed two tumblers of whiskey the night of his arrest. Sometime during the night, Browne awoke to take his nightly blood pressure medicine. However, instead of the blood pressure medicine, Browne testified that he mistakenly took Ambien, a common sleep aid that requires a doctor's prescription. Browne further testified that, because of his mistake, he did not remember driving his car. In fact, Browne claimed that he had no memory from the time he took the Ambien up to and until the nurse drew his blood.

During cross-examination by the state's prosecutor, Browne testified that the Ambien pills (white and round) were an entirely different color and shape than his blood pressure pills (green and oblong). On cross-examination, Browne also testified that he had been sternly warned by his doctor not to take Ambien in combination with alcohol.

REQUIRED TASKS

Task One: Motion Writing

Assume that you represent Browne in the above matter. At the close of the prosecution's case-in-chief, you make an oral motion for judgment of acquittal (MJOA) to dismiss the government's criminal case because it failed to prove an *actus reus*. The trial judge, however, requests that you place your oral motion and its supporting arguments in writing. Prepare an MJOA on behalf of Browne. You should use the law provided below to guide you in your argument that the government's criminal case against Browne should be dismissed and that he should be acquitted.

In preparing for this task, see the sample MJOAs in the online component for this Chapter. Remember that this task requires you to craft arguments as to the statutes' meaning, for that will control what the MJOA must address in claiming the government's failure of proof, specifically failure to prove an *actus reus*. Accordingly, review the jurisdiction's substantive law (both case and codified) provided below and in the online component regarding the charge of DWI. You should also use an online database to read the following cases:

- *Rogers v. State*, 105 S.W.3d 630 (Tex. Crim. App. 2003)
- *Williams v. State*, 630 S.W.2d 640 (Tex. Crim. App. 1982)
- *Hanks v. State*, 542 S.W.2d 413 (Tex. Crim. App. 1976)
- *Hearne v. State*, 80 S.W.3d 677 (Tex. App. 2002)
- *Lewis v. State*, 951 S.W.2d 235 (Tex. App. 1997)
- *Nelson v. State*, 149 S.W.3d 206 (Tex. App. 2004)
- *Torres v. State*, 585 S.W.2d 746 (Tex. Crim. App. 1979)

ESTIMATED TIME FOR COMPLETION: 90 minutes.

LEVEL OF DIFFICULTY (1 TO 5):

Task Two: Drafting Jury Instructions

Unfortunately for Browne, the trial judge denied your MJOA. Just before you and the prosecutor make closing arguments, the judge asks if either of you has any specific requests for jury instructions. You respond "yes" and request that the judge instruct the jury on "involuntary intoxication." The judge asks that you draft an appropriate jury instruction that will accurately capture and reflect the state's law.

In preparing for this task, see the supplemental materials regarding jury instructions in the online component for this exercise. Remember that this task, like all the others in this chapter, first requires you to craft arguments as to the statutes' meaning, for that will control what the jury instruction will, in accordance with the law, request. Accordingly, review the jurisdiction's substantive law (both case and codified) provided in the online component, and, if you have not done so already, use an online database to read the cases listed above for Task One.

ESTIMATED TIME FOR COMPLETION: 90 minutes.

LEVEL OF DIFFICULTY (1 TO 5):

PRACTICE SKILLS USED:

Skill 1: Motion Writing

Skill 2: Legal Argument; Integrating the Law and the Facts

Skill 3: Drafting Jury Instructions

Skill 4: Tactical Thinking

Skill 5: Motion Writing; Motion for Judgment of Acquittal (MJOA)

SKILLS GUIDES

For supplemental material relevant to the skills practiced in this Exercise, see the materials provided in the online component.

SKILLS GUIDE #1: Motion Writing

Please refer to Chapter 8, Skills Guide #1.

SKILLS GUIDE #2: Legal Argument; Integrating the Law and the Facts

Please refer to Chapter 8, Skills Guide #2.

SKILLS GUIDE #3: Drafting Jury Instructions

Please refer to Chapter 2, Skills Guide #1.

SKILLS GUIDE #4: Tactical Thinking

Please refer to Chapter 1, Skills Guide #4.

SKILLS GUIDE #1: Motion Writing; Motion for Judgment of Acquittal (MJOA)

A trial court can enter a judgment of acquittal in both state and federal courts if the prosecution fails to introduce sufficient evidence from which a reasonable jury could find proof beyond a reasonable doubt. In order to make a motion for acquittal, all counsel needs to do is allege that the evidence is insufficient to sustain a conviction. No other reasons or grounds need be stated. MJOAs are generally oral and often considered perfunctory. However, where there is a significant legal question that must be decided in order to determine if the prosecution introduced sufficient proof on each element, consider filing a short written motion. A written motion requesting a judgment of acquittal can send a signal that there is a real issue in the case. Writing it also helps prevent the common mistake of forgetting to argue a point while on your feet.

To be successful, the MJOA should allege more than that the prosecution's proof failed. The issue is whether the prosecution has introduced sufficient proof on each element of the offense. As such, a MJOA is fact-dependent. That does not mean, however, that the legal standard should be ignored. In order to determine whether the prosecution has introduced sufficient proof on each and every element, it is necessary to determine what the elements are. Therefore, the legal standard can sometimes be the most important section in a motion for judgment of acquittal. In fact, judgment of acquittal is probably most common when the prosecutor and the judge do not agree on the elements of the offense.

How do you draft an effective written MJOA? The best time to prepare a written motion is when jury instructions are being drafted. Counsel will be researching the elements anyway, and the requested jury instructions can be incorporated into your MJOA.

Make it short. As Justice Scalia pointedly advises, the amount of time a judge spends reading a brief is often inversely proportionate to its length. While it should not be a tome, if there is strong authority indicating that the case should not proceed, it should be set out in writing.

When you begin to write, keep in mind to whom you are writing and speak to that audience. Additionally, you should also keep in mind your secondary audiences (e.g., a supervisor, a reviewing court on appeal). It is entirely possible (and in some cases, likely or desirable) for another judge or judges to review your motion and the trial court's ruling on it.

Identify your motion's objective(s). The motion's job is to explain to the court the purpose and necessity of the motion, justify the motion's request for relief, elaborate on the rational for the requested relief, and persuade the court that it appropriately has (via the motion) the legal bases upon which to grant the motion. The motions drafter has to understand the problem (e.g., the government failed to prove one or more elements beyond a reasonable doubt), request the proposed solution (e.g., dismissal), and be conversant regarding the legal issues or problems connected with the solution (because there will be argument against the motion by the opposing attorney). You must bring your understanding to your motion and communicate why it should be the understanding that prevails. Usually, organize your motion's legal arguments based on the statutory language or rule of law; these will often provide the necessary, most consistent, and most helpful organization. Sometimes, however, your strongest legal argument may come later or is buried deeper within the statute's provisions. Do not worry. You will almost certainly want to start with your strongest point and move toward your weakest (or omit the weakest point altogether).

If you have multiple arguments or legal points to make, divide and identify the motion's argument sections into subparts. Create a definitive, declarative statement to head each section, announcing that part of the argument to your reader. Again: keep it short and simple; shorten the sentences and omit unessential points. Keep the paragraphs short and to the point. If there is a need for additional argument, you may either request oral argument (which is, more accurately, a question and answer session with the judge) or it will be requested of you and your opponent.

As in any legal document, provide your reader references where necessary, directing them to the specific page numbers ("pin cites" or "pin citations") upon which your argument relies. Conclude your motion with the requested relief from the trial judge. Do not be shy; ask for exactly what you want from the judge.

ADDITIONAL MATERIALS FOR THE EXERCISE — AVAILABLE IN ON-LINE COMPONENT

TEX. PENAL CODE ANN. § 6.01: Requirement of Voluntary Act or Omission

TEX. PENAL ANN. § 6.04: Causation: Conduct and Results

TEX. PENAL CODE ANN. § 49.01: Definitions

TEX. PENAL CODE ANN. § 49.04: Driving While Intoxicated

Chapter 4

MENS REA BASICS

Mens rea refers to the cognitive, mental component of a crime. Specifically, the *mens rea* describes the blameworthy mental state associated with criminalized conduct. For practical purposes, it is the state of mind that the prosecution must prove a defendant had when committing a crime. We do not criminally punish mere thoughts. Rather, and as the U.S. Supreme Court explained in *Morrissette v. United States*, "crime, [i]s a compound concept, generally constituted only from concurrence of an evil-meaning mind with an evil-doing hand."[1] The *mens rea* is determined when the actor's mental state coincides with his *actus reus* (*see* Chapter 3). The *mens rea* requirement is satisfied when, at the time the actor committed the *actus reus*, the government proves that the actor possessed the requisite mental state required by law.

Mens rea is not the same thing as motive. The *mens rea* refers to the mental state with which the defendant acted when committing a criminal act. Motive refers to the reason why the defendant committed his entire criminal act. For example, if D purposely kills V, that means D wanted V dead. Purpose is the mental state. But there could have been many potential motives for having that mental state: D's jealousy of V dating another man, D's being able to inherit money from V under V's will once V is dead, or D's hating V for winning an award to which D believed D was entitled.

Proving an intangible thing such as a "guilty mind" — the literal meaning of *mens rea* — is easier said than done, especially where the standard is proof beyond a reasonable doubt. Courts over time have commented on the difficulty of a proper definition of the *mens rea* required for any particular crime. Perhaps the day will come when science and technology will allow for the discernment of thoughts with certainty. For now, we must rely on circumstantial evidence, because direct evidence of the accused's state of mind is rarely available. Even a confession is circumstantial evidence because the person confessing might be lying, hallucinating, coerced, or confused.

At common law, *mens rea* fell into two categories: general intent and specific intent. But the distinction between these two concepts is confusing. Different courts, sometimes even different judges in the same jurisdiction, define the term differently. Sometimes they use the terms without defining them, leaving lawyers to guess at the intended meaning. Confusion reigns, and this can be especially difficult for those new to the study of criminal law. One common and useful definition of "specific intent," restated in a non-technical fashion, is this: a specific intent is a desire to bring about a state of affairs that is not an element of the crime. With these crimes, the *actus reus* is done with the objective of accomplishing a particular result. But the result itself

---

[1] Morissette v. United States, 342 U.S. 246, 251 (1952) (emphasis added).

need not be achieved to prove the crime. So, for example, common law burglary is a specific intent crime, as it prohibits the trespassory breaking and entering of the dwelling house of another at night *with the intention to commit a felony therein.* (Some common law jurisdictions instead require merely an intention to commit any crime therein, rather than only a felony.) The defendant need not, however, succeed in committing a felony therein. He may or may not do so. Yet he is guilty so long as he wanted to commit a felony inside the home at the time that he broke and entered into it without the owner's consent. It is, therefore, not enough that a defendant had the intention or purpose to do something. The thing that he wanted to do must not itself be an element of the crime if that intention is to be labeled "specific intent." Common law larceny offers another example. Common law larceny prohibits trespassory taking and carrying away of the personal property of another *with the intent to permanently deprive the owner* of the property. The defendant need not succeed in permanently depriving the owner. That is not an element of the crime. He just has to want to succeed. Thus, a defendant who steals a car planning to use it forever as his own but who is caught, the car being returned to its owner, has failed in his plan to achieve the result of permanently depriving the owner of the property. Nevertheless, because the thief wanted permanently to deprive the owner, that is sufficient to render the thief guilty of larceny.

A general intent crime is everything that is not a specific intent crime. More precisely, a general intent crime is one where the relevant mental state or mental states relate to other elements (non-mental state elements: the act, attendant circumstance, or result). So, unlike with a specific intent crime, all the things that are desired must, in fact, occur. Thus, imagine the following crime: "It is a felony intentionally (purposely) and trespassorily to enter the dwelling house of another." This type of crime is often called "criminal trespass." Notice that it requires intent. But the things that you must intend — entering another's home without their permission — must in fact occur. It is different from burglary because wanting one of these things is not enough. They must all actually happen. Intent is thus a necessary but not a sufficient condition to label a crime "specific intent." The intent must be to bring about something that need not happen — that is not itself an element of the crime — in order for the intent to be "specific." Any other intent is general.

Crimes involving mental states less culpable than intent are usually also general intent crimes. Thus, common law rape generally required a merely negligent mental state by the defendant in believing that the woman consented. In other words, if a defendant unreasonably believed that the woman consented to sexual intercourse, the defendant would have the mental state necessary to be convicted of rape. That mental state would be one of general intent.

The purported policy justification for the specific versus general intent distinction is that specific intent crimes are worse than general intent crimes of the same class. Thus, criminal trespass is bad, but trespassing with the purpose of committing a crime such as rape upon entry (burglary) is worse even if you never commit that crime. It is worse because it shows that the defendant is both more morally culpable and more dangerous than the simple trespasser. Specific intent crimes thus generally receive harsher sentences than general intent crimes.

The common law also varied certain substantive rules of criminal law based upon whether those rules were applied to a general or specific intent crime. For example, the rules for when "mistake of fact" is a defense (discussed in a later chapter) are different when applied to a general intent versus a specific intent crime.

This distinction, however, has been the source of much confusion, and legal reform began to replace this dichotomy with an alternative analysis, thanks to the American Law Institute's Model Penal Code and its approach in delineating — while streamlining — the mental states associated with criminal culpability. Broadly and at common law, *mens rea* was synonymous with blameworthiness, i.e., conditions that make a person's behavior sufficiently wrong or culpable to merit criminal conviction condemnation. Today, *mens rea* describes the required mental state of mind — along with the codified *actus reus* — that defines a criminal offense. Except for certain minor or strict liability (*see* below) offenses, jurisdictions require that there be a specified *mens rea* for a criminal offense. It is important to recognize, however, that mental state can embrace cognitive or intellectual thinking and affective or emotional thinking. As one illustration, the common law declares one of the elements of voluntary manslaughter to be acting in the "heat of passion," an emotion. Model Penal Code ("MPC") manslaughter embraces a broader array of emotions than just heat of passion. Acting with "knowledge," however, has more of an intellectual component than an emotional one, such as being aware of a practical certainty that your actions will kill someone — regardless of how you feel about the matter.

The Model Penal Code (MPC) embodies the modern meaning and distinguishes the concept of *mens rea* from the common law by substituting the term "culpability" for "*mens rea*."[2] The MPC simplified common law offenses in two significant, radical ways: (1) it limited *mens rea* to only four (versus the common law's numerous) mental states: purpose, knowledge, recklessness, and negligence and (2) it adopted an elemental analysis. The highest level of MPC culpability is "purposely." A person acts "purposely" if it is his/her "conscious object to engage in conduct of that nature or to cause such a result."[3] The next level of MPC culpability is "knowingly." A person acts "knowingly" if s/he is "aware that his conduct is of that nature" and "practically certain that [his/her] conduct will cause such a result."[4] The next MPC culpability level is "recklessly." A person acts "recklessly" if s/he "consciously disregards a substantial and unjustifiable risk" that is "a gross deviation from the standard of conduct that a law-abiding person would observe in the actor's situation."[5] Finally, under the MPC, a person acts "negligently" if s/he is unaware of a substantial and unjustifiable risk of which s/he should have been aware and that the "failure to perceive it . . . involves a gross deviation from the standard of care that a reasonable person would have observed in the actor's situation."[6]

Nearly all states have adopted the MPC culpability language, verbatim, largely, or

---

[2] *See* MODEL PENAL CODE § 2.02.

[3] *See* MODEL PENAL CODE § 2.02(2)(a).

[4] *See* MODEL PENAL CODE § 2.02(2)(b).

[5] *See* MODEL PENAL CODE § 2.02(2)(c).

[6] *See* MODEL PENAL CODE § 2.02(2)(d).

in part. Some have adopted the MPC legislative history and interpretation when assessing the state's own provisions or when engaging in statutory interpretation. The Multistate Bar Examination tests the MPC's states of mental culpability and, because again, states have fully or partially adopted the code's provisions, applicants are tested on the MPC during the essay and (where relevant) performance portions of many state Bar examinations. These facts make the MPC a highly influential body of law, relevant beyond a first year Criminal Law class.

Finally, it is important to understand that a criminal statute is not faulty or unenforceable solely because it does not contain a *mens rea* element. Such crimes are designated "strict liability" offenses. Strict liability crimes do not require proof that the *actus reus* of the offense be committed with any *mens rea*; rather, the crimes are *malum prohibitum* crimes, i.e., criminal because they have been criminalized and constitute so-called "public welfare offenses." There are also *malum in se* (inherently wrong) crimes that are strict liability; however, there is a presumption against such crimes omitting a culpability element. Still, these crimes do not contain a *mens rea* element, given public policy concerns (e.g., statutory rape is more concerned about preservation of children and their bodily integrity than adult perpetrators).

The Model Code does not jettison strict liability crimes; rather, it limits them to "civil offenses," i.e., violations punishable only by fine, forfeiture, or other civil penalty. They also include offenses defined by statutes other than the Code where legislative purpose plainly intended absolute liability.[7]

---

[7] *See* MODEL PENAL CODE § 2.05(2).

EXERCISE

Strategies to Prepare: If you prepared the tasks in Chapter 3, you may notice that Chapter 4 provides you with an identical overview as that found in Chapter 3, as well as similar case and codified law. However, in Chapter 4, you are required to make different legal arguments. This is not unusual in the "real life" practice of law. Law school casebooks seek to introduce relevant legal concepts without too many complications. They often do so by presenting one legal proposition or concept per case, excerpt, or chapter. Although helpful to your early learning, the practice can also be a bit misleading. Criminal law (and other) cases often present multiple and overlapping issues.

This chapter's overlapping and distinct tasks based upon the same facts and law are much more consistent with what happens in real life and legal practice. In practice, you do not have the luxury before a senior colleague or a judge to shrug off the "additional" issues or "different" legal analysis required. Your job is to work with the law and facts to come to cogent legal conclusions via anticipatory issue-spotting. That anticipatory issue-spotting allows you to present legally sound conclusions or relevant questions that may lead to legally sound conclusions as well as the satisfactory disposition of the case in its entirety.

Accordingly, begin to train yourself to look beyond one issue or holding. Begin also to train yourself to identify the different areas of law that may be present in criminal law (and other) fact patterns (e.g., when identifying whether the state may bring a criminal assault case against a defendant, assess also the possibility of the victim bringing a civil law assault case against the defendant). These are good habits to get into, given the reality of legal practice.

Overview

Stanley, while driving down a residential street, observed Browne driving toward him in an unsafe manner. Hoping to avoid an accident, Stanley pulled his car over to the curb and came to a complete stop. However, as Browne began to pass, he hit Stanley's car, clipped a tree, and crashed into a ditch.

Five minutes later, when police arrived at the scene, they performed field sobriety tests on Browne. Browne failed the tests and admitted to the police that he had been drinking. Subsequently, the police took Browne to the local hospital where his blood-alcohol content measured .09. Browne was placed in custody and charged with Driving While Intoxicated ("DWI").

At trial, the government introduced evidence of Stanley's eyewitness testimony, police officer testimony of what he observed post-accident at the scene, emergency responder and hospital medical personnel testimony, and the blood-alcohol test results into evidence in their case-in-chief against Browne.

Browne, after consulting with his defense attorney, decides to take the witness stand and testifies on his own behalf. On the stand, Browne testified that he had consumed two tumblers of whiskey the night of his arrest. Sometime during the night, Browne awoke to take his nightly blood pressure medicine. However, instead of the blood pressure medicine, Browne testified that he mistakenly took Ambien, a common sleep aid that requires a doctor's prescription before disbursement. Browne further testified that, because of his mistake, he did not remember driving his car (which he had). In fact, Browne claimed that he had no memory from the time he took the Ambien up to and until the local hospital nurse drew his blood.

During cross-examination by the state's prosecutor, Browne testified that the Ambien pills (white and round) were an entirely different color and shape from his blood pressure pills (red and oblong). On cross-examination, Browne also testified that he had been sternly warned by his doctor not to take Ambien in combination with alcohol.

REQUIRED TASKS

Task One: Motion Writing

Assume that you represent Browne in the above matter. At the close of the prosecution's case-in-chief, you make an oral motion for judgment of acquittal (MJOA) to dismiss the government's criminal case because it failed to prove beyond a reasonable doubt the *mens rea* requirement. The trial judge, however, requests that you place your oral motion and its supporting arguments in writing. Prepare a written MJOA on behalf of Browne.

You should use the law provided below to guide you in your argument that the government's criminal case against Browne should be dismissed and that he should be acquitted. Additionally, in preparing for this task, you also should consult the supplemental materials for Task One found in the online component (that distinguish *mens rea* from *actus reus*).

Additionally, you should also use an online database to read the following cases for guidance regarding the application of the substantive law in this task:

- *Aliff v. State*, 955 S.W.2d 891 (Tex. App. 1997)
- *Hanks v. State*, 542 S.W.2d 413 (Tex. Crim. App. 1976)
- *Hearne v. State*, 80 S.W.3d 677 (Tex. App. 2002)
- *Nelson v. State*, 149 S.W.3d 206 (Tex. App. 2004)
- *Peavey v. State*, 248 S.W.3d 455 (Tex. App. 2008)
- *Solomon v. State*, 227 P.3d 461 (Alaska Ct. App. 2010)
- *Torres v. State*, 585 S.W.2d 746 (Tex. Crim. App. 1979)

Remember that this task, like all the others in this chapter, first requires you to craft arguments as to the statutes' meaning, because that will control what the MJOA must address in claiming the government's failure of proof. Accordingly, review the skills guides the jurisdiction's substantive criminal law (both case and codified) provided in the online component regarding the charge of DWI.

ESTIMATED TIME FOR COMPLETION: 90 minutes.

LEVEL OF DIFFICULTY (1 TO 5):

Task Two: Motion Writing

Now assume you are the prosecutor in this matter. Rebut and refute Browne's MJOA by drafting the government's opposition to defendant's MJOA. This will, necessarily, require you either to pair with a classmate who has written Browne's MJOA and/or anticipate what Browne's attorney will argue. Remember that this task, like all the others in this chapter, first requires you to craft arguments as to the statutes' meaning, because that will control what the MJOA opposition must address. Accordingly, if you have not done so already, review the skills guides below and the jurisdiction's substantive law (both case and codified) provided in the online component regarding the DWI charge. Additionally, in preparing for this task, you also should consult the items found in the online component of this text (which include sample MJOA Oppositions).

ESTIMATED TIME FOR COMPLETION: 90 minutes.

LEVEL OF DIFFICULTY (1 TO 5):

Practice Skills Used:

 Skill 1: Motion Writing

 Skill 2: Legal Argument; Integrating the Law and the Facts

 Skill 3: Tactical Thinking

 Skill 4: Motion Writing; Motion for Judgment of Acquittal (MJOA)

SKILLS GUIDES

For supplemental material relevant to the skills practiced in this Exercise, see the materials provided in the online component.

SKILLS GUIDE #1: Motion Writing

Please refer to Chapter 8, Skills Guide #1.

SKILLS GUIDE #2: Legal Argument; Integrating the Law and the Facts

Please refer to Chapter 8, Skills Guide #2.

SKILLS GUIDE #3: Tactical Thinking

Please refer to Chapter 1, Skills Guide #4.

SKILLS GUIDE #4: Motion Writing; Motion for Judgment of Acquittal (MJOA)

Please refer to Chapter 3, Skills Guide #1.

ADDITIONAL MATERIALS FOR THE EXERCISE — AVAILABLE IN ON-LINE COMPONENT

TEX. PENAL CODE ANN. § 6.02: Requirement of Culpability

TEX. PENAL CODE ANN. § 6.03: Definitions of Culpable Mental States

TEX. PENAL CODE ANN. § 49.01: Definitions

TEX. PENAL CODE ANN. § 49.04: Driving While Intoxicated

TEX. PENAL CODE ANN. § 49.10: No Defense

TEX. PENAL CODE ANN. § 49.11: Proof of Mental State Unnecessary

Chapter 5

MENS REA COMPLICATIONS AND FAILURE OF PROOF DEFENSES

OVERVIEW

Criminal defenses are legal strategies used by defendants who, essentially, cede the government's *prima facie* case, but offer a legally recognized excuse or justification for their conduct that either exonerates (eliminating a defendant's liability entirely) or mitigates (decreasing the criminal culpability to that of a lesser crime). Defenses provide a legally defined and accepted basis upon which a defendant may avoid or minimize criminal culpability. **Affirmative defenses** do so without controverting the government's evidence of criminal culpability. Instead, the criminal defendant asserting an affirmative defense advances a theory of the law that will exempt or exculpate the proven criminality. Some affirmative defenses, e.g., self-defense, provide the accused with a full and complete exoneration from criminal culpability. However, not all affirmative defenses exonerate. Some, such as provocation or intoxication, offer only mitigation, i.e., partial defenses. Still, a successful partial defense can reduce the severity of the charges, such as reducing murder to manslaughter.

At common law, the burden of proving affirmative defenses rested on the defendant. This burden accords with the general evidentiary rule that burdens of producing evidence and of persuasion with regard to any given issue are both generally allocated to the same party. Common law courts generally adhered to the rule that the proponent of an issue bears the burden of persuasion on the factual premises for applying the rule.

More recently, however, the U.S. Supreme Court decided in *Dixon v. United States*, 548 U.S. 1 (2006), that, absent an act of Congress on the issue, federal criminal defendants are required to prove by a preponderance of the evidence the elements of an affirmative defense that do not negate an element of the offense (i.e., failure of proof defenses). Similarly, in most states, affirmative defenses must be raised by the accused and proved by a preponderance of the evidence. Once raised, the prosecution must disprove the affirmative defense beyond a reasonable doubt.

Failure of proof "defenses" do not advance a defense theory of justification or excuse with the goal of exculpation or exoneration. Nor do failure of proof defenses concede that the government has carried its burden. Instead, failure of proof defenses insist that the prosecution did not meet its constitutionally imposed burden to prove a *prima facie* case against the defendant. Failure of proof defenses are asserted when the accused challenges as insufficient the prosecution's *prima facie* evidence. This is the crux of such a defense: it represents, maintains, and seeks to enforce the fundamental proposition that the defendant is entitled to be found not guilty because the government failed to satisfy its burden of proof. Failure of proof defenses, then, really are better described and regarded as failure of proof defects (in the government's case). Unlike affirmative defenses, an accused who makes a failure of proof defense does not concede sufficiency of the government's *prima facie* case. Rather, when asserting a failure of proof defense, the accused contests the government's case by asserting how the government failed to prove one or more elements.

A common way to challenge the prosecution via a failure of proof defense is to attack the government's *mens rea* evidence. Even the U.S. Supreme Court has proclaimed: "[f]ew areas of criminal law pose more difficulty than the proper definition of the *mens rea* required for any particular crime."[1] Given the challenges in this realm, proving — or disproving — mental states of criminal culpability, practitioners will undoubtedly encounter **mens rea complications**. Though this area has been aided by the Model Penal Code's ("MPC") reform (which included an overhaul of the former myriad of common law *mens rea* states via a streamlining of culpability to a mere four states), there remains a good deal of confusion.

I. MISTAKE OF FACT

Despite popular misunderstanding, mistake of fact defense is not an excuse. It is a failure of proof defense.

A defendant's mistake of fact is relevant to criminal culpability only if it shows that the defendant lacked the *mens rea*, i.e., state of mind required for the crime. So, for specific intent crimes, mistake of fact could negate the intent element and the defendant is not culpable for that specific crime. For example, assume that a person who buys a stolen car believes that the car actually belonged to the seller. Given the mistake, it is impossible to convict the defendant because the government failed to establish the requisite mental state. The mistake of fact negatives the criminal intent necessary to be convicted of receiving stolen property, and the buyer would not be held criminally liable.

The defendant must raise his/her mistake of fact defense. Once raised, the government must disprove it beyond a reasonable doubt, providing evidence that the defendant was not mistaken or that the defendant's mistake of fact did not negative the crime's *mens rea*. For specific intent crimes, the mistake of fact need not be reasonable; any mistake — reasonable or unreasonable — will suffice. A defendant is not guilty if his/her mistake of fact negatives the requisite mental culpability. For general intent crimes, however, the defendant's mistake of fact must have been reasonable.

Similarly, under the MPC, mistake of fact is not a defense unless "the ignorance or mistake negatives" the mental culpability of the charged offense.[2] A mistake of fact

---

[1] United States v. Bailey, 444 U.S. 394, 403 (1980) (italics added).

[2] MODEL PENAL CODE § 2.04(1)(a).

defense is not as complicated as it might seem. Either the government proves that the defendant had the proscribed mental state of culpability or it does not. Thus, mistake of fact is a defense that rejects and rebukes the prosecution's *mens rea* evidence. A defendant cannot be criminally convicted and must be acquitted when s/he did not possess the proscribed mental state.

II. MISTAKE OF LAW

Generally, ignorance of the law is no excuse or defense. When, however, the defendant's mistake of law was supplied by — and s/he reasonably relied upon — an erroneous interpretation of the law by an appropriate governmental agent (e.g., responsible for interpretation and official statement of the law), mistake of law is a defense. Essentially, the mistake of law is not the defendant's; rather, the defendant is offering an interpretation from an official charged with interpreting the law; the mistake of law, then, is not the defendant's, it is the official's. Note, however, that in nearly all American jurisdictions, reliance upon "mere" law enforcers such as police officers, will not usually suffice as a valid mistake of law defense, nor will reliance upon private counsel's interpretation.

Under the MPC, mistake of law is a defense when the law "is not known to the actor and has not been published or otherwise reasonably made available prior to the conduct alleged" or the actor acts "in reasonable reliance upon an official statement," subsequently determined to be in error. (MPC § 2.04(3)). Such a defense is not as easily made as it may sound. In some jurisdictions, an official statement of the law may only come from a statute (that has been later invalidated), a judicial decision from the jurisdiction's highest court, or a public official responsible for the law's interpretation, administration, or enforcement.

III. TRANSFERRED INTENT

Under the doctrine of transferred intent, the actor is assigned the requisite intent for the resultant social harm he causes and remains criminally responsible because of his/her "bad aim." Essentially, transferred intent is a *mens rea* substitution doctrine. The intention to, e.g., assault, harm, or kill person M(issed) substitutes for the intention to assault, harm, or kill Person A(accident). The doctrine of transferred intent does not transfer intentions across types of social harms (e.g., intent merely to assault — cause an unconsented to criminal contact — does not transfer to intent to kill when death results). In other words, when a defendant targets a specific victim but accidentally harms an unintended third party, the criminal law will transfer the defendant's criminal intent when the third party suffered the same or similar harm the defendant intended to inflict upon the missed target. So, if D intended to assault M(issed) but, instead, harms A(ccident), the criminal law considers D just as culpable as if he had actually harmed M(issed).

The transferred intent doctrine helps the prosecutor's burden of proof. That an unintended entity or individual is harmed — and not the intended — is not a defense under the doctrine, given that the criminal law presumes that one intends the natural and probable consequences of his/her actions. Intent to assault, injure, or even kill does not disappear merely because, in the course of the defendant's conduct, s/he assaults, injures, or kills the wrong victim. The intent to commit a crime is the same. The volitional act that causes the social harm is the same.

The MPC also recognizes transferred intent, which is governed by § 2.03:

> **Purposely or Knowingly**: culpability "is not established if the actual result is not within the purpose or contemplation of the actor unless . . . the actual result differs from that designed or contemplated" (different person or property injured; lesser injury caused than that contemplated)

> **Recklessly**: culpability "is not established if the actual result is not within the risk of which the actor is aware unless . . . the actual result differs from the probable result" (different person or property injured; probable injury would have been more serious than that caused)

> **Negligently**: culpability "is not established if the actual result is not within the risk of which [the actor] should be aware unless . . . the actual result differs from the probable result" (different person or property injured; probable injury would have been more serious than that caused).

IV. WILLFUL BLINDNESS/DELIBERATE IGNORANCE/"OSTRICH DEFENSE"

In determining whether a criminal defendant acted with the requisite mental state of criminal awareness and knowledge, a jury may consider whether the accused deliberately closed his/her eyes to what would have made the accused aware. This purposeful avoidance of a mental culpability and contrivance to avoid awareness so as to be able to assert a defense in the event of a criminal prosecution is often referred to as "the Ostrich Defense."

A deliberate effort to avoid guilty knowledge is often all that the law requires to establish a guilty state of mind. There are two types of evidence that can illustrate a defendant's deliberate attempts to remain ignorant: (1) evidence that the defendant committed overt physical acts to avoid the knowledge and (2) evidence that the defendant thwarted or shuttered her normal curiosity by an effort of will. When a defendant claims lack of the requisite guilty knowledge, and the facts and evidence support an inference of deliberate ignorance, that defendant will be accused of a conscious avoidance if the evidence allows a rational juror to reach the conclusion that the defendant was aware of a high probability of the fact in dispute and consciously avoided confirming that fact. Although a jury may be instructed, under proper circumstances, that knowledge of a criminal fact may be established where the defendant consciously avoided learning the fact while aware of the high probability of its existence, the court must include a proviso advising the jury that it may not find knowledge of the fact if the defendant actually believed the contrary.

The Model Penal Code's definition of "knowledge" was designed to include the "willful blindness" of defendants who act like "ostriches." Under MPC § 2.02(7), "[w]hen knowledge of the existence of a particular fact is an element of an offense, such knowledge is established if a person is aware of a high probability of its existence, unless he actually believes that it does not exist." The actor who is aware of a high probability of a fact's existence is "put on notice;" s/he has the opportunity, if s/he cares, to investigate and eliminate any doubt before acting (or refrain from acting). By engaging in conduct while aware of a high probability that such conduct is criminal, the accused has manifested indifference to the values underlying the criminal prohibition in much the same way as the actor who is certain the conduct is criminal.

V. INFANCY

The U.S. Supreme Court has recognized that "during the formative years of childhood and adolescence, minors often lack the experience, perspective, and judgment to recognize and avoid choices that could be detrimental to them."[3] The infancy defense is an essential component of a fair legal system. Children go through developmental stages before achieving both the intellectual capacity and moral maturity to understand the wrongfulness and consequences of even their intended conduct and purposely risky behavior. Maturity (of the sort upon which legal responsibility may be premised) usually emerges only with the onset of adolescence, when the person achieves an internalized morality[4] (thereby bolstering jurisdictions' rationale for treating certain adolescents as adults for some crimes committed).

Whether a child understands the consequences and wrongfulness of an action constitutes a prerequisite inquiry into to the existence of *mens rea*, as the U.S. Constitution requires capacity to form criminal intent before punishment may be imposed upon a defendant. The defense of infancy presumes a lack of criminal capacity in children. Historically, the government had to overcome the presumption of infancy when attempting to prosecute children under the age of majority. Today, jurisdictions rely upon statutes that determine whether children, i.e., those who have not yet reached the age of majority, should be criminally prosecuted in the adult criminal justice system or via juvenile adjudication (which, essentially, manifests recognition of the defense of infancy). Unless an accused child has the capacity to be held as culpable as an adult (again: via statute), a defense of infancy presumes the impossibility of a child to form or maintain the *mens rea* required for commission of a criminal offense.

The infancy defense, then, can be seen as a failure of proof defense, as the accused may legally be unable to form a sufficient mental state of culpability. This is especially true if the accused is quite young. However, the infancy defense may be better understood as an affirmative defense of excuse, i.e., one that does not controvert wrongness of the deed, but excuses the actor because conditions suggest that the actor is not responsible for the deed. Here, an actor is not excused merely because s/he is an infant, but because the effect of the infancy may create a condition that renders the actor blameless for his/her conduct constituting the offense.

---

[3] Bellotti v. Baird, 443 U.S. 622, 635 (1979).

[4] "In the first stage, moral judgment takes the form of an automatic, unreflective response to rules set out by adults. . . ." Andrew Walkover, *The Infancy Defense in the New Juvenile Court*, 31 UCLA L. Rᴇᴠ. 503, 540–41 (1984).

EXERCISE

Overview

On October 2, 2012, defendant and appellant Michael Gnome was indicted for possession of a firearm by a felon. Specifically, years ago, on July 24, 2009, Mr. Gnome pleaded guilty to felony attempted robbery in the federal District of Colorado. In that proceeding, Mr. Gnome and the government's prosecutor filed papers with the court in support of the plea agreement and stipulation for a deferred judgment and sentence. The sentencing judge's order granted the motion and stipulation, and stated that entry of judgment would be deferred for a three-year period.

The agreement contained an express provision that "the Defendant shall not possess any firearms, destructive or dangerous devices or weapons." Both Mr. Gnome and his attorney signed the agreement and Mr. Gnome's signature line was directly underneath a sentence stating, "I swear or affirm that I have read and understand this entire document, and every representation I have made is true." Mr. Gnome simultaneously filed a request to plead guilty. It contained the following language:

> *I understand that if the Court accepts my guilty plea to a felony I will stand convicted of a felony. I understand that this felony conviction may be used against me in any future proceedings under the criminal laws. I also understand that my felony conviction may be used against me in any future proceeding concerning my credibility. If I have entered into a Stipulation of a Deferred Judgment and Sentence, and I have not yet completed the terms of that agreement, my guilty plea may be used against me in any future proceeding. I understand if I have entered into a Stipulation of a Deferred Judgment and Sentence and I violate the terms of that agreement, I may stand convicted of a felony and then I will be re-sentenced by the Court.*

Mr. Gnome initialed this paragraph; both Mr. Gnome and his attorney signed the plea agreement. During the oral colloquy of the plea agreement in court, the following exchange took place:

SENTENCING JUDGE: Are you comfortable with understanding what you are giving up and what the consequences are of this plea so that you want to take this plea today?

THE DEFENDANT: Yes, ma'am.

SENTENCING JUDGE: Here is what will happen today, if I accept your plea today, hopefully you will leave this courtroom not convicted of a felony and instead granted the privilege of a deferred judgment, which means you will be supervised by the Department of Probation for a period of two years. But what I want you to understand is, because you are waiving your right to proceed to a jury trial for all time today, if something goes wrong during this deferred judgment and you don't do what we ask you to do, it is possible that you could be returned into court and at that time you can't ask me to go to a jury trial, do you understand that?

THE DEFENDANT: Ma'am?

SENTENCING JUDGE: Because you are giving that up for all time and the likelihood is that you may end up being convicted of this felony even though you don't have a trial. Do you understand that?

THE DEFENDANT: Okay, ma'am.

SENTENCING JUDGE: That also means it is a Class 5 felony if you end up convicted. So it is all up to you. As you can tell what I'm saying, if you end up convicted, the Court could impose a prison term between one and three years in the Department of Corrections with a two-year period of mandatory parole. Do you understand that that is the worst-case scenario and it could happen in this case?

THE DEFENDANT: Yes, ma'am.

SENTENCING JUDGE: Do you have any questions for me about how that works?

THE DEFENDANT: No, ma'am.

SENTENCING JUDGE: Have you spent enough time meeting with your attorneys so that you feel you understand what your options are?

THE DEFENDANT: Yes, ma'am.

. . . .

SENTENCING JUDGE: Was she able to answer all of your questions to your satisfaction?

THE DEFENDANT: Yes, ma'am.

SENTENCING JUDGE: Are you satisfied with her representation?

THE DEFENDANT: Yes, ma'am.

SENTENCING JUDGE: Are you thinking clearly this morning, Mr. Gnome?

THE DEFENDANT: Yes, ma'am.

After further discussion, the sentencing judge stated, "All right. Then I accept the plea of guilty. I find it knowing, intelligent and voluntary. I have made written findings consistent with that determination." Finally, the sentencing judge admonished Mr. Gnome to comply with everything required by the plea documents, which included the statement: "You shall not possess any firearm, explosive or other destructive device, or any other dangerous weapon, unless you obtain written permission from the Court." Mr. Gnome put his initials beside this sentence and signed the document.

On May 9, 2012, Mr. Gnome encountered members of the Denver, Colorado police force when he was walking away from a park where multiple gunshots had apparently just been fired. When the officers tried to talk to him, he fled. The police caught Mr. Gnome, who was holding one hand up in the air while his other hand held, by the barrel, a fully loaded .380 caliber pistol with an obliterated serial number. Mr. Gnome was taken into custody. Upon further investigation, police officers determined that he had been at the park with an individual whose gunshots hit another person. However, the caliber of the firearm recovered from Mr. Gnome did not match the caliber of the rounds found in the wounded individual. Nevertheless, this incident led to the felon-in-possession charge at issue in this case. On May 13, 2012, Mr. Gnome made an initial appearance before a magistrate regarding the felon-in-possession charge. The following exchange occurred in court:

MAGISTRATE: I want to tell you about the charges against you and the rights that you have in this court.

MR. GNOME: Yes, sir.

MAGISTRATE: You've been charged with one count of possession of a firearm by a previously convicted felon. The penalty on that count is not more than ten years' imprisonment, a $250,000 fine, or both, not more than three years' of supervised release, and a $100 special assessment fee. Do you understand the general nature of the charge against you?

MR. GNOME: Not really, sir, but . . .

MAGISTRATE: What part don't you understand?

MR. GNOME: Like why so much time with the charge? If I get caught with a firearm, that's the maximum or minimum . . . ?

MAGISTRATE: Yes, this is the penalty that applies for this charge, which is possession of a firearm by a previously convicted felon. Yes, it's not more than ten years.

MR. GNOME: But, I pleaded guilty in 2009. I thought that counted in my favor! I didn't think I was a felon! If I knew I was a felon, NO WAY would I have had anything on me, not even a water gun! How am I a felon if I didn't go to jail??!

REQUIRED TASKS

Task One: Motion Writing; Motions *In Limine*

ESTIMATED TIME FOR COMPLETION: 4 hours.

Assume that you represent Mr. Gnome in the above trial matter. On your client's behalf, file a motion in limine, requesting a pre-trial order requiring that the government prove — to obtain a conviction under 18 U.S.C. § 922(g)(1) — that Mr. Gnome knew he had a prior felony conviction. In preparing for this task, you should also use an online database to read the following cases for guidance regarding the application of the substantive law in this task:

- *United States v. Adkins*, 196 F.3d 1112 (10th Cir. 1999)
- *United States v. Capps*, 77 F.3d 350 (10th Cir. 1996)
- *United States v. Poe*, 556 F.3d 1113 (10th Cir. 2009)
- *United States v. Quarrell*, 310 F.3d 664 (10th Cir. 2002)

- *United States v. Langley*, 62 F.3d 602 (4th Cir. 1995) (en banc)

In addition, consult the relevant law provided in the online component as well as the skills guide and supplemental materials on writing a motion *in limine* provided in the online component.

LEVEL OF DIFFICULTY (1 TO 5):

◆◆◆

Task Two: Motion Writing; Opposition to Motions *in Limine*:

You now represent the government. Although you are quite confident about the jurisdiction's precedent against Mr. Gnome, you are troubled by the sentencing judge's musings from the bench after reading Mr. Gnome's motion in limine. The new district court judge now wants you to file an opposition to the defendant's motion in limine, given that she has "no doubt in this particular situation that Mr. Gnome has an extremely good mistake argument" and that "Mr. Gnome believed his attorney and he believed the sentencing judge." Using the material referenced in Task One (also provided in the online component), draft the substantive portion of your opposition to the defendant's motion in limine.

ESTIMATED TIME FOR COMPLETION: 4 hours.

LEVEL OF DIFFICULTY (1 TO 5):

◆◆◆

PRACTICE SKILLS USED:

Skill 1: Drafting and Using a Motion *in Limine*

Skill 2: Motion Writing

Skill 3: Tactical Thinking

Skill 4: Legal Argument; Integrating the Law and the Facts

SKILLS GUIDES

SKILLS GUIDES #1: Drafting and Using a Motion in Limine

The term motion in limine — Latin for "at the threshold;" pronounced *LIM*-in-nay or li-min-*NEE* — refers to motions made before or during trial (not afterward). Most motions *in limine* seek to exclude evidence. But that is not the only purpose. A motion in limine can also be used to obtain an advance ruling on the admissibility of evidence or a point of law. In one sense, a motion *in limine* is the evidentiary counterpart to a motion for summary judgment; it to eliminate evidentiary issues for trial. A motion *in limine*, when properly advanced, is one of the most useful weapons available to trial counsel. A successful motion can negate anticipated testimony or documentary evidence and, in the lucky few cases, eviscerate an opponent's case.

The motion *in limine* exists without explicit authorization in either statute or rule. Nonetheless, motions *in limine* serve as a convenient device for judges and lawyers to preview and decide certain evidentiary issues in advance of trial (or in advance of testimony) and facilitate the flow of the evidence at trial. Under Federal Rule 104(a) and its state law analogs, preliminary questions concerning the qualification of a person to be a witness, the existence of a privilege, or the admissibility of evidence shall be determined by the court. The rule adds that in making its determination, the court is not bound by the rules of evidence.

Courts prefer to address the preliminary matters that are the subject of motions *in limine* outside the presence of the jury. Pre-trial, inform your judge of your need to raise the issue regarding forthcoming evidence or legal issues regarding that forthcoming evidence. Evidentiary rulings are generally reviewed for abuse of discretion. In the context of the review of a ruling made on a motion *in limine* before trial, appellate judges may couch the standard of review as "abuse of discretion" but they may not mean it. In contrast, appellate judges are likely to be more deferential when reviewing rulings made in the course of trial precisely because the trial judge had the best vantage point when making the ruling. The trial judge had the chance to evaluate the credibility of witnesses, and to assess how the challenged evidence within the flow of the trial.

Writing a motion *in limine* is simple. Identify the evidentiary concern; describe the purpose for which you anticipate the evidence will be introduced; cite the applicable rules (and other directly applicable authorities); and explain why the evidence should be excluded or produced/accepted. Be specific. Do so in as short and concise a document as possible. Most motions *in limine* are quickly disposed of by trial judges orally and without written pleadings. Long theoretical or unduly argumentative diatribes will disserve your motion. The court may view your otherwise sound motion (or opposition) as unpersuasive hyperbole, and summarily deny it. Good advocates — advocates interested in winning not just the trial but also defending the victory on appeal — may opt to raise narrow evidentiary issues in the midst of trial rather than broad evidentiary issues before it. Very broad motions *in limine* are usually rejected because they exclude too many possibly relevant topics from the courtroom. A narrowly phrased motion *in limine* that focuses on certain specific facts is more likely to be granted, especially if the party making it can demonstrate that the specific facts are irrelevant, prejudicial, or against the rules of evidence. The best way to ensure that a trial judge will understand your case is to make your organizational plan overt. Put a summary of your point or points up front; write a one- or two-sentence summary of your point(s). Get right to the point; tell the judge the purpose of the motion, specifically, right at the beginning. (Virtually all analytical or persuasive writing should have a summary at the outset of the pleading. Whether you state the issue, summarize your position, or assert the correct result, you should do it up front. Yet too many court papers do not.)

Use short, boldface headings for each new section; this will allow the judge, at any point in the text, to refer to a subject heading and quickly know where s/he is in your argument and motion or opposition. The busy judge may want to skip ahead to the critical information, and the headings allow that. The busy judge may forget what's going on in your case, and the headings bring the judge's attention back into focus. In short, the headings make it easy for your reader: the busy judge.

Candor is essential. Be honest in characterizing the facts and the law, even where they may be less than favorable to your position. Do not omit relevant facts because they are unfavorable. Don't fudge, falsify, or fog. Be honest about the law, the entirety of it. Do not omit the sections or language that "harms" your position.

Though motions *in limine* do not often require written pleadings, placing your arguments (in support or opposition to) in a written pleading can be useful beyond the trial judge's ruling. A motion *in limine* is an evidentiary motion; placing the contested matter in writing is one way to ensure that any objections or evidentiary proffers made to the trial court are preserved in accordance with the jurisdiction's rules of evidence. Thus, for example, if the court denies your motion *in limine*, your motion, the court's ruling, and your objection are now in the trial court's record, available for appeal purposes.

The court may defer ruling on your motion, perhaps to evaluate the proffered evidence in the context of other evidence at trial, or initially deny it, reserving the right to revisit it and the court's ruling at an appropriate time. Whatever the reason, your motion will have sensitized the court to the evidentiary issues so that when the contested evidence surfaces, resurrection of any motion or opposition thereto can be held.

SKILLS GUIDE #2: Motion Writing

Please refer to Chapter 8, Skills Guide #1.

SKILLS GUIDE #3: Tactical Thinking

Please refer to Chapter 1, Skills Guide #4.

SKILLS GUIDE #4: Legal Argument; Integrating the Law and the Facts

Please refer to Chapter 8, Skills Guide #2.

ADDITIONAL MATERIALS FOR THE EXERCISE — AVAILABLE IN ON-LINE COMPONENT

18 U.S.C. § 922(g)(1): Unlawful Acts

18 U.S.C. § 924(a)(2): Penalties

Chapter 6

THE PROOF PROCESS: BURDENS OF PRODUCTION AND PERSUASION AND PROOF PLANNING

OVERVIEW

Criminal cases turn on proving facts as much as on proving law. But the law determines what facts must be proven (what facts establish the elements of the crime or defense). The law also establishes *how much* proof is required and by whom. Burdens of production and persuasion address these "how much" and "by whom" questions. Furthermore, not all evidence is admissible to prove all things. The law of evidence governs the admissibility question. Although an Evidence course addresses that law in detail, it is important for Criminal Law students to have some basic feel for a few evidence rules. The goal is simply to develop sensitivity to the ways in which evidence rules can affect proof planning.

Proof planning refers to the process of identifying what witnesses and physical evidence an attorney plans to offer at trial to prove the elements of a crime or defense. Proof planning also requires identifying what evidence will be used to challenge the opponent's case. Such evidence can be of two kinds: impeaching evidence offered to suggest that an opposing witness is lying or mistaken, and rebuttal evidence — other witnesses offered to contradict your opponent's claims or drill holes into her witnesses' testimony. Many lawyers use proof planning charts, which list each element of each crime and defense, what witnesses and physical evidence will be offered to prove each element, and what witnesses will be offered to challenge the opponent's case. Early in a case, when a lawyer does not know what proof is available, the chart also guides her in deciding what investigation to do and how (i.e., through formal discovery and informal investigation).

Proof planning might vary somewhat based upon whether the case is before a judge (a bench trial) or a jury. Understanding something about jury voting and the rules of jury selection helps in proof planning and in deciding whether to proceed before a judge or jury, or instead via guilty plea, in the first place.

I. BURDENS OF PRODUCTION AND PERSUASION

The burden of production is usually stated as the burden of producing "some" evidence. Some jurisdictions might phrase the burden differently, however, as the burden of establishing a *prima facie* case, that is, a case sufficient to enable a reasonable jury to find that the burden of persuasion has been met.

The burden of persuasion is also often called the burden of proof. It is the burden of convincing the fact finder. In criminal cases, the prosecution always has the burden of proving every case beyond a reasonable doubt.

Statutes determine who has what burden on which issues. For example, a defendant might raise a "failure of proof" or "derivative" defense. In common sense terms, this is a defense of this form: "Because of something I, the defendant, know, you the prosecution cannot prove this element beyond a reasonable doubt." One example is the mistake of fact defense. This defense essentially argues, "Because of my mistaken belief, you, the prosecution, cannot prove beyond a reasonable doubt the mental state(s) required for me to be guilty of this crime." But the prosecution does not have to disprove a defendant's mistake argument in every case. Rather, the prosecution must disprove a mistake claim only if the defendant first meets his burden of production (that is, he offers "some evidence") that he was mistaken. If he does not meet that burden, the government is freed from worrying about any mistake claim; the jury will never hear of it. But if he does offer some evidence of a mistake, the burden shifts to the prosecution to prove the absence of the mistake as part of its burden of proving the requisite mental state beyond a reasonable doubt.

The story is different with "affirmative defenses." Affirmative defenses, again in common sense terms, are of this form: "Even if you, the prosecution, can prove every element of the crime beyond a reasonable doubt, I, the defendant, am not guilty because I have a justification or excuse." Thus, someone who admits to purposely killing another person claims that he did so in self-defense, a complete defense to the crime of homicide. In many jurisdictions, the defendant has the burden of proving most affirmative defenses (here, self-defense, usually classified as a justification, meaning that under the circumstances it was better for society that he killed than that he did not) by a preponderance of the evidence. Sometimes statutes raise the burden even higher. Notably, the federal insanity defense statute (insanity being an excuse, roughly meaning that there was something that compromised the defendant's ability to make rational choices and act upon them) puts the burden of persuasion on the defendant by clear and convincing evidence.

Even if a defendant offers no evidence whatsoever in his defense, the defendant can still simply argue that the government has failed to prove all the elements of the crime beyond a reasonable doubt. But what does "beyond a reasonable doubt" mean? It is more than a preponderance of evidence and more than clear and convincing evidence, but less than beyond any doubt. It does not require proof to a mathematical certainty, but it does require a strong conviction that the element in question has been proven. Moreover, any doubts must be rooted in reason, based on the evidence presented at trial, and not in speculation. Beyond these general points, however, courts rarely define the term with any specificity. Even their vague explanations vary not only among jurisdictions but even among judges within a single jurisdiction. Pennsylvania judges long said something like this: "You have a reasonable doubt if you would hesitate to make a decision in a matter of great importance in your own life." The judges would then give examples of such matters, such as, "For example, if you would hesitate to marry a particular person, you would have a reasonable doubt about the wisdom of that marriage." Most prosecutors would consider this formulation unfairly slanted toward the defense, raising the burden too high. Defense lawyers, on the other hand, might argue in favor of such a definition. Lawyers and judges will indeed debate what "beyond a reasonable doubt" formulation should be contained in jury instructions, though many states have standard instructions on the point. Courts also often say that the term cannot be expressed in precise mathematical percentages. Yet most experts often illustrate the idea by assigning high percentages, perhaps 90% or higher, as meeting the beyond a reasonable doubt standard.

II.   THE LAWS OF EVIDENCE AND IMPEACHMENT

Sometimes, even if all prosecution witnesses are believed, the testimony still does not add up to beyond a reasonable doubt. More commonly, reasonable doubt may be created by challenging witness credibility. There are many ways to prove that a witness is lying or mistaken. On the lying side, under certain circumstances, a witness's prior criminal convictions can be used to show that he is not a credible person and thus should not be believed in this case. Typically, evidence codes distinguish between crimes that are "*crimen falsi*," those that involve dishonesty or false statement, and crimes that are not. *Crimen falsi* crimes, such as perjury or fraud, require proving intentional falsehoods as an element of the offense. In most jurisdictions, such crimes are always admissible to impeach the witness previously convicted of such crimes as having an untruthful character. For crimes that are not *crimen falsi*, impeachment is allowed typically only if the crime is a felony. By "felony," we mean that the crime was punishable by more than one year in prison or by death. The theory seems to be that anyone who could commit such a serious level of crime must have a flawed character, thereby suggesting a willingness to lie. But non-*crimen falsi* felonies are admissible only if they survive a balancing test where unfair prejudice does not substantially outweigh probative value. Many factors can enter into this balancing. Among the most important factors for your purposes are the age of the conviction (people change, so a nine-year-old conviction may say little about the person you are today) and the extent to which it involves some element of deception, even if not enough to rise to the level of *crimen falsi*. Thus, an assault is simply violent. But a robbery by people wearing masks involves both violence and some degree of deception.

Ways to show witness mistake, confusion, or lies also include introducing prior inconsistent statements (they said one thing at trial but told a different story earlier), eliciting contradicting testimony by a more credible witness, and suggesting an inability to perceive accurately. Perception problems could arise from not wearing prescription glasses, being too far away to see the crime clearly, or seeing it at night without much lighting. Witnesses may also have a bias or motive to lie or at least to remember things with a slant. For instance, a loving mother can be expected to testify for her son rather than against him.

III.   PROOF PLANNING CHARTS

Proof planning charts, mentioned above, are best explained by illustration. Here is the outline of a proof planning chart for a stranger rape case, using the traditional common law elements of that crime:

Elements of the Crime	Witnesses	Physical Evidence
1. Forcible	a. Mary, Victim, to describe being jumped from behind, mouth muffled, held down b. Nurse Ratchett to describe the victim's physical condition upon being admitted to the hospital and rape kit results	a. Photographs of injuries shortly after the incident (authenticated by the investigating detective arriving at the scene) b. Stitches
2. Non-consensual	a. Mary said "no" and physically resisted, punching her assailant and trying to scream b. Linda, Mary's best friend, to whom Mary reported the rape promptly after it happened c. John, a neighbor, who heard Mary scream for help and called the police	a. Mary's display of a scar from her stitches and injury b. Photograph of the crime scene and of Mary's torn clothes (authenticated by the investigating detective)
3. Sexual Intercourse	a. Mary to testify that it occurred b. Lab technician to testify that a substance submitted by Nurse Ratchett was semen c. Nurse Ratchett to testify about taking that substance from the victim as part of the rape kit in the hospital that night	
4. By a man	Mary	
5. With a woman	Mary	
6. Not his wife	Mary	

This proof planning chart is flawed. It is missing one critical element. One element of every crime, though not stated in the defining statute, is that *this defendant*, not someone else, did the crime. Like all elements of a crime, the identity of the offender must be proven by the prosecution beyond a reasonable doubt. In practice, identity can be a more or less important issue, depending upon the facts. Had this case been a date rape case between two students who knew each other from class, identity could not easily be contested. The more likely defense would be that the acts were consensual. But because this case involves strangers and clear evidence of much force, identity is the critical question. Yet nothing in the planning chart addresses identity. Calling a forensic scientist to testify to a DNA match between the semen and the defendant's DNA would be one way to prove identity. In most cases, however, scientific evidence will not be available. Identity might need to be proven based on eyewitnesses or based on the victim identifying the defendant as her assailant or based on circumstantial evidence. Defendants may also contest identity. They might do so by challenging the eyewitnesses' credibility. They also might offer an "alibi" defense, meaning they try to prove specifically that they were at a place other than the crime scene at the time the crime occurred. They also might try to rely on an "alternative perpetrator" defense, proving that someone else committed the crime.

IV. JURY, JUDGE, OR GUILTY PLEA

Most jurisdictions require juries to be unanimous in order to convict. If 11 vote to convict but one to acquit, that results in a hung jury. The defendant may usually be tried again, if the government wishes to do so. An acquittal also requires a unanimous verdict. If all the jurors vote to acquit, the government may neither appeal nor seek a new trial. The constitutional prohibition on exposing a criminal defendant to double jeopardy prevents those outcomes.

Jurors are selected from a broader array by a questioning process known as voir dire. Voir dire seeks to identify those jurors who cannot be fair and impartial. Prospective jurors may be dismissed "for cause" by the judge if he or she demonstrates bias or admits partiality. In addition, by rule of statute, each party is also allowed a number of "peremptory challenges," requests to dismiss jurors for no publicly stated reason at all. Peremptories are allowed up to the maximum number for each side unless the challenge is motivated by racial, ethnic, gender, or similar bias or stereotyping. For additional information on issues of jury selection, see Chapter 8, Skills Guide #5.

Jury trials generally occur in the same place where the crime itself happened. If, however, a defendant establishes that the local jury pool is so prejudiced against him that he presumptively cannot receive a fair trial in that location, then he may file a change of "venue" motion to move the trial elsewhere. Geography matters. Jury pools in different locations may at least seem to the lawyers to be more or less conviction-prone under certain sets of facts. Similarly, facts matter. A defendant may believe that, due to certain aspects of his case, for example, distasteful facts or an emotionally difficult crime, it would be difficult to find a truly impartial jury. If a defendant fears a conviction-prone jury and the case is scheduled before a judge whom the defense thinks will be more sympathetic to the case, the defendant may decide to waive a jury in favor of a bench trial. If a defendant is convinced that conviction is likely before either judge or jury, the defendant may instead seek to negotiate a guilty plea.

EXERCISE

Overview

Last year, on September 23, John Nicholas, a student at the University of Pennsylvania, in Philadelphia, Pennsylvania, had his home burglarized. John lived in a first floor apartment at 36th and Chestnut Streets. John had mostly closed the bedroom window — and fully closed all the other apartment windows — and locked the apartment door just before he went to sleep at midnight. The burglary occurred around 2:00 a.m. John was asleep when a noise awakened him. He looked up and saw a figure in his bedroom. John slept with a small orange night light near his bed. Some light also came though the blinds of his bedroom window from a streetlight nearby. The figure told John to be quiet. When John started to scream, the intruder held a knife to John's throat and told him, "I'll cut you if you don't shut up and do what I say." The intruder then pulled rope from his pocket, tied John's hands and feet, and stuffed rope into John's mouth to muffle his voice. John thought that he recognized what he could see of the intruder's face from the nearby Laundromat, having seen the intruder doing laundry there on several occasions. John was grateful that his girlfriend, with whom he lived, was out of town visiting family.

The intruder rifled through John's possessions and quickly walked through his house. Eventually, the intruder took John's mini flat-screen TV, which had on its back a small silver plate engraved with "Bunky loves Pooky." "Bunky" was John's girlfriend's nickname, and she called him "Pooky" when they were alone. She had given him the TV as a gift. The intruder also took from John's desk drawer all his cash on hand: $100. Finally, the intruder took John's expensive Movado wristwatch, then exited through the bedroom window. The night had been hot, and John had left the window open halfway — too small an opening for a person to enter unless he opened the window further — though John thought that the window might have been opened much more at the time that he saw the intruder leave.

John's girlfriend, Lola Sweet ("Bunky"), came home the next day to find John tied up. She released him, and John immediately called the police.

On September 25, Dave Marquee was stopped by police officer Robert Murdock, badge number 3472, at 38th and Chestnut Streets for speeding. When the officer approached Dave's car from the driver's side window, which Dave had opened to talk to the officer, the officer saw a mini flat-screen TV on the front passenger seat. The officer saw on the back of the TV a silver panel with the engraving, "Bunky loves Pooky." The officer recognized the phrase from the "Be on the Lookout" reports because of the phrase's oddity. Accordingly, the officer arrested Dave, read him his *Miranda* rights, and received a valid waiver of those rights. When Dave asked what he was being arrested for, the officer said, "for stealing that TV set in a burglary." Dave replied, "Look, I just bought this TV from a guy at 40th and Locust, who was selling it from the back of a truck. The truck had 'Mary's Furniture Discount Store' on the side of it. I figured that in this economy they thought bringing the furniture directly to the people was a good business tactic." When the officer seemed unconvinced, Dave asked for a lawyer and the two stopped talking.

Dave Marquee has now been charged with burglary, receiving stolen property, and aggravated assault in Pennsylvania state court. He has raised an alibi defense. John, however, had picked Dave's photo from a photo array of six photographs. The prosecutor's investigators managed to get statements from each of Dave's two alibi witnesses. Here is the first statement:

I am Dave Marquee's mother. On September 23 of last year, Dave was home with me all night and all morning. Dave lives with me in our first-floor apartment at 40th and Osage Streets. Dave is a student at Temple University and is living with me while he gets his degree. I remember that day well because Dave had his friend and study-buddy, Ronald Remus, sleep over that night. They were studying for an exam together. This was the only time that Ronald slept over. I liked Ronald. We watched a series of old Matlock reruns — they had a Matlock festival on TV after they finished studying. After that, the boys went to bed around 11:00 p.m. They had classes the next day. When they awoke in the morning, around 7:00 a.m., I made them pancakes. Then they went to class. So Dave couldn't have done this crime.

Signed,

Angelina Marquee

Here is the second statement:

My name is Ronald Remus. On September 23 of last year, I slept over at my friend Dave Marquee's house. Dave and I were study-buddies at Temple University. We are both economics students. We had an introductory calculus exam the next morning. I'm not real good at calculus, so Dave was helping me get through it. He's a good friend. We're sophomores, but we grew up together in West Philly, going to the same middle school. My parents moved to North Philly when I started college, but Dave and I stayed in touch, and he's helped me ever since we both started at Temple. I live with my parents in North Philly, and it's a long slog home from West Philly, so Dave and his mom let me stay the night after we studied. All we did was study all night, until about midnight. I slept on a sleeping bag in Dave's room. When we woke up, we wolfed down some cereal because we got up late and were afraid of missing our exam late that morning.

Signed,

Ronald Remus

The prosecutor's investigators also uncovered the following background information on these witnesses:

Remus had two prior convictions, one for perjury as a juvenile, at age 16, and one for the felony of burglary, at age 18, a crime he committed on his birthday. Remus received probation for the perjury conviction. Because it was his first adult offense, he spent only six months in jail on the burglary, and was released on five years probation. He is now age 21. Marquee's mother has a clean record and worked for 30 years for the United States Post Office. She is now age 50. She had to retire recently because she was diagnosed with early Alzheimer's. The disease is at such an early stage that most people who just meet her don't notice anything amiss. She is on medication to slow its course.

Here is an excerpt from the police report summarizing the photo array shown to John Nicholas by Detective Andrew Pinsky, at the local police station, on September 24 of last year:

> Showed 6-photo simultaneous array to burglary victim John Nicholas. All persons shown in the array were African-American and of approximately the same age, skin color, and facial features. Nicholas is Caucasian. Victim selected photo number 3, Dave Marquee. Asked Nicholas to sign a form acknowledging his selection of that photo and asking him to recite in his own words his degree of confidence in his choice. Victim wrote, "Looks like him, I think."

A forensic psychologist consultant, Jason Duncan, Ph.D., who specializes in eyewitness identifications, has told defense counsel in a report that simultaneous arrays (showing all photos at once to the witness) are less accurate than sequential ones (showing the photos one at a time). Duncan also explained the phenomenon of "own race bias," which makes inter-racial identifications less likely to be accurate than intra-racial ones. The defense has shared this report with the prosecution in an effort to promote a favorable plea agreement solely to the charge of receiving stolen property.

REQUIRED TASKS

Task One: Proof Charts

Prepare two proof charts, one for the prosecution, one for the defense, for each of the three charges.

ESTIMATED TIME FOR COMPLETION: 60 minutes.

LEVEL OF DIFFICULTY (1 TO 5):

Task Two: Cross-Examination

You are the prosecutor representing the State. Prepare potential cross-examination questions for each of the defense's alibi witnesses.

ESTIMATED TIME FOR COMPLETION: 45 minutes.

LEVEL OF DIFFICULTY (1 TO 5):

Task Three: Legal Research; Fact Patterns

Research case law in the relevant jurisdiction on the question whether there is sufficient evidence to present to the jury the charge of burglary or only the lesser crime of receiving stolen property. Prepare your answer under both of the following factual hypotheticals: (a) John Nicholas's in-court testimony identifying the defendant and any evidence offered by Nicholas or the detective about the photo identification are found admissible; and (b) none of this testimony is found admissible. Identify one or two controlling cases and be ready to explain how they support your conclusions.

ESTIMATED TIME FOR COMPLETION: 2 hours.

LEVEL OF DIFFICULTY (1 TO 5):

PRACTICE SKILLS USED:

      Skill 1: Preparing Proof Charts

      Skill 2: Cross-Examination

      Skill 3: Legal Research and Analogical Reasoning

SKILLS GUIDES

SKILLS GUIDE #1: Preparing Proof Charts

Little need be added to what has been said in the discussion of proof charts above. It is important to note, however, that a proof chart can help you to identify strengths and weaknesses in your case and to determine what further formal or informal discovery or legal research is needed. It is therefore desirable underneath a proof chart you have prepared to write a one or two-paragraph summary of your case's strengths and weaknesses, how to try to address the weaknesses, and what those weaknesses might imply as to tactics or strategy (for example, whether the weaknesses justify trying to craft a particular sort of guilty plea rather than going to trial). A separate proof chart is needed for each crime charged in the indictment, information, or complaint.

SKILLS GUIDE #2: Cross-Examination

It is not possible to give you a thorough explanation of cross-examination without first having studied Evidence and perhaps even basic trial practice. But we can give you enough guidance here to start working on a simple cross-examination. The content of a cross-examination is dictated by your theory of the case. Are you the government trying to prove the elements of the crime? Do you represent the defendant and are presenting an alibi defense? Every question you ask a witness during cross-examination must be guided by your overall theory of the case and the narrative you are presenting to the jury. Within that context, the purposes of cross-examination are at least twofold: first, to get the other side's witness to admit to any facts that help your theory of the case; and second, to impeach the opposing witness — that is, to temper or disprove any testimony that hurts your theory of the case. "Impeachment" is bringing out information suggesting to the trier of fact (typically, the jury) that the witness should not be believed, either generally, or as to a particular piece of testimony. A witness might be disbelieved because he is lying, mistaken, confused, biased, ignorant, or memory-challenged. Suggesting the witnessed is biased means bringing out reasons that a witness would want to give testimony favoring your opponent. Bias may arise from the possibility of receiving a financial gain from testifying or avoiding criminal or civil liability if the witness helps the government. But bias can also arise simply from liking or loving an involved party. People will sometimes lie for friends, family, or loved ones. Even when they do not consciously lie, however, their bias may skew their memory, the phrasing of their testimony, or how much information they mention and how much they exclude to slant the testimony more toward the person they are fond of, owe a debt, or anticipate giving them a future benefit.

Poor memory can be revealed by exploring details that you would expect someone to remember about an incident. If they cannot remember those particular details, that may suggest that they are misremembering when something happened, who was present, or how events truly developed.

Confusion and mistakes might be revealed by getting the witness to commit to statements that you can contradict through another witness or piece of evidence or to commit to statements that the witness herself has contradicted earlier through her own words. The first technique is called "contradiction." The cross-examiner simply gets the witness to say, for example, "the light was red." But the cross-examiner knows that on rebuttal she can call a more credible witness who will say, "No, I was there, and the light was green." Or perhaps there would be a record from the Department of Transportation that demonstrates that at that specific time the light was green. The second technique mentioned is impeachment by a prior inconsistent statement. For example, the cross-examiner has the witness say that the light was red. Thereafter, the cross-examiner gets the witness to admit that the day after the accident he told his mother that the light was green — a statement directly inconsistent with what the witness just testified to at trial.

Cross-examination cannot be done by thinking about the witness in isolation from other witnesses. For instance, a cross-examiner might try to get a witness to admit to a damaging fact that he did not admit to in any earlier statements. If the witness now admits this damaging fact, terrific. If, however, he denies the damaging fact, the cross-examiner knows that another witness will testify later that the damaging fact actually existed. Either way, the cross-examiner eventually ends up impeaching the witness. It is therefore safe to ask the question. Another way in which the cross-examiner must think holistically is that the cross-examiner might use the witness to lay the groundwork for impeaching another witness. Thus the witness now being cross-examined may reveal grounds for believing that another witness is biased, confused, mentally ill, or lying.

Witnesses can also be impeached by challenging their character for truthfulness. One way to do that is to bring out convictions for criminal offenses that suggest that the witness is the kind of person who lies more than most and, therefore, is probably now lying on the stand. Each jurisdiction has different rules for when impeachment with prior convictions is proper. Here, Pennsylvania's rules control.

Witnesses can also be impeached by showing that they did not have the opportunity or ability to observe events as accurately as they claim. Perhaps a robbery victim was frightened by his assailant's weapon, attacked quickly and in darkness, under great stress, and gave only tentative identifications of the assailant at a lineup or photo spread. Each of these factors would suggest that the witness is mistaken. He may believe that he has identified the right person, but his belief may be wrong because he just did not get an adequate chance to observe the facial features of his assailant.

SKILLS GUIDE #3: Legal Research and Analogical Reasoning

Legal research is covered thoroughly in a basic legal writing course. Here we just offer some reminders. First, the research must reveal the relevant governing legal principles. Second, here you are being asked to find similar cases to support your position, that is, to find cases whose facts and rationales are sufficiently similar to this case that they should control. In other words, you are arguing that the same outcome should be required in both cases. This type of argument is reasoning by analogy. You also must be attentive to similar cases that come out against the result you want. In such an instance, you must craft arguments that the case that seems to control is in actuality factually different in relevant ways, leading to a very different conclusion. You might even go so far as to use language from those cases suggesting that, on the facts of this case, the court in those cases indeed would have come out in your favor. This type of reasoning involves the process of distinguishing cases. In short, you analogize your case to similar good cases and distinguish your case from cases that reach the opposite result. It may be that you find no cases directly on point, or "on all fours" (i.e., with nearly the same relevant facts) or perhaps, not even close to your fact pattern.

When that is so, you must find the closest possible cases and at least explain why their logic or rationale requires the result you are requesting.

Starting with search terms that reasonably narrow your query is important. In addition, especially when you do research of the type discussed here — looking for cases with similar facts — you must carefully read the factual background of the case as well as the legal reasoning and holding in order to find caselaw sufficiently supportive of your position. You must also remember to check subsequent citation history to make sure that the case you rely on has not been overruled. The ideal case would be factually very similar to the current one, decided by the state's highest court, and decided as recently as possible. Where no such case can be found, the goal should be to find one as close to the ideal as possible. Sometimes you have to mix and match. For example, the most factually similar case might have been decided by a trial court. You should nevertheless cite and discuss it because of its similarity. But if you like its result, you should then discuss at least one case from a higher court that, while factually distinct, relies on legal reasoning, rules, logic, policies, or dicta suggesting that the higher court would reach the same result as the lower court were the higher court faced with the same factual situation.

ADDITIONAL MATERIALS FOR THE EXERCISE — AVAILABLE IN ON-LINE COMPONENT

18 PA. CONS. STAT. ANN. § 3502: Burglary

18 PA. CONS. STAT. ANN. § 3921: Theft by unlawful taking or disposition

18 PA. CONS. STAT. ANN. § 3925: Receiving stolen property

18 PA. CONS. STAT. ANN. § 2702: Aggravated assault

18 PA. CONS. STAT. ANN. § 2301: Definitions

PA. R. EVID. 609: Impeachment by evidence of a criminal conviction

Chapter 7

HOMICIDE I

OVERVIEW

Criminal homicide is often defined as the unjustified killing of another human being. At common law, criminal homicide was divided into murder and manslaughter. There were no degrees of murder or manslaughter. Manslaughter, however, was divided into voluntary manslaughter and involuntary manslaughter. Manslaughter at common law did not involve malice aforethought; however, it remained an unlawful killing without justification, excuse, or mitigation. This chapter covers first and second degree murder. Manslaughter and the doctrine of felony murder are discussed in Chapter 8.

I. COMMON LAW MURDER

At common law, **murder** was defined as the unlawful killing of one human being by another human being with malice aforethought. In order to be deemed a "human being," one had to be born alive.[1] Killing of the unborn (e.g., an embryo or fetus) may have been regarded as a criminal act (e.g., misdemeanor); however, it was not considered a criminal homicide.

At the other end of the spectrum, death was seen as the cessation of vital life cardiopulmonary functions such as respiration and circulation. Once one or more of those systems ceased functioning, a "human being" (and, therefore, human life) ceased to exist. Murder was also subject to the "year and a day rule": the accused killer could not be prosecuted unless his/her victim died within one year and one day of the conduct that allegedly caused the death. The rule arose from the difficulty of determining cause of death after an extended period. If the death occurred beyond a year and a day, it was conclusively presumed to be caused by something other than the defendant's conduct.

At common law, malice aforethought was a term of art for the mental state sufficient to establish murder. Malice was either express or implied and satisfied by evidence that the defendant had one of four mental states at the time of the killing: (1) an intent

---

[1] For example, the "born alive" rule was relied upon in *Keeler v. Superior Court*, 470 P.2d 617 (Cal. 1970), which held that "an infant could not be the subject of homicide at common law unless it had been born alive." The rule required that "[i]f a woman be quick with childe, and by a potion or otherwise killeth it in her wombe, or if a man beat her, whereby the childe dyeth in her body, and she is delivered by a dead childe, this is a great misprision [i.e., misdemeanor], and no murder; but if the childe be born alive and dyeth of the potion, battery, or other cause, this is murder; for in law it is accounted a reasonable creature, in *rerum natura*, when it is born alive."

(purpose or knowledge) to kill (express malice), (2) an intent (purpose or knowledge) to inflict serious/grievous bodily harm (implied malice), (3) a "depraved heart," i.e., extreme reckless disregard for the value of human life (implied malice), or (4) an intent to commit a felony, during the commission of which a human being dies (implied malice). Barring legal justification, excuse, or mitigation, each of these mental states manifested the accused's criminalized indifference to the value of human life.

Intent to kill murder at common law required the government to prove that the criminal defendant formed an intent to kill another human being without justification, excuse, or mitigation. This required evidence that the accused premeditated and deliberated before killing and that the accused's conduct was the legal cause of the victim's death. Premeditation evidence proves that the defendant's conduct was not spontaneous; rather, s/he thought about killing beforehand. How long of a thought or how long before acting upon the intent to kill has never been measured by a hard-and-fast rule. Historically, the length of premeditation was not long at all, given that "no time is too short for a wicked man to frame in his mind the scheme of murder."[2] Although it is often quite challenging to peer into the mind of anyone, and it is the rare defendant who, before killing, announces the intent to kill to witnesses or in a document, the criminal law has long accepted circumstantial evidence that allows jurors to infer that the defendant did have the requisite intent. Circumstantial evidence may include, e.g., the type of weapon used; lethal means employed; the severity, location of, or number of injuries inflicted; exploiting a victim's known weakness (e.g., startling to death a victim whose phobia includes snakes by placing several large ones in her bed) or dependency (e.g., disconnecting a premature infant's oxygen mask). If there is a defendant's confession or other statements that provide evidence of premeditation, they may also be introduced at trial to prove the defendant's intent to kill.

Proof of the defendant's deliberation — essentially, pondering and appreciating the significance of the premeditated intent to kill — is also required. Here, too, there was no specific length or amount of deliberation required at common law. The government was, however, required to prove that after the defendant premeditated, s/he also turned the matter over in his/her mind, giving it (a second) thought and some measure of rumination. However, what was required is that premeditation precede deliberation, i.e., the defendant must first have an intent to kill (premeditation) before its deliberation is possible. (Today, some modern courts require a significant lapse of time for there to be sufficient evidence of "premeditation." For these courts, "any amount of time, no matter how short," will not do because it makes it too hard to distinguish modern first and second degree murder, as explained below.)

Additionally at common law, one who acted with malice aforethought was guilty of murder if, with the **intent to cause grievous or serious bodily injury**, the defendant engaged in conduct that led to the death of a human being. This level of injury rises above mere or moderate harm. Instead, the level of injury inflicted and intended must imperil human life. This was often easily proven because the victim actually died from the injury inflicted. If the accused intends without justification, excuse, or mitigation

---

[2] Commonwealth v. Drum, 58 Pa. 9, 16 (1868).

to inflict this level and type of human harm, then s/he is guilty of murder if, as a result of the harm intended and inflicted, the grievously injured person dies. (Modern definitions of serious or grievous bodily injury/harm extend the definition to include injury intended or likely to cause permanent loss or disfigurement of a bodily organ or function. For example, throwing acid in another's face with the intent that it will cause facial disfigurement and death results would suffice.)

Extreme recklessness murder is also referred to as abandoned, malignant, or **"depraved heart murder."** Here, the defendant does not intend to kill his/her victim; s/he does not even intend to cause grievous bodily injury. Instead, this type of malice at common law was the result of a defendant's advertent and unjustifiable risk taking. The language often associated with such risk-taking at common law is "wanton indifference," "extreme recklessness," "wanton disregard," and "extreme indifference." Though the killing is unintended, the risk (taken and lost) was unjustified. This mental state constituted malice aforethought at common law because it was " 'so wanton, so deficient in a moral sense of concern, so devoid of regard of the life or lives of others, and so blameworthy' **as to render the actor as culpable as one whose conscious objective is to kill."**[3] Thus, when a defendant engages in such risky behavior that leads to the death of a human being, the trier of fact may infer that the defendant killed with malice aforethought. It is important to remember that ordinary criminal recklessness is often manslaughter but is not depraved heart murder. Though the latter term is often undefined or not clearly defined, common law courts required that the risk be far greater than that involved in ordinary recklessness, i.e., a very large risk in which the defendant fully appreciates the risk. Still others require extreme risk, full appreciation, and an "anti-social purpose." Such a purpose often includes escaping detection of the defendant's involvement in another crime (e.g., keeping a dog trained to viciously protect an illegal methamphetamine lab).

Defenses against common law murder or manslaughter include justifications and excuses such as duress, necessity, self-defense, defense of others, and defense of property. For example, the defense of duress occurs when the defendant is coerced by another to commit a crime via the threat of unlawful force (to be used against the defendant or someone with whom the defendant has a connection). The duress defense requires that the threat be "present, imminent, and impending" and must contain an apprehension or threat of death or serious personal bodily injury if the defendant does not comply and commit the crime. The defense of necessity, also known as a choice of evils, results when, in the face of a natural event (e.g., blizzard, tidal wave) the defendant must choose between killing and suffering substantial harm to him/herself and/or property. The necessity defense is generally not available for homicides under the common law. Self-defense at common law allows an individual to use whatever force is reasonably necessary to prevent the immediate unlawful imposition of equal or greater force upon the defendant. Deadly, i.e., a homicidal level of force, may be justified when resisting unlawful deadly force or the threat of imminent unlawful deadly force.[4] Defense of others justifies using a commensurate amount of force to protect a third person when the latter is threatened under circumstances that would

---

[3] People v. Suarez, 844 N.E.2d 721 (N.Y. 2005) (citation omitted; emphasis added).

[4] For a more detailed discussion of self-defense, see Chapter 13, Self-Defense.

allow the third party to protect him/herself and the defendant reasonably believes that intervention is immediately necessary. Defense of property, too, may justify a use of force; however, at common law, defense of property never justified the use of deadly force. To the extent that homicidal force was used within one's home in self-defense, however, the "Castle Doctrine" would justify such an amount of force, particularly when protecting oneself and loved ones.

II.   MODERN LAW

American reform of the common law included legislative codification and statutorily "grading" various types of criminal homicides. Pennsylvania began this trend in 1794 when it created in the state's criminal code degrees of murder (again: at common law and prior to this change, murder had no "degrees"). Other jurisdictions followed suit, leading to laws across the nation dividing murder into degrees. Today, most American jurisdictions divide criminal homicide into degrees that range from first degree to third, fourth, or higher. The purpose of grading these unlawful killings is to limit the most severe punishment (death penalty or life imprisonment without the possibility of parole) to the most criminally culpable.

Although the statutes and definitions vary across American states and federal jurisdiction, all grade the most culpable killings at the lowest degrees. The lower the degree of criminal homicide, the more serious the killing and punishment. Almost all American jurisdictions that rank criminal homicide by degrees include as **first degree murder** willful (desire to cause death), deliberate (appreciating the full significance of the killing), and premeditated (thinking about beforehand) killings, as well as killings that occur during the commission of inherently dangerous felonies (felony murder). Much like the formula at common law, modern statutes do not quantify the amount of time required to engage in either premeditation and deliberation. Today, they can occur within a moment's time, a matter of seconds, and even within the blink of an eye. The consistent requirement in many jurisdictions is that the government prove both that a defendant had time to premeditate and deliberate and the defendant, in fact, did both. Proving a sufficient amount of time to do both, standing alone, is legally insufficient evidence of the requisite *mens rea* elements. The evidence must show that the defendant had an intent (desire or purpose) to kill and actually premeditated and deliberated. Circumstantial evidence is often relied upon by the government to prove the codified elements of first degree murder.

First degree murder statutes also often identify "aggravating factors" that, if present, will increase the defendant's punishment (e.g., capital murder). Aggravating factors vary from state to state; however, some of the most common ones are killing of a police officer in the course of his duty, killing a judge, killing a witness slated to testify during a criminal trial with the intent to influence judicial proceedings, mass/multiple killings, and killing for hire. If a defendant is convicted of capital murder, s/he can be subjected to the death penalty in some jurisdictions.

The distinction between first degree and **second degree murder** also varies by jurisdiction. Most often, any of the traditional common law mental states that do not require premeditation or deliberation constitute second degree murder. Thus, second degree murder will be the appropriate criminal charge if the defendant did not kill with the intent codified in first degree statutes. Sometimes the charge of second degree murder is based upon the prosecutor's decision, given, e.g., insufficient evidence that the defendant premeditated or deliberated. Sometimes, a defendant is convicted of second degree murder because the jury determined that the defendant's killing did not rise to a first degree criminal homicide, given the victim's conduct or the defendant's misperception of the victim and the threat the victim posed. Additionally, modern modifications of the felony-murder rule sometimes codify killings that occur during the commission of an unenumerated felony as second degree murder.[5]

Third degree murder statutes exist in some American jurisdictions.[6] Third degree murder is defined most commonly as one of general intent killing. Although a specific

---

[5] For example, Missouri's second degree murder statute provides:

Second degree murder, penalty.

565.021. 1. A person commits the crime of murder in the second degree if he:

(1) Knowingly causes the death of another person or, with the purpose of causing serious physical injury to another person, causes the death of another person; or

(2) Commits or attempts to commit any felony, and, in the perpetration or the attempted perpetration of such felony or in the flight from the perpetration or attempted perpetration of such felony, another person is killed as a result of the perpetration or attempted perpetration of such felony or immediate flight from the perpetration of such felony or attempted perpetration of such felony.

2. Murder in the second degree is a class A felony, and the punishment for second degree murder shall be in addition to the punishment for commission of a related felony or attempted felony, other than murder or manslaughter.

3. Notwithstanding section 556.046 and section 565.025, in any charge of murder in the second degree, the jury shall be instructed on, or, in a jury-waived trial, the judge shall consider, any and all of the subdivisions in subsection 1 of this section which are supported by the evidence and requested by one of the parties or the court.

Nebraska's statute is much more pithy:

28-304. Murder in the second degree; penalty.

(1) A person commits murder in the second degree if he causes the death of a person intentionally, but without premeditation.

(2) Murder in the second degree is a Class IB felony.

[6] Florida, Minnesota, and Pennsylvania have third degree murder statutes. In Minnesota, third degree murder is codified at § 609.195 and defines murder in the third degree as follows:

(a) Whoever, without intent to effect the death of any person, causes the death of another by perpetrating an act eminently dangerous to others and evincing a depraved mind, without regard for human life, is guilty of murder in the third degree and may be sentenced to imprisonment for not more than 25 years.

(b) Whoever, without intent to cause death, proximately causes the death of a human being by, directly or indirectly, unlawfully selling, giving away, bartering, delivering, exchanging, distributing, or administering a controlled substance classified in Schedule I or II, is guilty of murder in the third degree and may be sentenced to imprisonment for not more than 25 years or to payment of a fine of not more than $40,000, or both. In Pennsylvania, third degree murder is defined as follows: Chapter 25: Criminal Homicide § 2502 (c) Murder of the third degree. All other kinds of murder shall be murder of the third degree. Murder of the third degree is a felony of the first degree."

Florida's statute § 782.04 provides:

intent to cause serious bodily injury is not required, malice — express or implied — is an element. Malice may be found if the accused consciously disregards an unjustified and extremely high risk that his or her actions might cause death or serious bodily injury. Given the lack of hard-and-fast rules across jurisdictions, the statutes must be consulted to determine the crime's defining and attendant circumstances.

III.   THE MODEL PENAL CODE

The MPC rejects degrees of murders and simply splits criminal homicide into three categories: murder, manslaughter, and negligent homicide.[7] Under the MPC or in a MPC jurisdiction (i.e., where a state has adopted the Model Penal Code definition and "legislative history"), a person is guilty of criminal homicide if s/he takes the life of another human being purposely, knowingly, recklessly, or negligently and without justification or excuse.[8]

Under the MPC, a **murder** occurs when the defendant purposely, knowingly, or recklessly kills another.[9] Again: there are no degrees. Nor under the MPC is there a

---

(4) The unlawful killing of a human being, when perpetrated without any design to effect death, by a person engaged in the perpetration of, or in the attempt to perpetrate, any felony other than any:

   (a) Trafficking offense prohibited by s. 893.135(1),

   (b) Arson,

   (c) Sexual battery,

   (d) Robbery,

   (e) Burglary,

   (f) Kidnapping,

   (g) Escape,

   (h) Aggravated child abuse,

   (i) Aggravated abuse of an elderly person or disabled adult,

   (j) Aircraft piracy,

   (k) Unlawful throwing, placing, or discharging of a destructive device or bomb,

   (l) Unlawful distribution of any substance controlled under s. 893.03(1), cocaine as described in s. 893.03(2)(a) 4., or opium or any synthetic or natural salt, compound, derivative, or preparation of opium by a person 18 years of age or older, when such drug is proven to be the proximate cause of the death of the user,

   (m) Carjacking,

   (n) Home-invasion robbery,

   (o) Aggravated stalking,

   (p) Murder of another human being,

   (q) Aggravated fleeing or eluding with serious bodily injury or death,

   (r) Resisting an officer with violence to his or her person, or

   (s) Felony that is an act of terrorism or is in furtherance of an act of terrorism,

is murder in the third degree and constitutes a felony of the second degree, punishable as provided[. . .].

[7] *See* MODEL PENAL CODE § 210.1 (Criminal Homicide), § 210.2 (Murder), § 210.3 (Manslaughter), and § 210.4 (Negligent Homicide).

[8] *See* MODEL PENAL CODE § 210.2(1). For a review of MPC culpability, see Chapter 3, Actus Reus.

[9] *See* MODEL PENAL CODE § 210.2(1). For a review of MPC culpability, see Chapter 3, Actus Reus.

requirement that the government prove premeditation, deliberation, or malice afore-thought. Proof of purposely or knowingly will suffice under MPC § 210.2; however, the MPC *does* draw "a narrow distinction between acting purposely and knowingly."[10] Conduct is not done purposely unless it was the defendant's conscious object to perform an action of that nature or to cause such a result. If s/he is simply aware that his/her conduct is of the required nature or that the prohibited result is practically certain to follow from that conduct, the defendant acted knowingly.[11] Under the MPC, criminal homicide constitutes **manslaughter** when it is committed recklessly.[12]

---

[10] *See* American Law Institute, Model Penal Code and Commentaries, Comment to § 202 (1985).

[11] *See* American Law Institute, Model Penal Code and Commentaries, Comment to § 202 (1985).

[12] *See* MODEL PENAL CODE § 210.3(1)(a). For a review of MPC culpability, see Chapter 3 Actus Reus. For more on manslaughter, see Chapter 8, Homicide II — Manslaughter and Felony Murder.

EXERCISE

Overview

In the early morning of October 1, the victim, Isaiah Visage, was shot to death. The government's case will rest primarily on the testimony of two witnesses present at the shooting: (1) George Gamma and (2) Larry Lowell. The criminal defendant charged with First Degree Murder is Tim Canova. The government has indicated that it will pursue a theory of deliberate premeditation in prosecuting Tim Canova; however, the issue at trial is identity, i.e., the government has to prove beyond a reasonable doubt that Tim Canova is the shooter. Tim has an alibi defense, i.e., that he was out of the state on the night of the shooting. The pretrial record consists of the following evidence, to be introduced via witness testimony:

Lowell is expected to testify that he witnessed the events on the night of the killing. Earlier that night and before the killing, Lowell spent time at his apartment where he, his girlfriend, Ashley Nunez, and the defendant all lived. At one point during the evening, the defendant, Tim Canova, and his unnamed "date" appeared at the apartment. The defendant talked on his cell phone with the victim, Isaiah Visage, about illegally selling a handgun, a felony in this state. Lowell watched the defendant pull out a gun at one point during the telephone conversation with the victim. The defendant began playing with the gun, putting bullets in the weapon and taking them out. At one point, the defendant passed the gun to Lowell, who held it briefly, but quickly passed it back to the defendant without incident.

Later, Lowell and the defendant left to meet the victim (Ashley Nuñez and the defendant's "date"). Lowell understood from the overheard telephone conversation that they were going to meet the victim so that the defendant could sell the victim a gun. However, en route, the defendant told Lowell that he planned to "end it" with the victim.

Lowell and the defendant arrived at the selling location. The defendant, according to Lowell, seemed surprised that Visage showed up with a friend, Gamma. While the defendant and Visage walked ahead to complete the sale, Gamma and Lowell hung back, walking behind the two men.

Suddenly, for no apparent reason to the witnesses, Visage turned and punched the defendant hard. The defendant pushed Visage. Both men then fell to the ground in struggle. Instead of selling the gun to Visage, the defendant shot him. Gamma raced from the scene. The defendant instructed Lowell to search Visage's pockets and take what money Lowell found. Lowell was fearful and did as he was told, given what he had just witnessed.

Nunez, Lowell's girlfriend, is also expected to testify. Nunez, with whom the defendant spent the pre-incident evening (along with Lowell), is expected to testify to some of the defendant's pre-incident conversations with the victim. She is expected to confirm that the defendant pulled out a gun and displayed it to Lowell, that the defendant left the apartment with Lowell, that the defendant and Lowell returned shortly thereafter, and that the defendant took "a lot of money" from his pocket.

Nunez is also expected to testify to the content of messages she received that were posted on her Facebook account's "wall." Facebook, a social networking site accessed via the Internet, allows communications between individuals who have Facebook accounts. Nunez is expected to testify that the defendant, in an attempt to thwart Nunez's trial testimony, placed several communications on her Facebook "wall." Nunez is expected to testify that the defendant has a Facebook account, that the Facebook name he used was "doit2it." She will testify regarding the following communications:

1. "Don't snitch."

2. "Pretend you're Forrest Gump!"

3. "Talk to Tim; don't talk to the judge."

Nunez is expected to testify that she: (a) did not respond to the above posts and (b) believed defendant Tim Canova urged her not to testify and, in the alternative, to feign a lack of memory.

REQUIRED TASKS

Task One: Evidentiary Problems

You are the prosecutor's law clerk, far more familiar with social media than the prosecutor himself. In fact, given your familiarity with social media, you have decided to help your prosecutor understand how to make use of the Facebook posting in this criminal homicide trial.

Decide how to use the potential social media evidence in the government's case that would support a theory of first degree murder, pursuant to the relevant Federal Rules of Evidence 401, 402, and 403 excerpted in the online component. Specifically, identify how the three Facebook postings, if taken for their truth, would be relevant to the prosecutor's first degree murder case. In preparing for this task, review the below-noted jurisdictions' substantive law, as **your jurisdiction has not yet ruled on the relevance and, therefore, admissibility of social media evidence.** Use an online database to read the following cases for guidance regarding the application of the substantive law in this task:

- *Targonski v. Oak Ridge*, 921 F. Supp. 2d 820 (E.D. Tenn. 2013) (*see* Q. (iv) Motion in Limine)
- *Clement v. Johnson's Warehouse Showroom*, 388 S.W.3d 469 (Ark. Ct. App. 2012)
- *Tienda v. Texas*, 358 S.W.3d 633 (Tex. Crim. App. 2012)
- *Griffin v. Maryland*, 19 A.3d 415 (Md. 2011)
- *Connecticut v. Eleck*, 23 A.3d 818 (Conn. App. Ct. 2011)

Additionally, in preparing for this task, you also should watch the Suggested Video Clips (SVCs) to be found in the Task One materials in the online component for this Chapter.

ESTIMATED TIME FOR COMPLETION: 3 hours.

LEVEL OF DIFFICULTY (1 TO 5):

Task Two: Statutory Interpretation

Again, you are the prosecutor's law clerk. Prior to this criminal prosecution, your state's murder statute read as follows:

> **PART 4, TITLE 1, CHAPTER 265, § 1: MURDER DEFINED:** Murder committed with deliberately premeditated malice aforethought, or with extreme atrocity or cruelty, or in the commission or attempted commission of a crime punishable with death or imprisonment for life, is murder in the first degree. Murder which does not appear to be in the first degree is murder in the second degree. The degree of murder shall be found by the jury.

Last week, however, your state's legislative body passed a revised criminal homicide statute that reads as follows:

§ 265.1. Murder

(1) Except as provided in Section 210.3(1)(b), criminal homicide constitutes murder when:

(a) it is committed purposely or knowingly; or

(b) it is committed recklessly under circumstances manifesting extreme indifference to the value of human life. Such recklessness and indifference are presumed if the actor is engaged or is an accomplice in the commission of, or an attempt to commit, or flight after committing or attempting to commit robbery, rape or deviate sexual intercourse by force or threat of force, arson, burglary, kidnapping or felonious escape.

There is no state case law yet regarding the new statute or any potential differences between the prior statute and the new one. The prosecutor you work for wants to be briefed on the new law. Prepare a list of discussion points you will rely upon during your next in-office meeting to explain the differences, if any, between the two statutes.

ESTIMATED TIME FOR COMPLETION: 60 minutes.

LEVEL OF DIFFICULTY (1 TO 5):

Task 3: Evidentiary Problems; Authentication

You remain the law clerk to the prosecutor. The prosecutor realizes that before she can introduce the wall posts, the Facebook evidence must be properly authenticated. Prepare a short how-to memo for the prosecutor, explaining why these items of Facebook evidence must be authenticated before being admitted as relevant evidence. Explain also how to authenticate this social media evidence. In preparing for this task, review Federal Rules of Evidence 104 and 901, provided in the online component. In addition, use an online database to read the following cases, as **your jurisdiction has not yet ruled** on the admissibility of social media evidence.

- *Tienda v. Texas*, 358 S.W.3d 633 (Tex. Crim. App. 2012)
- *Griffin v. Maryland*, 19 A.3d 415 (Md. 2011) (MySpace Evidence)
- *Connecticut v. Eleck*, 23 A.3d 818 (Conn. App. Ct. 2011) (Facebook)
- *Commonwealth v. Hartford*, 194 N.E.2d 401 (Mass. 1963)

Additionally, if you have not done so already, you also should consult the online component for Task One for additional SVCs to prepare you for this task.

ESTIMATED TIME FOR COMPLETION: 2 hours.

LEVEL OF DIFFICULTY (1 TO 5):

PRACTICE SKILLS USED:

Skill 1: Evidentiary Problems; Authenticating Social Media Evidence

Skill 2: Tactical Thinking

Skill 3: Legal Argument; Integrating the Law and the Facts

Skill 4: Statutory Interpretation

SKILLS GUIDES

SKILLS GUIDE #1: Evidentiary Problems; Authenticating Social Media Evidence

Social networking sites are rapidly becoming a standard method of communication for millions across the United States and the world. As social networking sites become more prevalent, litigators must understand how to authenticate evidence culled from the various electronic platforms provided by sites such as Facebook, Twitter, Google, and others. Social media provides the potential for bolstering witness or defendant credibility by proving real-time documentation of, e.g., alibi defenses, assessments, narratives, and other aspects of life and litigation. Social media also provides the potential for self-inflicted wounds with the inadvertent disclosure of visual, audible, or written evidence undermining a claim or defense. Increasingly, attorneys are mining these Internet sites for useful evidence to present at trial. Evidence from these sites may take the form of profile pages, postings, chats, private messages, photos, or video. This is so because the "@" symbol, used to pinpoint a person's digital presence on a social network, is a logogram that, once inscribed, represents digital — but not necessarily physical or actual — identity.

Authentication is a prerequisite to the admission of any form of evidence at trial. Authentication requires the proffering attorney to show that the evidence in question is what the proponent claims it to be. Authenticating evidence from these social networking sites may involve different methods, depending on the type of communication. Given the time and expense involved, the litigator must know how much foundational evidence a court will require for authentication.

Given the cloud-based, transient, and collaborative nature of social media, social networking sites present unique challenges for authentication. Social media is different from other types of electronic evidence because although users are encouraged to create individual profile pages and content for their personal use and Internet enjoyment, this understanding may not be completely or consistently accurate, despite indicia to the contrary. Although many users make identification and, ultimately, trial authentication easier by posting clearly personal information on profile pages (e.g., full name, date of birth, address) that assist a trial judge's determination that the proffered evidence is authentic, many others posts, pages, platforms, or "personas" are not that straightforward.

Many users are not interested in placing clearly identifying information on the Internet and will create profiles or accounts by using pseudonyms meant to conceal the user's true identity. To make matters more complicated, these users often change their pseudonyms, crossing gender lines and cultural understandings. Some of these same or other users will create social media accounts by using a self-portrait ("selfie"), which makes visual authentication possible for those who can compare the user with the photo. However, many users, again, do not. Instead, they use photos of famous people, pets, movie characters, shoes, nature, or anime or cartoon characters. Some users do not bother to associate any visual image at all with their accounts.

There is also a challenge regarding the veracity of social media communications and posted information. Users may exaggerate or create fictionalized information to post. So, for example, a user whose real name is Eli Wallace who resides in Kalamazoo, Michigan, and is an introverted 51-year-old cable technician may create a profile name of "King of the World," claim that he lives in Hollywood, California, is 31 years old, body builds for a living, and life guards at glamorous star-studded events on the side. Similarly, his postings of his "status" (where he is, what he is doing, what he has done, what he plans to do) will almost certainly consist of glamorous, dangerous, fascinating, but ultimately fictional, conduct.

One other authentication challenge unique to social media is the question of who accessed, used, and posted certain information on the platform's site. Increasingly, those who participate in social media have either experienced or are claiming that their social networking accounts have been hacked or wholly fictitious accounts have been created and proffered as if they originated from the hacked account holder. This issue can arise at trial. The proponent of the proffered social media evidence (e.g., a posted photograph, a three-sentence-long status update) must show that a particular person authored the communication, not simply that it came from a specific social networking profile. If, for example, Eli Wallace shares a computer with his brother, Stephen, and Eli's social networking sites are not secured or if Stephen has access to Eli's account, it is unclear that postings under Eli's social media accounts were authored by Eli (versus Stephen). Similarly, when individuals share homes, where computers, or mobile devices are left unattended, legitimate concerns arise when accounts are left open and unattended, vulnerable to others' input and postings. Additionally, if Eli's social media profile is "hacked," i.e., accessed by an unauthorized user (human or a computerized, automated "bot"), authentication of postings under his social media account may become not only compromised, but impossible.

If an attorney seeks to introduce such evidence at trial, authentication of social media evidence will involve a two-step process similar to the one found in the Federal Rules of Evidence ("FRE"). Under the FRE, the court must first make a preliminary determination of authenticity under FRE 901(a), which requires the proffering party to prove "evidence [of authenticity] sufficient to support a finding that the matter in question is what its proponent claims." The standard is low; the evidence need not be conclusive; it may also be circumstantial. However, the evidence must be sufficient to provide a rational basis for a jury to find that the proffered evidence is authentic. If the court has made a preliminary finding that the evidence is what the proponent claims, the evidence is introduced and subjected to cross-examination by the proffering party's opponent. The jury considers the evidence and makes the ultimate determination of authenticity, weighing the evidence accordingly.

The types of circumstantial evidence that tend to authenticate a communication are somewhat unique to each medium. FRE 901(b) provides an illustrative list of methods of authenticating various types of evidence. Based on the rule's extensive list and proffer possibilities, it seems that attorneys may certainly request that courts authenticate evidence from social networking sites by use of the proffered communication's distinctive characteristics. Depending on how a user chooses to access the Internet and his/her social media platform(s), s/he faces tracking by cookies, IP logging, or MAC address logging by Internet Service Provider (ISP, e.g., America

Online, Google, Internet Explorer, Firefox) or router, which can reveal his/her activities to the ISP(s), the online services used, advertising networks, and other third parties who have access to those locations, including, perhaps, state, local, and federal governments, all without a warrant. If the proffering attorney can gather evidence of such unique and genuinely distinctive characteristics, courts will likely allow circumstantial authentication based on content and context.

If, however, such evidence cannot be had and the characteristics of a communication in question are more general, courts will likely require additional corroborating evidence prior to authenticating. This additional corroboration may include, e.g., testimony of a witness with knowledge of the unique ISP address of the computer, that the communication originated from secured location or access that only the alleged account holder may access, or even testimony from a computer expert or the cable company technician who services the user's home or other connections to the Internet.

Rule 901(b)(1) also allows for authentication through testimony from a witness with knowledge that a matter is exactly what it is claimed to be. Social media evidence is most likely to be admitted at trial when it is obtained properly in the first place. The person who created the evidence may testify to authenticate it. That is the most obvious method for authenticating social media evidence. For example, profile pages and posts may require sufficiently distinctive data, such as references about which only the creator and purported "author" would have known. When this testimony is not possible, thoroughly documenting and verifying the process and results of social media data collection can help the evidence withstand authentication challenges. The simplest method is to capture and preserve a "screen shot" or "screen cap(ture)," i.e., printing a time- and date-stamped copy or saving as a file one or more static images taken while viewing any computer image of a social media (or other) website. However, these images may be difficult to authenticate without testimony based on personal knowledge of when, why, and how the images were captured, printed, or saved.

When a purported author is unavailable or uncooperative, proving that social media content was, indeed, created by the author can be a difficult task. Social networking site providers can also be the source of a wealth of information, some of which is not publicly visible but would help in an authentication quest. The social media websites themselves (check out their Terms of Service regarding, e.g., court-issued subpoenas for criminal and civil trials), law review articles, and experts can all provide information on this type of assistance. Rule 901(b)(4) provides that circumstantial evidence, including "appearance, contents, substance, internal patterns, or other distinctive characteristics of the item, taken together with all the circumstances," can help to authenticate evidence. Notably, the "characteristics of the offered item itself, considered in the light of circumstances, afford authentication techniques in great variety." Similarly, testimony also may be provided by a witness who has personal knowledge of how the social media information is typically generated. In such a case, the authenticating witness must provide factual specificity about the process by which the information is created, acquired, maintained, and preserved without alteration or change, or the process by which it is produced.

Beyond the unique issues of authentication, social media evidence also must clear additional evidentiary hurdles before it can be introduced: relevance, hearsay, and admissions. Luckily, these hurdles are generally amenable to traditional reasoning and evidentiary standards.

Relevance is the starting point for the introduction of evidence at trial. Evidence must be relevant before it is admissible at trial; irrelevant evidence is inadmissible, per FRE 402. Under FRE 401, relevant evidence is that which has any tendency — even the slightest — to make more or less probable a fact of consequence to the determination of the matter. Evidence can be relevant to the elements of the substantive law pertaining to trial action (e.g., murder, theft, negligence). Evidence can also be relevant to a criminal defense (e.g., duress, self-defense). If you cannot articulate what the evidence is offered to prove, either reanalyze what must be proven (i.e., what are the elements of the particular action), or creatively contemplate different ways that the elements can be proven or disproven (as FRE 401 contemplates the evidence making more or less probable). For example, in a criminal homicide trial the victim, V, is dead andthe defendant, D, is charged with V's murder. The prosecution discovers and seeks to introduce at trial evidence that D wrote a love letter to V's wife. The love letter is relevant evidence under FRE 401. The evidence of the love letter is evidence of D's desire for V's wife, and is ultimately probative of the element of criminal intent. The love letter is also evidence of D's motive to form a criminal intent and carry it out by killing V.

However, even if the evidence is relevant, its relevance must not, per FRE 403, be substantially outweighed by the danger of unfair prejudice, confusion of the trial issues, or mislead the jury. It also must not waste the court's time. Under evidence rules such as the FRE, the "cost" of admission of otherwise relevant evidence is to be balanced against its probative worth, or benefit. The cost may be too high. If photographs of the victim of a murder are offered to prove the fact of death or even its cause, the court would have to balance the probative value (proof that the victim is dead) against the potential for unfair emotional appeal to the jury that the pictures might have (traumatizing jurors with highly graphic images of a decapitation).

Similarly, social media postings also lend themselves to the rules regarding hearsay evidence at trial. Under FRE 801(c), hearsay is an out-of-court statement offered to prove the truth of the matter asserted. FRE 802 prohibits the use of hearsay, unless the FRE or other body of law (e.g., the Constitution) allows its admission. Out-of-court statements are hearsay only if offered to prove the truth of the matter asserted, and hearsay evidence is inadmissible when it falls outside an exemption or an exception to the rule. If the proffered social media evidence is a "statement" under the jurisdiction's rules, the first element of the definition of hearsay is met. FRE 801(a) defines a statement as: "(1) an oral or written assertion or (2) nonverbal conduct of a person, if it is intended by the person as an assertion." This definition requires that an intent to assert exists and can occur either in the form of an oral or written assertion; it may also occur in form of assertive conduct. But the focus of the definition is that the hearsay declarant must intend to assert. Most verbal evidence is easily determined to be a statement within the definition. However, sometimes people say or do something without intending to assert. Perhaps they ask a question, or give a direction, or just act in a way that communicates a belief, but is not a direct assertion. In such an instance, if the action was not intended as an assertion, then the evidence is not a statement within the definition of hearsay. It is not a statement because it is not intended as a statement.

On the other hand, statements may prove admissible, despite the rule against hearsay, if they fall within the meaning of an evidence code's hearsay exceptions or exemptions. Hearsay exceptions include such statements that can be deemed present sense impressions, excited utterances, and then-existing mental, emotional, or physical conditions. These statements may also fit a jurisdiction's definition of those exempted from the rule against hearsay. For example, FRE 801(d) exempts from the definition of hearsay two major categories of evidence: certain kinds of prior statements of witnesses (FRE 801(d)(1)) and admissions by a party opponent (FRE 801(d)(2)). Under the FRE, an admission is a statement made either by the party-opponent (explicitly, FRE 801(d)(2)(a)), co-signed by a party-opponent (FRE 801(d)(2)(b), made by his/her agent (FRE 801(d)(2)(c)), employee (FRE 801(d)(2)(d)), or co-conspirator (FRE 801(d)(2)(e)). These statements are generally relevant and admissible for their truth at trial, but only when they are introduced against the party opponent. Facebook status updates, public posts, chat transcripts, Tweets, and more lend themselves well to such exceptions. These codified exemptions and exceptions to the rule against hearsay allow the admission of out-of-court statements for their truth, given the circumstances under which the out-of-court statements were made.

The full and nuanced extent to which these evidentiary exceptions and exemptions may apply (or not) is beyond the scope of this skills guide, chapter, and volume. But, within a determination of whether social media evidence is properly authenticated at trial, the parties and presiding official will also need to determine whether, beyond relevancy requirements, the evidence — if in the form of out-of-court statements — implicates hearsay or admissions provisions.

SKILLS GUIDE #2: Tactical Thinking

Please refer to Chapter 1, Skills Guide #4.

SKILLS GUIDE #3: Legal Argument; Integrating the Law and the Facts

Please refer to Chapter 8, Skills Guide #2.

SKILLS GUIDE #4: Statutory Interpretation

Please refer to Chapter 2, Skills Guide #6.

ADDITIONAL MATERIALS FOR THE EXERCISE — AVAILABLE IN ON-LINE COMPONENT

Fed. R. Evid. 104: Preliminary Questions

Fed. R. Evid. 401: Test for Relevant Evidence

Fed. R. Evid. 402: General Admissibility of Relevant Evidence

Fed. R. Evid. 403: Excluding Relevant Evidence for Prejudice, Confusion, Waste of Time, or Other Reasons

Fed. R. Evid. 901: Authenticating or Identifying Evidence

Chapter 8

HOMICIDE II — MANSLAUGHTER AND FELONY MURDER

OVERVIEW

As discussed in the previous chapter, homicide can generally be divided into two main categories: murder and manslaughter. A murder conviction (whether first or second degree) requires proof of malice aforethought. If there is no malice aforethought, then a charge of manslaughter may be appropriate. In this chapter, we will first discuss felony-murder — a specific form of murder. Then we will discuss the crime of manslaughter.

I. FELONY MURDER

Stated in its simplest and broadest form, the felony-murder rule holds that a defendant is guilty of murder if death results from conduct undertaken during the commission of a felony. Most states today have some version of the felony-murder rule. Nevertheless, the felony-murder rule is the subject of much criticism and almost all jurisdictions have placed some limits on the rule and its application.

A. First Degree and Second Degree Murder

Felony-murder is a form of first or second-degree murder — that is, it is considered a murder with malice aforethought. In some jurisdictions, the malice required to sustain a felony-murder conviction is implied from the malice of the predicate felony (the felony during which the death occurred). In these jurisdictions, there is no *mens rea* requirement for the killing. A defendant is liable for the death regardless of whether that death occurred intentionally, recklessly, or negligently. For example, imagine that during the robbery of a jewelry store, the suspect pushes a security guard as he attempts to escape with stolen goods. Due to the suspect's actions, the security guard falls, hits his head on the ground, and dies. The suspect could now be charged with murder under the felony-murder rule, despite the fact that the death of the security guard was unintentional and perhaps even accidental. In its broadest application, the felony-murder doctrine is one of strict liability — if the defendant had the requisite *mens rea* to commit the predicate felony, the defendant is also responsible for the death that occurred during that felony's commission. Alternatively, some jurisdictions have narrowed the scope of the doctrine by requiring a particular mental state with respect to the felonious conduct that led to the death (i.e., the defendant must have *intentionally* committed the predicate felony).

Most jurisdictions distinguish a felony-murder that results in a first degree murder conviction from a felony-murder that constitutes second degree murder. Typically, first degree felony-murder is limited to murders that occur during the commission of an enumerated list of more serious predicate felonies. For instance, North Carolina defines murder in the first degree to include killings that occur during "the perpetration or attempted perpetration of arson, rape or a sex offense, robbery, kidnapping, burglary, or other felony committed or attempted with the use of a deadly weapon." N.C. Gen. Stat. § 14-17 (2012).

The definition of felony-murder resulting in a second degree murder conviction varies by jurisdiction. Some jurisdictions define second degree felony-murder as any murder that occurs during the commission of a felony, other than those listed under the first degree murder statute. In contrast, some jurisdictions limit which predicate felonies can serve as the basis for a second degree murder conviction, requiring a predicate felony that is considered "dangerous." There are generally two approaches to the "dangerous felony" limitation. In some jurisdictions, courts look at the predicate felony in the *abstract* to assess its dangerousness. For example, California limits the felony-murder rule for murder in second degree to felonies that are "inherently dangerous to human life." Other jurisdictions follow an *in-fact* approach, asking in each individual case whether the defendant committed the predicate felony in a manner that was dangerous to human life.

B. Limits to the Felony-Murder Rule

There are several additional limits to the application of the felony-murder rule. The independent felony rule is one common limitation (also called the "merger" doctrine). The independent felony rule states that, in order for felony-murder to apply, the predicate felony must be *independent* of the killing. In other words, if the predicate felony is a felony that involves the intent to injure, the predicate felony *merges* with the murder charge and cannot serve as a basis for a felony-murder conviction. For example, if a suspect and the victim are involved in a physical fight, in which the defendant then takes out a knife and kills the suspect, the charge of felony assault cannot serve as a basis for felony-murder. (The defendant may, however, be liable for the killing of the victim under another basis of liability such as a second-degree murder charge or manslaughter charge.)

The concept of "causation" also provides some limits to the application of the felony-murder rule. Sometimes referred to as the *res gestae* rule (Latin for "things done"), the requirement that the predicate felony *caused* the death places temporal and proximal requirements on the rule's application. In general, the predicate felony must be the "but for" cause of the death. For example, in the jewelry store hypothetical in which the suspect hits the security guard on the head, *but for* the suspect committing the robbery, the security guard would not have died. Many jurisdictions also include a consideration of "proximate cause" and hold a defendant liable only for a death that is a reasonably foreseeable consequence of the commission of the predicate felony.

Many jurisdictions also specify that the death must occur *during* the commission of the predicate felony. Nevertheless, this durational requirement has been interpreted as including the period of time immediately after the crime has occurred, and typically the time up until the suspect has reached a place of safety. For example, a suspect may be liable for the death of a security guard several blocks away if that death occurs as he is fleeing the crime scene. He may not, however, be liable for the death of the security guard if the security guard dies — albeit from the stress of witnessing the robbery — more than a week later.

In some jurisdictions, the felony-murder rule does not apply to deaths that are a result of actions by individuals other than the criminal suspects. Say, for example, that the security guard, upon witnessing the beginning of the robbery, fired his gun. Instead of hitting the defendant, however, the bullet killed a customer in the store. In many jurisdictions, the defendant would not be liable for the death of the customer. Similarly, if a co-defendant was shot by the security guard, the defendant would not be liable for his death under this limit to the application of the felony-murder rule.

The application of the felony-murder rule in tandem with the principles of accomplice liability may result in a defendant being convicted for murder even if the death was the result of his co-defendant's conduct. For instance, imagine that two suspects rob a jewelry store. If one suspect pushes the guard (who then dies) on his way out, both are liable for his death under the felony-murder rule. Some states have chosen to limit a defendant's liability for deaths caused by a co-defendant's actions. New York, for instance, provides an affirmative defense for liability for a co-defendant's actions if the defendant did not commit or aid in the killing, was not armed with a deadly weapon, and had no reason to believe the co-defendant was armed or would engage in conduct likely to lead to a death. *See* N.Y. Penal Law § 125.25(3) (McKinney 2006).

Critics of the felony-murder rule argue that it is unfair to punish someone for a murder he did not intend to commit. The Model Penal Code and a few jurisdictions reject the felony-murder rule completely. Some critics specifically decry the felony-murder rule when applied to an individual even though he was not the one who caused the death. Proponents of the felony-murder rule argue that the rule serves to deter people from committing felonies and from conducting themselves in a potentially deadly manner.

In practice, in the event that the facts of a case would support either a first-degree murder charge or a felony-murder charge, prosecutors may prefer to seek a conviction for felony-murder. The burden of proving only the predicate felony is likely viewed as less onerous than proving a willful, deliberate, and premeditated murder beyond a reasonable doubt.

II. MANSLAUGHTER

Manslaughter is generally defined as a killing that is committed without malice aforethought. Manslaughter is divided into two types: voluntary manslaughter and involuntary manslaughter.

A.   Voluntary Manslaughter

Voluntary manslaughter is broadly defined as a murder that occurs in "the heat of passion" as a result of "legally adequate provocation." Voluntary manslaughter is an intentional killing that is done without premeditation and deliberation, and without malice aforethought. Defendants who kill under these circumstances are viewed as less blameworthy than defendants who kill with malice, thus justifying a lesser homicide charge and typically a shorter prison sentence.

In order to warrant a manslaughter charge, the killing must occur in the "heat of passion." "Heat of passion" encompasses a broader range of emotions than simply anger; it can include other states of violent and extreme emotion, including fear and jealousy. Whether a defendant acted in the heat of passion usually includes a consideration of any potential "cooling off" period. Most jurisdictions will not find a killing to have been committed in the "heat of passion" if a reasonable person would have calmed down between the act of provocation and the killing. It is typically a question for the jury whether the defendant acted in the heat of passion.

A killing in the heat of passion in and of itself is not sufficient to reduce a murder charge to a charge of manslaughter. There must also be "legally adequate provocation." Such provocation is generally defined as provocation that would cause a reasonable person to act rashly and without deliberation. Under the common law, legally sufficient provocations were specified: observation of adultery, aggravated assault, mutual combat, commission of a serious crime against a close relative, and illegal arrest. Today, it is typically a question left for the jury — whether the provocation at issue in the case would be sufficient to make a reasonable person lose control and act without reflection. Judges in each type of jurisdiction (enumerated categories or general reasonableness question) must give the jury a manslaughter instruction where there is sufficient evidence to support it. In a categories jurisdiction, jurors would be told what is legally reasonable is only what is listed in the categories. In a general reasonableness jurisdiction, jurors are told they can, but are not required to, find any circumstance identified by the defense to be adequate provocation.

At common law, words alone did not constitute adequate provocation. The "mere words" doctrine meant two things: first, insults alone never constituted adequate provocation; and second, the acts by the victim that constituted the provocation had to be observed by the defendant personally, not merely heard about via someone else. For example, a man had to see his wife commit adultery. It would have been legally insufficient for someone to say to him, "Your wife just committed adultery." Today, some modern common law jurisdictions now permit these "informational words" — words conveying provoking information — to constitute adequate provocation. In other jurisdictions, however, the "mere words" rule has remained, though some jurisdictions do leave room for unusual circumstances or particular types of egregious verbal provocation.

The question whether a reasonable person would react to the provocation is an objective one. In this context, the reaction of a "reasonable person" is usually defined as how an "ordinary" person would have reacted under those circumstances. The objective standard does not ask if that particular defendant was more susceptible to the provocation. In contrast, the Model Penal Code and some jurisdictions permit the consideration of the defendant's personal characteristics when determining whether there was legally sufficient provocation. Under modern law, being *unreasonably* provoked into the heat of passion would render the killing a form of second degree murder.

B. Involuntary Manslaughter

Involuntary manslaughter is an unintentional killing and, as such, it is considered a lesser offense than voluntary manslaughter. There are typically two types of involuntary manslaughter: unlawful act manslaughter and criminally negligent homicide.

Unlawful act manslaughter is a killing that occurs during the commission of an unlawful act. In some jurisdictions, the predicate unlawful act is limited to misdemeanors or a narrower category of "dangerous misdemeanors." This type of involuntary manslaughter is called "misdemeanor manslaughter." Unlawful act manslaughter stands in contrast to a death that occurs during the commission of a felony, which would then serve as a basis for a felony-murder conviction.

A criminally negligent homicide is one in which the killing occurred as a result of a suspect's extreme or gross negligence or, in some cases, a low level of recklessness. Imagine a meat seller whose meat is infected with a food-borne illness. If the seller was unaware of the contamination but operated his store in a blatantly poor and unsanitary manner, he may be guilty of a criminally negligent homicide if a customer eats his meat and dies as a result. If, however, the seller was aware of the contamination and sold the meat anyway, this more extreme level of recklessness could arguably demonstrate malice aforethought and therefore be grounds for the charge of murder.

EXERCISE

Overview

Keith Ventnor and Ashley Jordan were boyfriend and girlfriend for five years, the last three of which they lived together in Apartment 2B at 643 Cedar Street in Charlotte, North Carolina. For those three years, they signed the rental agreement together and both names were on the lease. Last year, Ashley broke up with Keith and asked him to move out. Keith was devastated but moved out on May 1. At the time, he did not have his own place, so he did not ask to take any of the furnishings. After Keith moved out, Ashley changed the lease to be in her name only. Although she repeatedly asked for Keith to return his set of keys, he did not return the keys to her. Ashley did not change the locks.

In the months following the breakup, Keith's life hit a rough patch. He lost his job and was staying on a friend's couch. Keith also began to drink alcohol heavily. Six months after Keith moved out, Keith learned from a mutual friend that Ashley had a new boyfriend, Taylor Jackson, who was now living with her in Apartment 2B. According to Ashley, Keith was furious upon learning this information.

On November 14 at about 7:00 p.m., Keith called Ashley on her cell phone while she was at work. Ashley recounted the phone conversation as follows: Keith was very upset. He begged her to stop seeing Taylor and to get back with him. Ashley refused and told Keith to "get a life." Ashley admitted that she swore at Keith and called him several names including "a loser" and a "good-for-nothing." Keith was enraged by her response. He then yelled that he wanted his stuff back. Ashley told him to stop bothering her at work and hung up on him.

After the phone call, Keith got in his car and drove to 643 Cedar Street. Keith later admitted to the police that he was upset and that he "wanted to take something to get back at Ashley." When he arrived at the apartment, Keith used his set of keys to enter the apartment.

As Keith was attempting to get the flat screen television off the living room wall, he heard a voice yelling at him to stop. Keith turned and was confronted by Taylor Jackson. Taylor recognized Keith and immediately started yelling and swearing at Keith. According to Keith, Taylor began yelling and taunting him, including saying things like "Ashley loves me" and "we got together before you even left." The two men had a physical fight. In the midst of the fighting, Keith grabbed a large ceramic vase that was sitting on the nearby coffee table. He hit Taylor on the head, causing Taylor to stumble. As Taylor stumbled backwards, he hit his head on the edge of the fireplace and fell to the ground with a massive head wound. Keith, panicked and afraid, ran from the apartment. He later learned that Taylor died later that night in the hospital, after being interviewed by the authorities. According to Taylor, Taylor was merely yelling at Keith to get out of his house. Taylor admitted that a fight broke out and that Taylor swung the first punch, hitting Keith squarely on the jaw. The coroner listed blunt head trauma as the cause of death.

The police investigation included a crime scene investigation, the collection of DNA and fingerprints, and an interview with Ashley. Based on this evidence, the police arrested Keith for murder. Keith is now charged with first degree murder under the theory of felony-murder. The complaint lists the predicate felony as "the perpetration of burglary."

REQUIRED TASKS

Task One: Motion Writing; Motion to Dismiss

You are the prosecutor representing the State. At trial, the hypothetical as described above comprised the prosecution's case-in-chief. At the conclusion of your case, defense counsel orally moved to dismiss the felony-murder charge on the basis of insufficiency of the evidence. The judge has asked for written briefing on the motion.

For purposes of this task, you are not to consider issues of assault, merger, mutual combat, or provocation. Your argument is limited to the question whether there is sufficient evidence to support the charge of first degree murder on the theory of felony-murder based on the predicate felony of burglary.

To prepare for this motion, you should use an online database to review the following statute: N.C. Gen. Stat. § 15A-1227 (Motion for Dismissal). The legal standard for this motion is as follows:

> Upon defendant's motion for dismissal, the question for the Court is whether there is substantial evidence (1) of each essential element of the offense charged, or of a lesser offense included therein, and (2) of defendant's being the perpetrator of such offense. If so, the motion is properly denied.

> If the evidence is sufficient only to raise a suspicion or conjecture as to either the commission of the offense or the identity of the defendant as the perpetrator of it, the motion should be allowed.

For purposes of this task, you should focus only on part (1) of the above standard of review. The defense has conceded that Keith was the involved individual and therefore is not challenging his identity as the perpetrator.

The law governing the application of the felony-murder rule in North Carolina is as follows:

> When a killing is committed in the perpetration of an enumerated felony, murder in the first degree is established irrespective of premeditation or deliberation or malice aforethought.

> For felony-murder in the first degree to apply, the actual intent to kill may be present or absent; however, the actual intent to commit the underlying felony is required.

> A killing is committed in the perpetration or attempted perpetration of a felony for purposes of the felony murder rule where there is no break in the chain of events leading from the initial felony to the act causing death, so that the killing is part of a series of incidents which form one continuous transaction.

You should review the relevant jury instructions provided in the online component. Unless instructed otherwise, you should also review the supplemental law provided in the online component. This law will form the legal basis upon which you should write your opposition to the defense's motion to dismiss. You do not need to do any additional legal research.

ESTIMATED TIME FOR COMPLETION: 60 minutes.

LEVEL OF DIFFICULTY (1 TO 5):

Task Two: Oral Argument; Jury Instructions

You are the defense counsel representing Keith Ventnor. At trial, the jury heard the evidence as laid out in the hypothetical above. You are now preparing to ask the judge for your requested jury instructions.

Prepare your oral argument to support your request to instruct the jury on the charge of voluntary manslaughter. In order to warrant instructing the jury on this charge, you must persuade the judge that there is sufficient evidence to support the charge of voluntary manslaughter.

You should refer to North Carolina Pattern Jury Instruction Criminal-206.11 provided in the online component. This instruction provides the law regarding the definition of voluntary manslaughter and it is the instruction that you are requesting from the Court. Unless instructed otherwise, you do not need to address arguments regarding self-defense, initial aggressor, or excessive force. For purposes of this task, you do not need to conduct any additional legal research.

ESTIMATED TIME FOR COMPLETION: 45 minutes.

LEVEL OF DIFFICULTY (1 TO 5):

Task Three: Small Group Discussion; Jury Selection; Ethics

You are part of a team of lawyers representing Keith Ventnor. For purposes of this task, imagine that you are about to begin trial and you are preparing for jury selection. Meet with a partner or a small group of students. From your point of view as defense counsel, discuss the following questions:

- Is gender relevant in picking jurors in this case?

- To what extent may we legally use gender in picking or excusing jurors? May we exercise peremptory challenges in a way that reflects gender stereotypes or assumptions made on the basis of gender?

- In considering whether gender is a relevant characteristic of a potential juror, in what way specifically might a woman's or man's experiences be relevant to our theory of the case?

- Putting aside for the moment what we legally can or cannot do, should we be able to ask questions based on gender? Why or why not?

- What questions might we ask during jury selection that would illuminate potential jurors' opinions on subjects that we believe are relevant to the defense of our client and that may address some of our concerns related to the gender of potential jurors?

Before meeting with your co-counsel, you should read the applicable Skills Guide below, along with the supplemental materials provided in the online component. Then, take 10 minutes to jot down your own thoughts regarding the questions posed above. After you have completed that, join your co-counsel and have a group discussion.

ESTIMATED TIME FOR COMPLETION: 30 minutes.

LEVEL OF DIFFICULTY (1 TO 5):

PRACTICE SKILLS USED:

Skill 1: Motion Writing

Skill 2: Legal Argument; Integrating the Law and the Facts

Skill 3: Oral Argument; Motion Practice

Skill 4: Ethical Analysis

Skill 5: Jury Selection

SKILLS GUIDES

For additional material on the application of the felony-murder rule in practice, see the supplemental materials provided in the online component.

SKILLS GUIDE #1: Motion Writing

Motions are requests for a court to take action. A motion *in limine* — also called a pretrial motion — is a general term for a motion made during the beginning phases of the case, before the actual jury trial has commenced. Pretrial motions must typically be made in writing. Local rules govern the nature of a motion's content. In general, there are two substantive portions of any motion: the facts and the law. The extent to which you need to include certain facts or discuss the relevant cases varies by jurisdiction.

The facts of the case may be included in a short statement to the court or may be a lengthier and separate section of the motion (sometimes labeled "Factual Background" or "Statement of Facts"). The motion should provide sufficient factual background to enable a reader familiar with no other documents to follow the legal argument being made. The purpose of the fact section is to give the judge a basic overview of the relevant facts. This could include a brief procedural history as well as the facts to which you will later cite in your legal argument. In addition, any specific facts relevant to the exact nature of the motion should be included (for example, in a motion to dismiss for violation of speedy trial rights you would want to include all the pertinent dates). If you are citing to evidence from the factual record of the case (e.g., a preliminary hearing transcript), you should follow the applicable citation rules. These citations enable the judge to verify and review the facts that you have included. Beyond this background material, however, the motion should allege no more facts than are necessary to support the requested relief.

The fact section of your motion is not simply a neutral recitation of the facts of the case. It is part of your overall motion and should be written from the point of view of an advocate. Which facts are relevant to your position? What are the facts you would like to emphasize to the judge? Consider the tools of narrative, tone, and rhetoric in constructing a fact section that presents the facts in a light that is favorable to your position. A skilled legal writer presents the facts in an ethical and credible way without forgetting his or her position as an advocate for a particular outcome.

The legal argument portion of a motion varies by jurisdiction. In some jurisdictions, there is no discussion of the legal basis of the motion, and in other areas only a brief cursory mention of the legal grounds for relief is necessary. A more extensive discussion of the caselaw might be contained in a separate written document. In contrast, in some jurisdictions, a discussion of the law, including relevant cases, is contained in a subsection of the Motion itself. Labels for the legal discussion vary. In practice you may see titles such as, "Memorandum of Law," "Argument," or "Memorandum of Points and Authorities." Whatever its title or placement, the legal argument presents the applicable law and your argument regarding the application of your facts to that law.

The motion should finish with the requested relief. Sometimes, the moving party will attach to the motion a proposed order for the court to sign if the court grants the requested relief.

As with the content, the format of the motion also varies by court and jurisdiction. Some motions are drafted using a longer paragraph-by-paragraph narrative form. Other motions will be written in the form of a series of short numbered paragraphs. In this latter style, each paragraph should contain a single sentence or brief series of closely related sentences. Finally, although we have discussed the fact section and legal argument sections separately, you may also see a motion that does not distinguish between the request for relief and the legal and factual argument justifying that relief. A variety of types of motions are provided in the online component. You will find additional motions in the online component for Chapter 9 and in the supplemental materials for Chapter 12, Task One.

For this exercise in Chapter 8, you need only draft the legal argument portion of the motion. This section focuses on the relevant law and applies the facts of your case to that law in a manner that supports the legal outcome you are requesting.

SKILLS GUIDE #2: *Legal Argument; Integrating the Law and the Facts*

A successful legal argument persuades the decision-maker that the application of the facts of your case to the relevant law mandates that the decision-maker rule in your favor. Every legal argument is made from the position of an advocate. The presentation of the law and the facts is not neutral. Rather, legal argument is a credible and ethical, yet positioned, statement of the law and the facts from your party's position (and the outcome you desire).

A good starting place in preparing a legal argument is to outline the law that is relevant to the legal question at hand. What do you have to demonstrate in order to have the judge rule in your favor? Does the law require four factors to be met? Is there an evidentiary burden? A requisite act and mental state? After this step, then determine whether there are questions of legal interpretation that may arise when applying this law. For instance, what have courts found to be sufficient inducements by the police to support an entrapment defense? You will likely need to do legal research to give the court legal authority that supports your argument and interpretation of the legal principles at hand.

Next, brainstorm the facts of your case that apply to the law. How will you argue that the facts of this case apply to the applicable law? A strong legal argument also incorporates factually similar cases that support your legal argument. For example, have courts prohibited an entrapment defense under similar facts? The comparing or contrasting of other cases provides support for your interpretation of the facts and the law in your case.

After completing this part of the planning process, the next steps are to prepare the presentation of the relevant law and the applicable facts. Remember the goal: a legal argument presents the law in such a way, that upon applying the facts of your case to that law, the judge will rule favorably for the party you represent. In preparing your argument, consider the tools of narrative and rhetoric. What is the narrative of your case? Is there a story or theme that you want to communicate to the decision-maker that will be persuasive? What exact words or style of speech will help you effectively and persuasively communicate your position? For instance, if you are the defense counsel, do you call your client the "Defendant?" Or would you refer to him by his name?

With respect to the technical aspects of preparing for oral argument, many practicing lawyers find that preparing argument bullet points or a detailed outline of your argument is more helpful than writing out the argument word for word. The argument should be clear in its structure and organization. Written arguments, in addition to being structured and clear, should also be carefully proofread and should use correct citation rules for the jurisdiction. The citation of authority communicates to the judge that your argument is supported by the law and adds to its persuasiveness. In contrast, an argument not supported by legal authority (or appears not to be due to a lack of citations), not proofread, or disorganized has the potential to hurt your credibility as an advocate and your ability to argue effectively for your client.

SKILLS GUIDE #3: Oral Argument; Motion Practice

At the trial court level in many jurisdictions, much of legal argument takes place orally and in the context of arguing for or against a motion. While you likely will file a written motion requesting particular relief or an opposition to a request, a judge will often ask to hear from both parties before making a decision on the motion. Oral arguments in motion practice require a concise explanation of the law, the relevant facts, and why the court should rule in your favor. You should clearly state the relief you are requesting (or the denial of relief). In practice, the judge may ask you questions about particular portions of your argument and you may get a chance to "rebut" your opposing counsel's argument. Thus, the skill of oral argument for motion practice — as is true for all oral arguments — is a blend of preparation, organization, and flexibility. For more optional reading on the skill of oral argument in motion practice, see the supplemental materials provided in the online component.

SKILLS GUIDE #4 and #5: Ethical Analysis; Jury Selection

Although the many skills required by jury selection cannot be addressed in a few pages, for purposes of Task 3, you should begin with an understanding of the basics of jury selection and the use of peremptory challenges.

The rules of jury selection vary among jurisdictions. Generally, counsel for both sides are given the opportunity to question potential jurors during a process called "voir dire." Voir dire is a time for both sides to ask potential jurors about their backgrounds, preconceived notions or biases, and any personal experiences that would prevent them from being a fair and impartial juror. Voir dire is not a time to directly try your case in front of those who may eventually comprise the jury. That said, a skilled lawyer does use jury selection as an opportunity to advance aspects of his or her theory of the case in an effort to select a jury that will be both fair and receptive to their side of the case. For instance, if you are defense counsel and your theory of the case is that your client has been falsely accused by a neighbor, you may want to question potential jurors about whether they believe a person can be wrongly accused or if they have ever been involved in a dispute with their neighbors. Another example might be if you are prosecuting a gun crime, you may want to question potential jurors about their beliefs on private gun ownership.

After voir dire, both sides ask the Court to excuse those jurors they believe should not be on the jury. There are two types of challenges to potential jurors: challenges for cause and peremptory challenges. Challenges for cause are made for potential jurors who, due to some relationship, belief, or experience, cannot serve as a fair and impartial juror. A challenge for cause is requested by counsel and the judge will grant or deny that request. A peremptory challenge may be made on any ground other than a specified impermissible ground such as race or gender. Peremptory challenges are typically limited in number by local court rules. Each side will get an equal number and, unless counsel believes it was made on the basis of an impermissible ground, cannot be challenged by the other party. If you would like more background information on peremptory challenges, take a moment to read the optional supplemental material in the online component.

As noted above, a peremptory challenge cannot be made on the basis of gender. The Supreme Court held such peremptory challenges unconstitutional in *J.E.B. v. Alabama*, 511 U.S. 127 (1994). However, a peremptory challenge can be made for any reason other than race and gender.

For additional guidance on the skills involved in jury selection, consult the optional documents listed in the online component for Task Three.

ADDITIONAL MATERIALS FOR THE EXERCISE — AVAILABLE IN ONLINE COMPONENT

N.C. Gen. Stat. § 14-17 (Murder in the First and Second Degree Defined; Punishment)

North Carolina Pattern Jury Instructions-Criminal 206.15 (Relevant Excerpts) First Degree Murder in Perpetration of a Felony (Burglary)

North Carolina Pattern Jury Instructions-Criminal 206.11 (Relevant Excerpts) Voluntary Manslaughter

Chapter 9

RAPE

OVERVIEW

I. SUBSTANTIVE LAW

At old common law, rape was defined as forcible, non-consensual sexual intercourse by a man with a woman not his wife. Force in most jurisdictions had to be force sufficient to overcome the utmost resistance by a woman. "Utmost resistance" meant resistance "unto death." This strange formulation determined whether the defendant engaged in the act of using force by focusing on the victim's degree of resistance. Many more modern common law jurisdictions moved to define force in terms of "reasonable resistance" by the female victim rather than her resisting with such a degree that it is obvious that she would prefer death to "violation." Some modern jurisdictions require only the slightest amount of force. Others purport to do away with the force requirement entirely, but force or its absence still seems relevant to juries in practice.

The requirement of lack of consent is likewise problematic. The term "consent" is rarely defined, or at least not in any comprehensible way, in statutes or jury instructions. "Non-consensual" might mean that the woman subjectively, in her own mind, did not agree to sexual intercourse. Another definition of "non-consensual" requires that she expressed by words or actions her unwillingness to engage in sexual intercourse. Alternatively, the determination of consent, or lack thereof, might contain both subjective and objective components: proper words or actions combined with the requisite mental state. When the term is undefined, however, the jury will ultimately give it meaning based upon its own, everyday understandings of the term in the context of sex. Apart from how it is defined, ordinary lay interpretations of a woman's actions will be central to the jury's analysis of whether the absence of consent was proven in the case before it. Some jurisdictions try to finesse these issues by eliminating any requirement that consent be absent. Instead, they use terms suggesting that the woman's will must be "overborne" or that her submission must be "compelled." In practice, however, jury decisions about whether a defendant's actions showed that he overbore the victim's will or compelled her to submit are probably not much different from the determination of whether consent was lacking. Nevertheless, the language of will and compulsion attempts to prod juries toward focusing on the defendant's conduct more than the victim's. The success of such efforts in affecting verdicts is up for debate.

"Sexual intercourse" generally occurs if there is penetration, "however slight," but otherwise fits commonsense definitions of the term. Forcible sex short of intercourse may constitute another kind of sex crime, but is not rape. Indeed, although we focus on the crime of rape here, it is important to remember that there are a host of other potential sex crimes.

The traditional element that the sexual intercourse be between a man and a woman is largely self-explanatory. Most modern statutes have been redrafted to be gender-neutral: either a man or a woman can commit rape. Many statutes still require that the assailant and the victim be of different sexes. Where this is so, other statutes make it a separate sort of crime for penetration that occurs between persons of the same sex.

Many jurisdictions have eliminated the requirement that the woman not be the man's spouse. Jurisdictions that have retained that requirement sometimes have a separate crime of "spousal rape." That crime may have different elements from the crime of rape in addition to a spousal connection. For example, a complaint to authorities may be required within 90 days of the event to prove the crime of spousal rape.

As with all crimes, the burden of proving each element of the crime of rape beyond a reasonable doubt lays with the prosecution. The defense most commonly relies on one of three arguments: (1) identity (someone else did the crime); (2) consent; or (3) lack of the required mental state. Note that arguments 1 and 3 turn on elements not expressly recited in the common law definition of the crime. Argument 1 arises because every crime assumes as an element proof beyond a reasonable doubt that it was the defendant who did the crime. A defendant might, therefore, argue that the eyewitness was mistaken, perhaps from stress, darkness, or not wearing her glasses. This defense becomes difficult where there is scientific evidence, such as DNA testing, of identity or where the victim knew the suspect for a significant amount of time. The third argument arises because nearly all crimes require proving a mental state beyond a reasonable doubt. When a statute is silent about the requisite mental state, the courts will engage in statutory interpretation or use other rules of law to discover what mental state the legislature intended. Where the potential punishment is large, rarely will a court find that mental state to be strict liability, that is, no requisite mental state at all.

At old common law, mistake of fact was a defense to a general intent crime such as rape if the mistake was honest (i.e., the defendant is not lying about making the mistake) and reasonable. Overcoming that defense requires proving that the mistake, generally about the existence of consent, was unreasonable, that is, the defendant was negligent in his beliefs. But what the defendant reasonably could believe always turns on what is reasonable under the circumstances. Modern courts have wrestled with what standard to apply when deciding whether the defendant's belief was reasonable. For example, should the standard be the "reasonable man," "reasonable woman," or "reasonable person?" Should the jury be instructed further on what factors may enter into reasonable beliefs, or should we let it decide without further instruction?

The Model Penal Code (MPC) definition of rape is also silent about mental state. Under MPC Section 2.02, however, that silence is interpreted as the requisite mental state of recklessness. Recklessness first requires negligence. Recklessness also requires conscious awareness of the risk. In cases of rape, the risk is that the woman is not consenting. Specific state statutes are often vague about the required mental state but may sometimes be drafted in a way that can be interpreted as requiring that the defendant acted at least "knowingly." The statutes can be fuzzy about just what the defendant must know. Is it enough for him to know that he engaged in sexual intercourse? That he used force? Or must he also know that the woman consented? Knowledge of consent would require the prosecution to prove beyond a reasonable doubt not merely that the defendant was aware of a risk of non-consent but additionally prove that he was actually aware that the victim in fact did not consent. The willful blindness doctrine may sometimes help in this regard. Willful blindness occurs when a defendant is aware of a high probability that the element (here, lack of consent) exists but does not seek to confirm his suspicions because, if caught, he wants to be able to deny knowledge. The law generally treats willful blindness as if it were true knowledge, though it is not, because of the policy decision to not encourage culpable ignorance.

II. PROCEDURAL LAW

Old common law followed several important procedural rules. First, conviction required corroboration. A conviction could not occur based solely upon the victim's testimony — physical evidence or additional witnesses were needed. Jurisdictions differed on what constituted sufficient corroboration. Second, juries were to be given the "Lord Hale instruction," roughly an instruction to be skeptical of women claiming rape because it is an accusation easily made and hard to disprove. Third, evidence codes often prohibited evidence of prior non-consensual sex acts by the defendant. Such acts fit under the general prohibition on propensity evidence — using prior acts to suggest a defendant's character and propensity to commit the charged act. But evidence of a woman's prior consensual sexual activity with other men was admissible to prove her consent in the case on trial and to attack her credibility. The reason for this admissibility was a common exception to the bar on propensity evidence, namely, the defendant was allowed to offer evidence of a pertinent trait of character of the alleged victim. "Promiscuity" was thought to be "pertinent" to consent and to credibility. The assumption was that any woman having consensual sex outside of marriage was likely to consent with other men, as well as likely to lie. The fourth common procedural rule was that the prosecution of rape required proof of prompt complaint by the victim.

Some modern jurisdictions retain some or all of these common law procedural rules. The MPC retains most of them. See MPC § 213.6 — a link is provided in the online component. But other jurisdictions have modified them. "Rape shield statutes" commonly prohibit much evidence of prior sexual conduct or behavior of the victim from coming in at trial. States vary widely in the specifics of their rape shield laws. Some states bar prior victim sex evidence unless the court concludes that it is substantially more probative than prejudicial. Others are more specific, typically banning evidence of prior acts by the victim of sex with other men unless offered to prove that they (the other men), rather than the defendant, were the source of semen or injury (essentially an identity defense). These jurisdictions may also allow evidence of prior sex between the victim and the defendant if offered to prove consent in the case at trial. These codes usually bar any opinion or reputation evidence about the victim's sexual character. Some state codes are similar to those described above but instead of speaking in terms of "prior acts," they prohibit evidence of prior sexual "conduct" or "behavior." That raises questions about whether conduct other than acts, such as sexual thoughts, dreams, dress, or dancing, are covered. Federal Rule of Evidence 412 has the most protective rape shield law, though it is rarely precisely copied by states. Federal Rule of Evidence 413, on the other hand, permits evidence of prior non-consensual sex acts by the defendant to prove his use of force in the current case if those prior acts involved genital contact or being sexually aroused from injuring another person. This rule has been somewhat more influential with the states.

EXERCISE

Overview

Janice Flower was an 18-year-old college freshman at Indiana University, Bloomington. Janice attended the school on a need-based scholarship. Her parents earned just enough money to pay for rent and food and really could not afford to pay for Janice to go to college. Janice's mother was quite ill, but insisted that, rather than staying home, Janice take the scholarship and attend Bloomington.

Robert Kennedy Stith and Janice were in the same Economics 101 class. Robert was the 21-year-old famous son of a wealthy member of the Indiana state legislature, and from an old Indiana family known for decades for its wealth, power, and love of Indiana Democratic Party politics and elected office. Robert was a senior who had already received early admission into Harvard Law School. He was classically handsome, and the local press covered his every move. He was believed to be in training as the next popular politician from the Stith family.

On several occasions after class, Robert approached Janice, a straight "A" student, to ask for her help in clarifying certain economic concepts. Shortly before the first midterm, he asked if he could come to Janice's house so that she could tutor him. She agreed. One Tuesday night, Robert spent several hours at her house studying. At the end of that night, Robert asked her out on a date the following Saturday night. Janice happily agreed. She told her parents, who were delighted.

That Saturday, at 6:00 p.m., Robert picked Janice up from her home in his expensive Porsche Targa. Janice was dressed in her most expensive dress, one low-cut in front and extending only to her upper thighs. Robert was dressed in expensive pants, a matching jacket, and a silk tie. Robert took her to dinner at the finest French restaurant in town, Chez Louis. They shared a bottle of champagne, ate a fine meal, and laughed often. At Robert's suggestion, they then went to a local club, Roots, to dance and drink. Janice was already a bit tipsy. She rarely drank alcohol. The two danced and each had two more drinks. By 11:00 p.m., Janice suggested they call it a night. But Robert asked her to come to his family's home for a moonlit walk on their spacious property and gardens. She agreed.

When they arrived at his home, no one else was there. The two walked awhile around the gardens, then Robert suggested that they sit and talk. Once they sat, Robert kissed her. They kissed for approximately 10 minutes. At this point, the stories diverge.

Janice later told police the following: After approximately 10 minutes of kissing, Robert started touching her breasts, but she told him to stop. He said he would but in fact did not. Janice then pulled away and said, "I like you, but not on a first date," and asked him to drive her home. Robert's face turned red and his voice angry. He said, "I didn't spend all this money on you for nothing. You know you want it. You've been flirting with me for months. You're not going home until I get what I earned." He then threw her on the ground. She started crying. She was frightened but softly asked him to please stop. He told her to shut up. He then unzipped her dress, pulled it off of her, pulled off her underwear, and had intercourse with her. Afterwards, he drove her home. Robert kissed her again at the door and told her he would really like to see her again. Again afraid, Janice told him she would like that. She then ran to her room and cried. She felt ashamed. She did not believe anyone would believe that the wealthy Robert would do such a thing, and so at first told no one. But she had trouble living with what had happened and so four days later asked her professor, Professor Allbright, for advice. Professor Allbright convinced Janice to contact the police, which is exactly what she did. The police arrested Robert two days later, though he immediately made bail. Once the story got out during the days following Robert's arrest, Janice confided in her friend, 19-year-old Rhonda Sampson, while the two were in Janice's bedroom. Rhonda and Janice had long talked about Robert, and Rhonda had a crush on him. Rhonda got angry about Janice's version of events and stormed out. Shortly thereafter, Janice noticed that her diary was missing. She believes that Rhonda stole it.

Robert, after his arrest, agreed to talk to the police. Robert said that the kissing led to sexual intercourse, but it was all consensual. He admitted that Janice said that she did not want to go "all the way" on a first date. But he told her he would be gentle, and kissed her while softly leading her to lie down. She cried a bit, but he thought those tears were tears of pleasure. He had heard around the school that she "got around" with lots of guys, especially with those on the football team, and he knew she liked him. She never once said no, and he never threatened her. It was a great night, he really enjoyed himself, and he drove her home and asked her to go out with him again. She smiled, said yes, and kissed him goodnight. In his point of view, he was suddenly and out of nowhere, arrested, and is completely surprised by any claim of rape.

Janice's "friend," Rhonda, turned over Janice's diary to the police after taking it from Janice's room. Here is one excerpt from the diary:

> Dear Diary: Today Bobbie asked me out. I can't believe it. He is so gorgeous. I've had dreams about him making love to me. And he's so rich. I wonder if he could help out my mom. Better be coy, though. I don't want to make the same mistake with him that I made in the fall semester with Johnny Blaine. If guys think you're easy, they just dump you once they're done. Lesson learned.

Based on the diary entry, the police interviewed Johnny Blaine, who told them that he had consensual sexual intercourse with Janice in the fall, on an October Saturday night. He said that she was very flirtatious and always wore "sexy" clothes. He never really liked her. He thought she was arrogant and easy. Right after sex, he thanked her but said he didn't think he wanted to see her again. She got furious and threatened to get back at him. He was therefore really surprised when she made these wild claims about his best friend, Robert.

The police turned over this case to the local prosecutor's office and Robert has now been charged with the crime of rape. Prosecution investigation revealed that Robert has a juvenile perjury conviction from when he was 15 years old from another state (Massachusetts). Blaine has a felony burglary conviction from last year, in which he received probation. The investigation also revealed that, when asked about Johnny Blaine by her friends, including Rhonda, Janice lied and said that she had never had sex with Johnny.

REQUIRED TASKS

Task One: Small Group Discussion; Case Theories

Meet with at least one other student to discuss the strengths and weaknesses of the case for each side. Pick a side you want to represent — prosecution or defense — and brainstorm case themes and a possible theory of the case.

ESTIMATED TIME FOR COMPLETION: 30 minutes.

LEVEL OF DIFFICULTY (1 TO 5):

Task Two: Motion Writing; Evidentiary Problems

You are the prosecutor in the case. Draft the motion *in limine* seeking exclusion of the following evidence:

1) the diary entry;

2) Robert's statement that Janice "got around" with other guys;

3) Rhonda's statement that Janice lied to her about having sex with Johnny Blaine;

4) Johnny Blaine's testimony.

ESTIMATED TIME FOR COMPLETION: 60 minutes.

LEVEL OF DIFFICULTY (1 TO 5):

Task Three: Drafting Legislation

In reaction to Robert's arrest, several local leaders and community groups are arguing that Indiana's outmoded rape laws might lead to Robert's acquittal. In response, the Indiana state legislature is considering changing the substantive rape statute. Prepare an outline for arguments concerning what amendments might address the concerns of these constituents and draft a proposed new rape statute in your role as an aide to an Indiana legislator. Be sure to read Skills Guide #3, which lists additional materials you will need to complete this task, as well as additional guidance in completing this task.

ESTIMATED TIME FOR COMPLETION: 90 minutes.

LEVEL OF DIFFICULTY (1 TO 5):

Task Four: Ethics; Dealing with the Media

Assume for the purposes of this task that that the motion *in limine* from Task Two was denied. You are now the senior prosecutor in the office that is prosecuting the case against Robert Stith. The junior prosecutor has told you that he plans to hold a press conference to reveal Robert's and Johnny's prior criminal records, their status as best friends, and Rhonda's crush on Robert. Outline what advice you would give the junior prosecutor on the case concerning what he or she may say in a press conference about the case and why.

ESTIMATED TIME FOR COMPLETION: 60 minutes.

LEVEL OF DIFFICULTY (1 TO 5):

PRACTICE SKILLS USED:

      Skill 1: Brainstorming: Themes and Case Theories

      Skill 2: Motion Writing

      Skill 3: Drafting Legislation

      Skill 4: Counseling a Client

Skill 5: Ethical Analysis; Dealing with the Media

SKILLS GUIDES

In the online component you will find links to several videos that should be viewed as background material for the tasks of this chapter. There are also optional supplemental materials on issues that frequently arise in the prosecution and defense of rape cases. For additional reading, use an online service to download and read the following article: Deborah Denno, *Why the Model Penal Code's Sexual Offense Provisions Should Be Pulled and Replaced*, 1 Ohio St. J. Crim. L. 207 (2003).

SKILLS GUIDE #1: Brainstorming: Themes and Case Theories

Brainstorming with colleagues is one way to decide upon case strategy, theory, and tactics. Such brainstorming is especially wise once the facts of the case have sufficiently been developed but it is still early enough in a case to form working case themes and theories. A case theory, simply put, is the story you want to tell the jury. For example, in a purse-snatching case with a victim and a suspect of different race, imagine the following facts: the defendant may suffer from some serious emotional problems, have been identified in a suggestive lineup, claim to have been home with his mother at the time of the crime, and have a low IQ.

Several defense narratives might be suggested by this brief set of facts. Story One: The defendant was legally insane at the time of the crime; that is, he suffered from a mental disease or defect that made him incapable of knowing the nature and quality of his actions, or knowing right from wrong, or that rendered him incapable of staving off an irresistible impulse to steal. Whether this story is viable will depend upon further fact investigation, such as by consulting an expert to determine whether the defendant's emotional problems were so severe as to meet the legal test of insanity.

Story Two: A Caucasian victim, frightened and having had only a brief chance to see her assailant, had trouble clearly differentiating African-American faces and, while truthful and well-meaning, wrongly identified the defendant because of some minor facial similarities to the true wrongdoer. This story's viability might also require consulting an expert on cross-racial identification and studies that demonstrate the greater accuracy in witnesses identifying those of their own race relative to those of other races.

Story Three is an alibi defense. The defendant was home with his mother, a home so distant from the crime scene that, at the time the crime occurred, he could not have been the thief. This story might be combined with Story Two on misidentification based on race. This theory also requires investigation to determine whether there are other witnesses, hopefully less biased than a mother testifying about her son, to corroborate the alibi. Additional study of the exact distance between the crime scene and the defendant's whereabouts would also be required.

Story Four: The defendant's IQ was so low that he was incapable of forming the specific intent to permanently deprive another of their property, an element of larceny; thus, the defendant should only be found guilty of some lesser offense, if any crime at all. Like the defense theory of insanity, this theory would likely require an expert to testify about the impact of an extremely low IQ on the ability to form the relevant mental state as well as a mental health evaluation of the defendant by one or both parties.

Which of these stories to choose will turn on judgments about the relative credibility of prosecution and defense witnesses, whether it is wise to call the defendant to the stand (then exposing him to cross-examination, perhaps about his prior crimes, if any), which story is likely to be most persuasive to the jury, and which story is best supported by the evidence. Telling conflicting stories is usually not the best option in criminal cases, for instance, saying, "My client was not there, but if he was there, he was legally insane." Juries typically will not believe inconsistent stories. Ethical rules also place limits on which story you can tell. A lawyer cannot knowingly offer perjured testimony. Nevertheless, if a client insists on perjuring himself, some states permit this to happen but require the lawyer to limit the damage, for example, by letting the client tell his extended narrative without too much lawyer questioning and by prohibiting the lawyer from relying on his client's testimony in closing argument.

Real-world cases of course offer many more complex facts than the sketchy ones outlined in these examples. As such, the narrative and complexity of case theories will vary case by case. Nevertheless, the examples given above demonstrate the importance of picking a working case theory early on and potentially modifying it later as the investigation proceeds. In short, the case theory may impact almost everything you do as a lawyer assigned to a particular case: discovery, investigation, witness choice, witness questioning, as well as opening argument and closing argument to the judge or jury.

A case theme is a one-sentence encapsulation of the case theory (two sentences at most) that captures in a gripping way the core of the story or narrative. Stated differently, the case theme is a sentence(s) that communicates the emotional tone of the case. Because the potential case theories listed above are fairly simple, they may seem like case themes. The distinction might be clearer in a more complex fact pattern. Nevertheless, here are a few examples that try to point out the distinction. Assume the alleged thief is John Merrick. One possible case theme (if the facts support it and we are adding some facts to make the point) would be this: "John Merrick has long suffered from paranoid schizophrenia, a disease that led him to believe that a demon had taken over his body and forced him, against his will, to steal that purse." This one sentence personalized the defendant — his name rather than role is used — and tried in a vivid, common-sense way to encapsulate the core of an insanity defense. A different case theme might be this: "John is a young man without a car or bike, was home with his mother and the family priest at the time of the crime — a home over twenty miles away from where the theft took place." This theme tries to develop sympathy for the defendant as well as build credibility for the case theory of an alibi defense.

The best way to decide on case themes and theories is to sit down with colleagues familiar with the case and begin to brainstorm. Brainstorming may take the form of simply writing down every possible idea — however strong, weak, or nonsensical. Then, after all the ideas are written down, you can proceed to discuss each and determine the strengths and weaknesses of each one. The brainstorming session might start by outlining the strengths and weaknesses of each side's case. Some case themes and theories might naturally arise from this conversation. Each theory and theme can then be tested against the evidence, credibility concerns, beliefs about the jury's likely composition and biases, and common sense. This brainstorming process will lead to a decision on what case theory and theme to choose.

SKILLS GUIDE #2: Motion Writing

Please refer to Chapter 8, Skills Guide #1. In addition, you should examine the Sample Narrative Motion provided in the online component.

SKILLS GUIDE #3: Drafting Legislation

Drafting legislation can be a very time-consuming and complex task. Extensive research would be required into all the legal issues relevant to the statute. Sample and model statutes and existing statutes in other states on the same topic would need to be consulted. A reporter or staff member might be assigned to write an extensive memorandum. Relevant empirical evidence and experts might need to be consulted. An initial draft would then be critiqued by other individuals and debated among a group, with numerous changes repeatedly made from one meeting to the next until a final product results. Statutory drafting also raises political questions about what the legislature will in fact be willing to pass, not just what provisions serve the best or desired policies. A variety of books also lay out stylistic concerns in drafting legislation. Drafting a relatively simple piece of legislation can often take years.

Here, we ask you to engage in a much simpler exercise just to get the flavor of the drafting process. Use the MPC Article 13 provisions on rape as an initial guide to format and style. These MPC sections are listed in the online component. Do not be afraid, however, to make your statute a better model of "plain English" than some might think true of the MPC. Meet in a small group of ideally five students (but if not five, then another odd number of students) and try to come to an agreement on the underlying policy questions. What mental state(s) should be required for rape? Should force be required? Lack of consent? What act(s) should be required? Decide what policy positions to take on these and any other relevant matters. Decide what reasons you have for the position you choose. Your group should then craft statutory language (you might assign each member to individually draft a portion of each provision, then the group can critique it and begin the editing process together).

Here are the steps to follow:

1. Review the various rape statutes and background information provided in this Chapter. Pay special attention to the article by Deborah Denno cited at the beginning of the Skills Guide section.

2. Brainstorm, using the MPC as an initial guide, a list of all potential provisions the statute might need. These provisions should include at the very least a definitions section (if you use any terms that you believe require definition); a provision defining rape; and a provision addressing the procedures noted in MPC § 213.6.

3. Decide via group discussion what position you want to take on each of these provisions.

4. Return to the Indiana statute and redraft it — changing wording, adding or deleting provisions — as you see fit. Use only the MPC, the Indiana statute, any other sample statutes provided to you by the professor. Do not do independent research.

5. Meet as a group again to finalize the statute.

6. If there is group disagreement on any provision, majority rules.

7. Prepare a written outline of your group's reasons for changing the substantive content or style of any provision of the Indiana statute or for not doing so, as well as for any provisions that you add. If there is dissent as to any provision, the dissent and its reasons should be noted in the outline.

SKILLS GUIDE #4: Counseling a Client

Lawyers play different roles in different contexts. One of the lawyer's roles is as client advisor. An advisor should have previously completed all the necessary factual and legal research. The advisor must then meet with the client and lay out for the client various options, as well as brainstorm with the client (as well as with others in the office prior to meeting with the client) about whether additional options should be considered. The lawyer should then lay out for the client the pluses and minuses of each course of action, then offer the lawyer's opinion about how best to proceed. Visual aids can sometimes be helpful in advising a client. For example, a lawyer might prepare a chart of the various options, listing under each option its pluses and minuses.

Advice need not be limited to legal advice. The client wants a problem solved and thus needs to know what course of action to take to achieve that goal. Economic, reputational, and moral concerns might all matter. To the extent that the lawyer is competent to address these things, they should be raised with the client or, if experts in those areas are needed, they should be consulted. But a client will usually insist on a bottom-line lawyer recommendation, which the client might reject. The client should be told, where appropriate, that the decision is ultimately the client's to make.

We use the words "where appropriate" because ethical codes often distinguish between ends and means. Choices of ends are for the client, whereas choices of means are for the lawyer, at least as a general matter. The line between ends and means, however, is not always clear. Furthermore, a lawyer who ignores a client's insistence on a course of action contrary to the lawyer's advice may not have that "client" for long. The lawyer may try to persuade the client to the lawyer's view. If that fails, the lawyer certainly should reject any unethical course of action. But an ethical choice concerning means insisted upon by a client creates pressure on the lawyer to comply with the client's wishes. The lawyer must thus gauge how strongly she feels about the issue and how much damage the client's approach to the case could cause. The lawyer must then decide whether to risk the client's anger or accept the client's perhaps reasonable but different judgment. It is important to remember that in some areas of the law, the client has the final say and therefore the lawyer must cede to the client's desired course of action. Ideally, however, lawyer persuasion and a strong attorney-client relationship should avoid any conflict in individual opinions.

SKILLS GUIDE #5: Ethical Analysis; Dealing with the Media

The *lawyer* may not herself engage in any conduct that violates the relevant code of ethics. These ethical rules also prevent the lawyer, including when serving as a prosecutor, from using a host of other persons as surrogates for the lawyer. In other words, the prosecutor cannot avoid discipline by using these other listed persons to engage in conduct barred to the lawyer. The rules governing all lawyers — defense and prosecution — also simply say that the lawyer cannot use others associated in the lawyer's firm to make statements that the individual lawyer would be prohibited from making. But the rule is silent about clients doing so.

Clients are, of course, not lawyers. Thus they are not subject to the lawyers' disciplinary codes. But can a lawyer advise a client to make public statements prohibited to the lawyer? In the materials for this Chapter, the rule text in Indiana does not address the matter, and the answer to the question is ambiguous. Nevertheless, some jurisdictions have answered the question "no," and a lawyer takes a grave risk by offering such advice. Moreover, even if a lawyer were not facing potential discipline for such conduct, client statements that a lawyer could not herself make are likely to be damaging to the case, perhaps inappropriately tainting the jury pool. Even worse, such statements under the Indiana rules seem to create a right of measured response by the opposing party to overcome any prejudice caused by the client. This right of response is a narrow one, but it may entitle the prosecutor to make statements damaging to your client that the prosecutor might otherwise be barred from making or would choose not to make. Clients may also just say things or phrase things in ways that damage the client's case or the client's reputation rather than repair them. If you are considering a public statement about the case, sometimes, depending upon the goals of that statement, it is most persuasive coming from the client, other times most persuasive coming from the lawyer. Furthermore, the news cycle is rapid, and the news media may have little tolerance for covering overly long statements. Accordingly, in general, in advising the client you should:

1. Decide whether to recommend that you, the lawyer, make the statement or that the client does so.

2. Determine the goals of any statements to be made.

3. Determine what level of detail and length of statement to make.

4. Determine the content of any statement.

5. Avoid making, or counseling the client to make, any statement that violates the ethics codes.

6. Anticipate how to avoid or minimize responsive statements by the opposing party.

Sometimes it is best to give a client written advice in the form of a client letter, especially if the legal issues are complex. More often, advice is given orally in a face-to-face meeting with the client or, if necessary and to save costs, via telephone or Skype.

For the Task of this Chapter, some of the issues discussed above do not arise because the prosecutor is considering making the statement, and the prosecutor's only client is "the People" — that is the State or jurisdiction the prosecution represents. Nevertheless, the same basic principles of not using others to evade the lawyer's ethical limits on dealing with the press apply to the prosecutor. The prosecutor should also go through a similar process to that described above in deciding whether and what she may say to the press. For the state rules relevant to this Task, Rule 3.6 governs all lawyers in dealing with the press. In addition, Rule 3.8 imposes special obligations on the prosecutor's dealings with the media and the public. Therefore, in analyzing the ethics questions of this Task, both rules must be consulted.

ADDITIONAL MATERIALS FOR THE EXERCISE — AVAILABLE IN ON-LINE COMPONENT

IND. CODE § 35-42-4-1: Rape

Indiana Rules of Evidence:

IND. R. EVID. 403. Exclusion of Relevant Evidence on Grounds of Prejudice, Confusion, or Undue Delay

IND. R. EVID. 404. Character Evidence Not Admissible to Prove Conduct; Exceptions; Other Crimes

IND. R. EVID. 405. Methods of Proving Character

IND. R. EVID. 412. Evidence of Past Sexual Conduct

IND. R. EVID. 608. Evidence of Character and Conduct of Witness

IND. R. EVID. 609. Impeachment by Evidence of Conviction of Crime

Indiana Rules of Prof. Conduct:

IND. RULES OF PROF'L CONDUCT R. 3.6: Trial Publicity

IND. RULES OF PROF'L CONDUCT R. 3.8: Special Responsibilities of a Prosecutor

Chapter 10

ATTEMPT AND SOLICITATION

OVERVIEW

Generally, we understand a crime as engaging in a statutorily prohibited course of culpable conduct that leads to a social harm. Specifically, the prosecution gathers evidence that the accused conceived, evaluated, resolved (*mens rea*), prepared (which falls somewhere between the *mens rea* and *actus reus*), commenced (closer to the *actus reus*), and completed one or more course(s) of conduct (*actus reus*) that caused social harm. Luckily, our criminal justice system does not waste resources prosecuting those who merely think about committing crime. There are not enough jails to contain those of us who ponder the most violent criminal conduct after, e.g., being cut off by an aggressive driver or rudely treated by a customer service representative.

However, American criminal codes do criminalize various preliminary acts intended to cause harmful conduct or results. When an individual moves beyond thinking about committing a crime into the realm of preparing to commit a crime, one has bridged the *mens rea/actus reus* "divide," coupling culpable thought with action. Here, at this juncture, a government may properly prosecute. Why is that? The government should not have to wait until the crime is completed before it is able to intervene and punish; at this point, conduct manifests criminal intent. Concern for society's safety and well-being authorizes criminalizing the actor's "preparatory steps" before the harm that s/he seeks to inflict occurs.

Criminal statutes define conduct committed with the purpose of accomplishing some further crime as inchoate crimes. Inchoate crimes are defined by laws that prosecute and punish a defendant's preparation to violate the criminal law. These laws criminalize steps taken toward committing the intended crime; they provide a basis upon which to find a criminal defendant guilty even if s/he does not accomplish his/her ultimate criminal goal. Thus, an inchoate criminal defendant must have been in the pursuit of a course of criminal conduct that — had s/he been successful — would have culminated into a completed crime. Because inchoate criminal statutes punish those defendants whose conduct did not reach their intended level of "success," inchoate crimes are also referred to as "non-result," "incomplete," or "anticipatory" crimes.

Arguably, inchoate crimes allow governments to impose criminal culpability for acts that result in no social harm at all. While no actual harm typically results from these crimes, they nevertheless represent a potential for harm that is legitimately within the scope of the criminal law's prohibitions. Identification of those whose overt behavior manifests criminal propensities offers a significant societal benefit; those willing to perform the steps leading up to a crime are not benign actors. Thwarting their dangerousness benefits society, because the closer the actor gets to successful execution, the more likely s/he will be successful unless someone or something prevents the intended social harm.

Inchoate crimes include attempt, conspiracy, and solicitation. Most criminal codes punish inchoate offenses less severely than the intended crime. Others, including the Model Penal Code, punish inchoate crimes as severely as the intended crime.

I.   ATTEMPT

A criminal attempt occurs when the defendant with the specific intent to commit a crime commits some act toward carrying out that crime. Though the focus in criminal attempts seems to be only on the defendant's state of mind, *actus reus* does matter; s/he has accomplished one or more steps. How many steps s/he must take and how close to committing the intended crime s/he must come varies among jurisdictions. At minimum, the accused must have done something directly moving toward and bringing him/her nearer to the crime s/he intends to commit. Mere preparation, however, is not enough. Instead, the defendant must have taken a "substantial step" in furtherance of the crime. It is more than mere preparation. In fact, identifying it takes mere preparation into the realm of execution. The "substantial step" corroborates the defendant's criminal purpose, but is less than the last act before object/intended crime completion. Identification of a defendant's substantial step shifts the emphasis from what remains to be done to what the actor has already done; that more "steps" need to be taken before the crime can be completed does not preclude finding a substantial has occurred.

In some cases, it will be difficult to determine when an attempt begins and when mere preparation ends. Acts consistent with innocent behavior may, in the eyes of those with knowledge or belief of the actor's criminal design, be connected to the commission of a crime. There are three tests generally used across American jurisdictions to determine whether a person committed a criminal attempt:

1.   The defendant had the physical proximity necessary to have completed the crime (with the emphasis being on what steps remain to be taken);

2.   Whether any ordinary person witnessing the acts of the perpetrator would undoubtedly conclude that s/he was intending to commit the crime in question; and

3.   Whether the perpetrator has taken a significant or substantial step that clearly indicate intent to commit the crime (this is the Model Penal Code test).[1]

Whether the actions taken by a defendant charged with criminal attempt amounted to mere preparation or constituted an overt act directed toward the accomplishment of the basic offense is a question for determination by the jury. According to one legal commentator, "[u]ntil the Model Penal Code was drafted, most states punished, but

---

[1] *See* MODEL PENAL CODE § 5.01(c).

did not define, criminal attempts."[2] Nevertheless, common law criminal attempts were considered misdemeanors, irrespective of the seriousness of the crime the defendant sought to commit. The Model Penal Code defines criminal attempt as follows:

§ 5.01 Criminal Attempt.

(1) Definition of Attempt. A person is guilty of an attempt to commit a crime if, acting with the kind of culpability otherwise required for commission of the crime, he:

    (a) purposely engages in conduct that would constitute the crime if the attendant circumstances were as he believes them to be; or

    (b) when causing a particular result is an element of the crime, does or omits to do anything with the purpose of causing or with the belief that it will cause such result without further conduct on his part; or

    (c) purposely does or omits to do anything that, under the circumstances as he believes them to be, is an act or omission constituting a substantial step in a course of conduct planned to culminate in his commission of the crime.

Subsection (1) sets forth the general requirements for an attempt, dividing the cases into three types: those where the actor's conduct would constitute the crime if the circumstances were as he believed them to be; those where the actor has completed conduct that he expects to cause a proscribed result; and those where the actor has not yet completed his own conduct, and the problem is to distinguish between acts of preparation and a criminal attempt (liability depends upon the actor having taken a substantial step in a course of conduct planned to culminate in commission of a crime). In all three situations, purposely is the requisite *mens rea*, with two exceptions: with respect to the circumstances under which a crime must be committed (the culpability otherwise required for commission of the crime is also applicable to the attempt) and with respect to offenses where causing a result is an element, a belief that the result will occur without further conduct on the actor's part will suffice.

MPC § 5.01 continues:

(2) Conduct That May Be Held Substantial Step Under Subsection (1)(c). Conduct shall not be held to constitute a substantial step under Subsection (1)(c) of this Section unless it is strongly corroborative of the actor's criminal purpose. Without negativing the sufficiency of other conduct, the following, if strongly corroborative of the actor's criminal purpose, shall not be held insufficient as a matter of law:

    (a) lying in wait, searching for or following the contemplated victim of the crime;

    (b) enticing or seeking to entice the contemplated victim of the crime to go to the place contemplated for its commission;

    (c) reconnoitering the place contemplated for the commission of the crime;

---

[2] *See* Joshua Dressler, Understanding Criminal Law at 374 (2012).

(d) unlawful entry of a structure, vehicle or enclosure in which it is contemplated that the crime will be committed;

(e) possession of materials to be employed in the commission of the crime, that are specially designed for such unlawful use or that can serve no lawful purpose of the actor under the circumstances;

(f) possession, collection or fabrication of materials to be employed in the commission of the crime, at or near the place contemplated for its commission, if such possession, collection or fabrication serves no lawful purpose of the actor under the circumstances;

(g) soliciting an innocent agent to engage in conduct constituting an element of the crime.

This subsection elaborates on the mere preparation/criminal attempt divide, indicating what is meant by § 5.01(1)(c)'s "substantial step." Substantial step conduct must be strongly corroborative of the actor's criminal purpose. The kinds of conduct that fit with what has been seen via patterns in the common law are provided, with the requirement that the issue of guilt be submitted to the jury if one or more of them occurs and strongly corroborates the actor's criminal purpose.

(3) Conduct Designed to Aid Another in Commission of a Crime. A person who engages in conduct designed to aid another to commit a crime that would establish his complicity under Section 2.06 if the crime were committed by such other person, is guilty of an attempt to commit the crime, although the crime is not committed or attempted by such other person.

Subsection (3) fills what would otherwise be a gap in complicity liability. (MPC § 2.06 covers accomplice liability in situations where the principal actor actually commits the offense. In cases where the principal actor does not commit an offense, however, an accomplice will be liable if he engaged in conduct that would have established his complicity had the crime been committed.)

(4) Renunciation of Criminal Purpose. When the actor's conduct would otherwise constitute an attempt under Subsection (1)(b) or (1)(c) of this Section, it is an affirmative defense that he abandoned his effort to commit the crime or otherwise prevented its commission, under circumstances manifesting a complete and voluntary renunciation of his criminal purpose. The establishment of such defense does not, however, affect the liability of an accomplice who did not join in such abandonment or prevention.

Within the meaning of this Article, renunciation of criminal purpose is not voluntary if it is motivated, in whole or in part, by circumstances, not present or apparent at the inception of the actor's course of conduct, that increase the probability of detection or apprehension or that make more difficult the accomplishment of the criminal purpose. Renunciation is not complete if it is motivated by a decision to postpone the criminal conduct until a more advantageous time or to transfer the criminal effort to another but similar objective or victim.

Subsection (4) provides a defense of renunciation, which can be claimed if the defendant abandoned or otherwise prevented the commission of the target crime(s), under circumstances manifesting a complete and voluntary foregoing of his criminal purpose. The provision's second paragraph defines "complete and voluntary." The defense is an affirmative defense.

Attempts may be incomplete. They may also be complete, i.e., "successful" attempts. Complete attempts occur when the defendant takes every necessary step in the commission of the targeted/intended crime, yet is unable to commit it. Incomplete attempts occur when the defendant takes some, but not all, steps toward committing the target crime, but is prevented by an intervening force outside of his/her control and before completing the attempt.

Factual impossibility is not a defense. There, the defendant attempts a crime, but could not complete the target offense due to facts not known to him. A classic hypothetical of factual impossibility is a defendant's attempt to kill an individual by shooting a gun at the targeted person, but the gun is unloaded. The criminal attempt has occurred, despite the defendant not knowing that the gun lacked ammunition.

At common law, legal impossibility was a defense to a criminal attempt charge. Legal impossibility occurs when the defendant does what s/he intends, but the result does not constitute a crime (e.g., accepting goods that s/he believed to have been stolen, but were not; offering a bribe to a person whom he believed to be a juror, who was not; shooting a stuffed deer believing it to be alive). The primary rationale of legal impossibility (of receiving stolen property, jury tampering, poaching) is that, judging the actor's conduct in the light of the actual facts, what he intended to do did not amount to a crime. Whatever the defendant did, it was not criminal, despite his/her wanting and intending it to be.

Legal impossibility, however, is not a defense under the MPC. The actor's criminal purpose has been clearly demonstrated; s/he has gone as far as s/he could in implementing that purpose, based on his/her purpose and considered in the light of his/her beliefs, not on what is actually possible under existing circumstances. The defendant's criminal dangerousness has manifested.[3]

Finally, a criminal attempt may be renounced or abandoned if the defendant withdraws from the criminal enterprise. Jurisdictions have differed on whether a defense of "withdrawal" or "renunciation" were available to those charged with a criminal attempt. Where available, once the defendant was within "striking distance" of the completed crime, i.e., within the zone of target crime completion, withdrawal was unavailable as a defense. However, in jurisdictions that follow the Model Penal Code, withdrawal is a defense if it is both voluntary and successful.[4] The defendant must inform all of the parties of his intent to withdraw and must thwart the target offense by informing the authorities. Withdrawal, however, is not voluntary and successful if it is motivated in whole or part by belief of law enforcement detection or capture of the perpetrator(s). Nor does it serve to absolve the accused of any criminal acts that occurred before s/he withdrew from the criminal attempt.

---

[3] *See* MODEL PENAL CODE § 5.01(1)(a).

[4] *See* MODEL PENAL CODE § 5.01(4).

Criminal punishment of such preparatory conduct occurs in lieu of punishment for the substantive crime. When, however, the defendant successfully commits the target crime, attempt merges with the substantive crime. In these cases, the defendant cannot be convicted of both the target offense and the attempt to commit it. Merger applies to a continuing course of conduct; it does not apply to multiple attempts. For example, if unsuccessfully D attempts to poison V to death in one year and two years later, tries and succeeds in killing V by shooting him to death, the attempted murder by poisoning does not merge with the murder by shooting; however, the attempt to kill by shooting merges with the killing by shooting.

II. SOLICITATION

Solicitation occurs when one individual requests or encourages another to commit crime. Solicitation may also be thought of as a criminal attempt to conspire. Examples of solicitation include hiring someone to commit a murder, offering a sex worker money to prostitute, bribing a judicial officer to render a desired verdict. Solicitation involves no more than asking someone to commit a crime in exchange for something of value. Unlike attempt, historically, solicitation requires no overt act other than the offer itself. Accordingly, the risk of imposing an unduly harsh punishment is greater because — unlike attempt — no steps beyond the asking need be taken or are required.

To establish solicitation, the solicitor must intend that another person engage in conduct constituting a crime. There must be an affirmative request, command, or other type of communication aimed at causing the solicited person to commit the crime. Actual communication from the defendant to either an intermediary or the solicited person, indicating the subject matter of the solicitation, must be proven. Similarly, evidence of the accused acting toward the commission of a crime — not a mere intent to commit a crime — must be shown. The evidence may consist of any conduct conveying the idea of an invitation to commit a crime. Words alone may constitute solicitation.

Proof of solicitation requires evidence that the defendant has the intent to solicit, induce, convince or entice *another* to commit a crime. Thus, criminal solicitation requires more than one person and it requires an intent to promote commission of the solicitor's criminal aspiration(s) via another's conduct. Though there are situations in which the conduct solicited would not constitute a crime, solicitation manifests a "dangerous" personality and is, therefore, criminally culpable. It is necessary, then, that in all cases the actor has the requisite purpose of "promoting or facilitating" commission of the intended crime.

The harm of solicitation is fully realized when the solicitor offers something of value to another person to facilitate the crime's commission. By offering something of value to another person so that they commit a crime, a solicitor supplies a motive that otherwise would not exist, thereby increasing the risk the criminal conduct will occur. A solicitation can be thought of as an attempt to conspire, i.e., the first step in a criminal conspiracy.[5] The crime of solicitation is completed even though the person solicited does not accept the offer or is an undercover police agent who would never have accepted the solicitation under any circumstances. If the solicitation to the unlawful scheme is accepted, it may spawn a criminal conspiracy and, itself, may be charged by the government. Solicitation is complete at the time of the solicitation. Once the target offense is committed, the solicitation merges with the target offense. However, as in attempt, the target crime need not be carried out for the crime of solicitation to be committed. The solicitor is guilty of solicitation whether the solicited crime is committed or not.

Whether the solicitation to commit a crime constitutes an attempt by the solicitor is a question that, historically, has been answered in several ways:

1. treat every solicitation as a specific type of criminal attempt to be governed by that law, the solicitation being an overt act that — alone or together with other overt acts — may surpass preparation and result in liability;

2. punish only solicitations accompanied by other overt acts (e.g., offering money, furnishing weaponry, providing means and material);

3. punish the solicitor for overt acts that go beyond what would be called preparation if the solicitor planned to commit the crime himself; or

4. do not punish solicitations, as it is not the solicitor's attempt to commit the desired and ultimate criminal offense personally (i.e., simply punish those who actually commit crimes).

The Model Penal Code defines solicitation as follows: "[a] person is guilty of solicitation to commit a crime if with the purpose of promoting or facilitating its commission he commands, encourages or requests another person to engage in specific conduct which would constitute such crime."[6] Interestingly, the MPC definition of a "substantial step" in a criminal attempt, outlined in § 5.01(2)(g), identifies "soliciting an innocent or agent to engage in conduct constituting an element of the crime." Evident also in the MPC's provision pertaining to the doctrine of impossibility as a defense unilateral solicitation and conspiracy doctrine: "[I]t is immaterial to the liability of a person who solicits or conspires with another to commit a crime that the person whom he solicits or with whom he conspires is irresponsible or has an immunity to prosecution or conviction for the commission of the crime."[7] (This is unlike most American jurisdictions, which still regard solicitation as a bilateral enterprise.)

Under the MPC, renunciation is a defense to solicitation. "It is an affirmative defense that the actor, after soliciting another person to commit a crime, persuaded him not to do so or otherwise prevented the commission of the crime, under circumstances manifesting a complete and voluntary renunciation of his criminal purpose."[8]

---

[5] If the other person accepts the solicitation, and someone commits an overt act, then the crime of conspiracy has been committed.

[6] MODEL PENAL CODE § 5.02(1).

[7] MODEL PENAL CODE § 5.04(1)(b).

[8] MODEL PENAL CODE § 5.02(3).

Because impossibility is no defense to the crime of attempt, the MPC seems also to reject such a defense to a charge of solicitation, although no specific code section speaks to this point. As is true with attempt under the MPC, liability of the actor turns on his purpose, considered in the light of his beliefs, and not on what is actually possible under existing circumstances. The actor's liability is to be determined by reference to his state of mind and does not depend upon external considerations, though it is still necessary that the result desired or intended by the actor constitute a crime. If, according to his beliefs as to facts and legal relationships, the result desired or intended is not a crime, the actor will not be guilty of an attempt even though he firmly believes that his goal is criminal. The great majority of American jurisdictions have also abolished impossibility as a defense to the criminal charge of solicitation.[9]

Today, nearly every jurisdiction permits the defense of renunciation to a charge of criminal solicitation, given that the solicitor is often in the best position to avoid the commission of the offense. Additionally, since the solicitor had the means to provide the motivation for the commission of the offense, s/he is also likely to have the means to thwart, supplant, or eliminate it. Most state criminal codes follow the MPC's requirement that the actor have "persuaded [the person he solicited] not to do so or otherwise prevented the commission of the crime. . . ." Some jurisdictions permit renunciation as a defense when the defendant does not prevent the offense, but only makes "a reasonable effort" or a "substantial effort" to prevent the conduct. This requirement is satisfied by giving "timely warning to law enforcement authorities." The solicitor must have also notified the person solicited. Most jurisdictions also require that the defendant affect a "complete and voluntary" renunciation by dissuading the solicited agent or otherwise prevented the offense "under circumstances manifesting a complete and voluntary renunciation of his criminal purpose." Note that under the MPC, impossibility as a defense is rejected (as criminal guilt focuses upon the circumstances as the actor believed them to be, rather than as they actually existed).

Criminal codes have, increasingly, defined other and newer inchoate crimes. These codes have also allowed prosecution upon proof of a similar "dangerousness assessment," i.e., the state must show the prohibited act would have occurred had it not been for the incompetence of the perpetrator(s) or the competence of law enforcement. Again: one of the dangers of these other and newer inchoate crimes — often pejoratively regarded as "anticipatory," incomplete, or unconsummated — is the same risk implicit in the punishment of the classic inchoates: false charges.

---

[9] United States v. Hsu, 155 F.3d 189, 199 (3d Cir. 1998).

EXERCISE

Overview

MEMORANDUM

To:	Summer Intern
From:	Trial Attorney
Re:	Briefing Memorandum re: State v. Viggio, aka, "Eye-Baby Prosecution"

Thank you in advance for your assistance in this matter.

Carla Viggio is currently a junior at a small, private college in Virginia. Prior to the incident discussed below, Carla wanted to transfer from her private college to the new, governmentally run, Roanoke County College (RCC), located in Roanoke, Virginia. RCC is the brainchild of the Virginia legislature, i.e., RCC was created not from private funding or sources, but conceived and funded by members of the Virginia state legislature who wanted to establish a very specific type of college environment within the state.

RCC is the newest jewel in a crown of quality state-run colleges and universities; however, it is unique in that it is an "environment controlled" college, one of a few (but increasingly popular) in the United States.[10] Accordingly, RCC's campus regulations are quite strict. For example, genders are segregated in public and private spaces and may only "mix" while in the presence of an RCC chaperone. Shaking hands with the opposite sex is against the rules. RCC students (1) may not sing too loudly, (2) must, while enrolled in their freshmen year, go to bed no later than 8:00 p.m., (3) must never make physical contact with the opposite gender, (4) may not date under any circumstances, (5) must only use gender-appropriate stairwells and elevators, and (6) may never view or possess video games, DVDs, or use the Internet outside of what RCC offers and authorizes. As a condition of admission, matriculation, and graduation, all students are required to live on campus during the entire four-year undergraduate program.

Violation of RCC's regulations will result in school expulsion and, where appropriate, prosecution, as the school has been authorized to conduct business as if it were a self-governing jurisdiction with full power to condemn certain conduct via criminal conviction and punishment. The promulgating state legislators credited with founding RCC believed that students should be saved from themselves, particularly given that institutions of higher learning are increasingly being held legally responsible for students' well-being. Accordingly, these legislators determined that the school's administrators would be given the power to regulate all aspects of campus life.

---

[10] *See, e.g., Ten Incredibly Strict College Campuses*, COLLEGE TIMES, Apr. 26, 2010, http://www.collegetimes.tv/10-unbelievably-strict-college-campuses/.

Carla believed that studying while a student on RCC's campus would be a dream come true. However, transferring from her private college to RCC would have required Carla to forfeit her lacrosse scholarship, which she was financially unable to do. Nevertheless, Carla longed to associate with a more chaste, moral, and sober student body than the one at her college. Carla's RCC dream, however, soon became a nightmare last August, when she decided that she would forego a social life and study for her classes every weekend of the academic year not at her college, but at RCC.

Carla's routine was simple: she packed her books, drove to Roanoke (stopping along the way to buy foods permitted on RCC's campus), parked her car in the space marked "Visitors," walked to the School of Biology's library, and studied in the section marked "Women." Carla's study plan worked quite smoothly and she continued to follow her plan throughout the month of September.

However, on a Sunday in October, Carla met David, a young man who was not an RCC student, but seeking the same "controlled environment" as Carla. David bumped into Carla when David unsuccessfully attempted to locate the "Males Only" stairwell. Carla pointed David to the proper stairwell. David was quite grateful for Carla's kindness, asked Carla her name, and introduced himself. She told him her name, but also quickly let him know that she was not enrolled as an RCC student. David admitted also being a visitor to RCC's campus and was happy to learn that he was not the only visitor on campus.

Carla asked David if he would like to get a coffee together; David said "yes." Given their awareness of RCC's rules, Carla and David walked separately to the parking lot, got into their respective cars, and drove off, meeting a few miles away from RCC's campus to get a coffee together.

Shortly after their encounter, approximately one month later, Carla and David began dating while off and away from RCC's campus. They also continued to study at RCC, scheduling their sessions to occur at the same time. They studied into the night in separate parts of the library, with the understanding that once the library closed at midnight, they would meet off-campus for coffee or dinner.

On a night in December, Carla and David walked separately to their parked cars after concluding another successful RCC study session. While walking, David sent Carla the following text message: "CU@ car." Carla sent a text message back: "OK." Upon reaching her car, Carla decided — on a whim — to pull her car up to David's car in a way that would allow their driver's side windows to nearly touch and also allow them to say "good night" face-to-face (albeit sitting in their respective cars). However, when Carla did so, she was startled to see sadness on David's face. Carla asked David what was wrong; David sat silently, eyes downcast. Carla tried to figure out what was going on and continued to ask David what was wrong; David continued to avoid her eye contact. Carla loudly pleaded with David to "Look at me!"

Carla sat, awaiting a clue as to what was wrong. She looked at David's face for any expression. After approximately ten seconds had passed, Carla put her car in reverse and, suddenly, David finally looked up and at Carla. Immediately, both Carla and David heard a loud police whistle. Unbeknownst to Carla and David, campus security had observed their encounter and, subsequently, converged upon Carla and David's cars. Campus police arrested both Carla and David. Carla was charged with scopophilia, a violation of RCC's Criminal Code. David was ultimately released and not charged.

RCC has indicated that it plans to criminally prosecute Carla in the state of Virginia (where it is located) for: (1) criminal attempt and (2) criminal solicitation, per RCC Criminal Code § 501 and § 502. The government will introduce testimony from campus police that, on the evening in question, they observed Carla and David from the time they left the library and witnessed Carla intentionally pull her car up to David's so that they could be physically close and violate RCC Criminal Code, § 101, which provides:

RCC CRIMINAL CODE, § 101: SCOPOPHILIA: "Every person who purposely casts a prolonged gaze into the eyes of another person for the purpose of obtaining or receiving intimate visual gratification shall be guilty of scopophilia. Scopophilia is punishable as a criminal misdemeanor."

Again: Carla is not being prosecuted for the above statute, but for the following crimes:

RCC CRIMINAL CODE, § 501: ATTEMPT: "A person is guilty of an attempt to commit a crime if, acting with the kind of culpability otherwise required for commission of the crime, s/he: a. purposely engages in conduct that would constitute the crime; b. does or omits to do anything with the purpose of causing or with the belief that it will cause such result without further conduct on his/her part; or c. purposely does anything which, under the circumstances as s/he believes them to be, is an act constituting a substantial step in the course of conduct planned to culminate in the commission of the crime."

RCC CRIMINAL CODE, § 502: SOLICITIATION: "A person is guilty of solicitation to commit a crime if with the purpose of promoting or facilitating its commission s/he commands, encourages or requests another person to engage in specific conduct that would constitute such crime or an attempt to commit such crime."

As far as we have been able to tell (given the dearth of legislative history and record of this criminal statute), RCC's Criminal Code was implemented as a part of the RCC Mandate of 2005. The general legislative intent regarding RCC's Criminal Code was "to create a mini-society whose environment would foster and reward responsible living, civility, chastity, and marriage." Legislators believed that practices such as alcohol abuse, illicit drug use, and sexual exploration would minimize RCC students' abilities to develop proper social relationships and disrupt the educational process. Accordingly, these legislators believed that by outlawing, banning, and restricting such practices, they would never take root, much less flourish, on RCC's campus.

REQUIRED TASKS

Task One: Writing Legal Memoranda; Supporting Indictment

You are the summer intern for the district attorney who will prosecute Carla in this criminal matter. Assess the strength of the government's *criminal attempt* case against Carla in a legal memorandum. In preparing for this task and all other tasks in this chapter, review the proffered substantive (both case and codified) criminal law. Also use an online case law database to read the following case for guidance regarding the application of the substantive law in this task: *In re Banks*, 244 S.E.2d 386 (N.C. 1978).

Additionally, in preparing for this task, you also should consult the SVC and supplemental materials to be found in the online component.

ESTIMATED TIME FOR COMPLETION: 2 hours.

LEVEL OF DIFFICULTY (1 TO 5):

Task Two: Writing Legal Memoranda; Opposing Indictment

You are the summer intern for the public defender who will represent Carla in this criminal matter. Assess the strength of the government's *criminal solicitation* case against Carla in a legal memorandum. In preparing for this task and all other tasks in this chapter, review the proffered substantive (both case and codified) criminal law. Also use an online case law database to read the following cases for guidance regarding the application of the substantive law in this task:

- *In re Banks*, 244 S.E.2d 386 (N.C. 1978)
- *United States v. Chong Lam*, 677 F.3d 190 (4th Cir. 2012)
- *Kolender v. Lawson*, 461 U.S. 352 (1983)

Additionally, in preparing for this task, you also should consult the supplemental materials found in the online component of this text.

ESTIMATED TIME FOR COMPLETION: 2 hours.

LEVEL OF DIFFICULTY (1 TO 5):

PRACTICE SKILLS USED:

Skill 1: Planning and Brainstorming

Skill 2: Legal Argument; Integrating the Law and the Facts

Skill 3: Professional Writing

SKILLS GUIDES

For sample legal memoranda, consult the documents provided in the online component.

SKILLS GUIDE #1: Planning and Brainstorming

Please refer to Chapter 1, Skills Guide #3.

SKILLS GUIDE #2: Legal Argument; Integrating the Law and the Facts

Please refer to Chapter 8, Skills Guide #2.

SKILLS GUIDE #4: Professional Writing

Please refer to Chapter 16, Skills Guide #3.

Chapter 11

CONSPIRACY

OVERVIEW

A "conspiracy" is defined in criminal law as an agreement between two or more people to commit a criminal act or acts — "the combination of minds in an unlawful purpose." *Smith v. United States*, 133 S. Ct. 714, 719 (2013). Conspiracy is a type of inchoate crime. Criminal liability attaches to the beginning stages of an offense. The planned offense (often called "the target offense") need not be completed or even attempted in order to sustain a conspiracy charge. Conspiracy is a substantive criminal offense in its own right — that is, a person can be convicted of conspiring to commit a target offense. Although subject to much debate, attaching criminal liability to conspiracy in its own right is generally understood to be a means of addressing the increased potential danger of group criminality.

I. ACTUS REUS

The *actus reus* of the conspiracy charge is an agreement between two or more people. The agreement does not need to be explicit or in writing. Rather, a "meeting of the minds" can be inferred from the parties' conduct and the factual circumstances surrounding the commission of the target offense. The prosecution must demonstrate that there was a common understanding as to the target offense and may do so using circumstantial evidence. Some jurisdictions require that the target offense be a felony whereas other jurisdictions include agreements to commit any level of criminal offense.

In common law and in many conspiracy statutes today, a conspiracy requires at least two people, both of whom are "true" parties to the agreement. If one party, for instance, due to mental capacity or insanity, is not able to form the mental state required to make an agreement, the elements of the conspiracy charge are not met. Relatedly, if one party is simply pretending to agree to the planning of the target offense, he may not qualify as a "true" co-conspirator. The requirement of two parties is often labeled the requirement of a "bilateral" agreement. Some jurisdictions, as well as the Model Penal Code, follow a "unilateral" approach, meaning that the "true" conspirator is liable under conspiracy theory even if the second person in agreement is not a true co-conspirator. The difference in these two approaches is seen in conspiracy cases involving an undercover police officer. In jurisdictions that require a bilateral agreement, an agreement between an undercover officer and one defendant would not on its own support a conspiracy charge. However, in jurisdictions that follow the unilateral approach, a defendant who makes an agreement solely with an undercover officer is able to be charged with the substantive offense of conspiracy.

Some state conspiracy statutes require proof of an *overt act* in furtherance of the conspiracy. Federal conspiracy laws generally do not require such proof. An overt act can be a very minimal act in the process of the planning for, or commission of, the target offense; such an act does not need to rise to the level of an "attempt" to commit the target offense. Overt acts can include otherwise innocent conduct if those acts are done in furtherance of the conspiratorial agreement, such as making a phone call or renting a car. In addition, an overt act of one member of the conspiracy satisfies the requirement for all members.

II. MENS REA

Conspiracy contains two distinct *mens rea* requirements. The first is the intent to agree to commit a crime. Proof of this intent is intricately related to the proof of the agreement itself. The second required mental state is the knowledge of the target offense (the goal of the conspiratorial agreement). The defendant must have knowledge of the general nature of the target offense but is not required to know all of its specific details. The defendant does not need to know the entire scope of the planned offenses or the identity of all co-conspirators. In addition, proof of the deliberate failure to learn details in order to claim lack of knowledge can satisfy the knowledge requirement.

III. THE SCOPE OF LIABILITY

In addition to being liable for the conspiracy itself, a member of a conspiracy is also criminally liable for the target offense. In other words, a party to the conspiratorial agreement need not personally commit the target offense in order to be found guilty of that offense. For example, if Todd and Megan agree to rob a store, and then Megan stands outside while Todd enters the store and commits the robbery, both can be charged with the offense of conspiracy and the offense of robbery.

In some jurisdictions, a member of the conspiracy is also liable for *any* crime committed by a co-conspirator, if that crime was reasonably foreseeable as part of the underlying agreement and was committed in furtherance of the conspiracy. First recognized by the Supreme Court in *Pinkerton v. United States*, 328 U.S. 640 (1946), the *Pinkerton* rule dramatically expands the scope of liability under the conspiracy charge. To continue with our previous example, if Todd, while committing the aforementioned robbery, also shoots a security guard in order to escape the store, in a jurisdiction that follows the *Pinkerton* rule, Megan may also be held criminally liable for that shooting. A prosecutor would argue that the shooting of a security guard was reasonably foreseeable as a crime that would occur during a robbery and that the shooting was done in furtherance of the robbery they conspired to commit. The *Pinkerton* rule is the subject of much criticism; the Model Penal Code and several state jurisdictions have declined to adopt this expansion of criminal liability.

IV.　THE STRUCTURE OF THE CONSPIRACY

In assessing a suspect's liability under conspiracy doctrine, it is essential to first assess the nature of the conspiracy itself. Is the defendant a part of one large conspiracy or are there are several smaller separate conspiracies? For example, imagine a national drug trafficking operation. Is the drug courier in one east coast town liable for all the drug sales completed across the country? Or is he merely part of a smaller agreement to sell drugs in his individual locality? As you might imagine, questions of the size and scope of the conspiratorial agreement can have drastic consequences on a suspect's criminal liability.

To answer these questions of size and scope, the central question is whether there is one unifying agreement that encompasses all of the members. Although it is not necessary that a conspirator know all the details of the target offense or even all the individual members of the conspiracy, there does have to be an agreement to one unifying criminal enterprise. In complex conspiracies, the extent of an individual conspirator's knowledge (and as a consequence, his criminal liability) can be difficult to determine. Visual and descriptive metaphors of a "wheel" conspiracy and a "chain" conspiracy are sometimes used to help diagram the organization of a conspiracy. A "wheel" conspiracy is comprised of a hub, spokes, and the connecting circular frame. For example, the drug distributer is considered the hub and the other individuals (i.e., the drug sellers) with whom he has separate agreements to sell drugs are considered the spokes. In order to have a true wheel, however, there also needs to be a frame connecting all the spokes together. Therefore, for a wheel conspiracy, there is typically evidence that the "spokes" were aware of the common plan or purpose, for example, to sell drugs for a particular gang throughout a particular neighborhood. For a conspiracy to be considered one wheel — that is one conspiracy in and of itself — there must be evidence of a common scheme, plan, or goal.

In comparison, a "chain" conspiracy is comprised of linear links. Although each link may not know the actual identity of every party above or below them, they have knowledge of the other members in the chain and there is a common agreement to be a part of that particular course of crime. A chain conspiracy may describe a drug distribution conspiracy (e.g., a seller, a distributor, a wholesaler) in which, although the wholesaler might distribute to other sellers (and thus be a part of *additional* chain conspiracies), there is no evidence that the seller is part of any common plan or scheme to sell drugs with the other sellers.

A conspiracy may not neatly fit the visual depiction of a "wheel" or a "chain." More significantly, a large conspiracy may have parts that are wheels and parts that are chains. The goal of assessing the structure of the conspiracy and the knowledge of the various participants is to determine the extent of each defendant's criminal liability and the proper offenses charged.

V.　DEFENSES TO CONSPIRACY

The Model Penal Code and some jurisdictions recognize a limited defense of "withdrawal" from the conspiracy. Although typically not a defense to the charge of conspiracy itself, if the defendant withdraws from the conspiracy, he may not be prosecuted for any crimes committed by members of the conspiracy post-withdrawal. The defense of withdrawal (sometimes called "renunciation") is considered an affirmative defense and the defendant bears the burden of proving his withdrawal by a preponderance of the evidence. An affirmative act of withdrawal is typically required. Such an act could include communicating the withdrawal to co-conspirators or notifying the authorities of the conspiracy and its plans.

The applicable statute of limitations also serves as another possible defense to a conspiracy charge. The statute of limitations is a time limit after which the bringing of claims is barred. For example, in the federal system, a prosecution must begin within five years of the charged offense date. With respect to the conspiracy charge, the statute of limitations "clock" begins ticking on the date the conspiracy ends (due to either abandonment, completion of the target offense, or arrest). In jurisdictions that recognize a withdrawal defense, the statute of limitations clock begins on the date the defendant withdraws from the conspiracy. The government bears the burden of proving the timing of the conspiracy. To illustrate, imagine Defendant Ben withdrew from the conspiracy on June 5, 2005. On September 5, 2012, the prosecution charged Defendant Ben with conspiring to distribute drugs from 2001-2007. If the applicable term of the statute of limitations was five years and Defendant Ben met his burden of proof with respect to his withdrawal, this prosecution would be barred under the statute of limitations. On these facts, Defendant Ben's withdrawal, in combination with the statute of limitations, serves as a complete defense to the charge of conspiracy.

VI. THE CONSPIRACY CHARGE IN PRACTICE

In general, the charge of conspiracy is considered an effective, and often controversial, tool for prosecutors to expand the scope of criminal liability. A prosecutor does not need to convict, or even charge or identify, all parties to the conspiracy. In order to bring charges of conspiracy against an individual defendant, the prosecutor simply needs to prove the existence of at least two parties to the agreement. Given the nature of a conspiracy itself, a trial on a conspiracy charge often involves multiple defendants. A co-defendant trial likely means that more evidence will be relevant for admission and the prosecutor might have her choice of the jurisdiction in which to file charges.

In addition, the co-conspirator exception to the hearsay rule has emerged as an important tool in the prosecution of members of a conspiracy. As you may know, hearsay statements (out-of-court statements admitted for their truth) are generally inadmissible in a criminal trial. The co-conspirator exception allows the government to introduce in its case-in-chief hearsay statements of co-conspirators made during the course of, and in furtherance of, the conspiracy. These statements can be introduced as evidence against any member of the conspiracy, whether or not that member was present when the initial statement was said out of court. The act of withdrawal and the statute of limitations provide some limits to the introduction of co-conspirator hearsay statements. Statements made by a co-conspirator are not admissible against a defendant if they were made after the defendant's withdrawal from the conspiracy. Similarly, statements made by a co-conspirator are not admissible against a defendant if the statements were made after the statute of limitations term applicable to the defendant has expired.

EXERCISE

Overview

Nick Jones was indicted for crimes connected to his alleged role in an organization that has sold and distributed crack cocaine and heroin in Pennsylvania and Maryland for the past 10 years. All the arrests were made one month prior to the indictment. There are eight co-defendants:

- *Robert Manning*: Alleged distributor of drugs for Philadelphia. Evidence against him includes phone calls between himself and Nick Jones.

- *Thomas Manning*: Brother of Robert Manning and his roommate; alleged distributor for Philadelphia and Baltimore. Known as "Big Tom." Evidence against him demonstrates he receives his drugs directly from Nick Jones.

- *Cyril Pontiff*: Caught selling drugs in Philadelphia to an undercover officer posing as a street-level buyer. Cyril told the police that he received his drugs from Thomas Manning. Cyril stated that he had once met Thomas at Thomas's apartment. Cyril stated he knows Thomas also lives with his brother.

- *Celia Bishop*: Caught selling drugs to an undercover officer in Baltimore. Celia told the police that she gets her drugs from a guy she calls "Big Tom." She has never seen anyone else besides "Big Tom" and has always met him on a street corner.

- *Paul England*: Alleged seller at the street level in Philadelphia. Paul was caught on video entering the Manning brothers' apartment at least once a month. He told the police he receives his drugs from Robert. Paul was initially caught selling to an undercover officer.

- *Dave Bartels*: Alleged distributor for Pittsburgh. Evidence against him includes photos of a meeting between him and Nick Jones. The police conducted a search of Dave's apartment pursuant to a warrant and found narcotics, money, and a black book with what appears to be a customer list.

- *Eli Mears*: An individual listed in Dave's black book. Eli is a transient but lives on the streets of Pittsburgh. The local police stopped Eli on the street; money and drugs were found in Eli's pocket.

- *Jennifer Walters*: Alleged distributor in Harrisburg. Evidence against her includes photographs of her receiving alleged packages of narcotics from Nick Jones.

Nick Jones and his eight alleged co-conspirators have been charged with conspiracy to distribute narcotics and to possess narcotics with the intent to distribute them, in violation of 21 U.S.C. § 846 and 21 U.S.C. § 841(a)(1). In addition to the evidence listed above, here is a brief summary of the evidence the government has collected to use in its case-in-chief:

- The conspiracy began on August 5, 2004 and remains active today.

- On April 14, 2012, Thomas was recorded on a phone call stating, "Harrisburg is booming. We have tons of business there." He was speaking to an unidentified male.

- Cyril's told the police in a post-arrest interview: "Yeah, I've seen Big Tom's brother. Does he sell drugs? We all do. That's how we all make money."

- Paul and Nick grew up as children together in Philadelphia. On a recorded phone call between Nick and Paul from May 26, 2006, the following conversation took place:

  o Paul: "How's it going down there?"

  o Nick: "I've got Baltimore now. It's all mine."

  o Paul: "Cool, cool."

- Jennifer is cooperating with the government and will testify that at an in-person meeting in February 2011, Nick, Robert, Thomas, and she discussed state-wide operations and future prospects of their drug business in Maryland and Pennsylvania.

- Paul went to prison on an unrelated domestic assault charge in January 21, 2009. He served a three-year term and was released on December 18, 2011. At the same time he was facing the assault charge, he was also charged with selling drugs on January 4, 2009. He was not convicted of the drug charge due to the agreed-upon plea bargain.

- At the drug transaction that led to Cyril's arrest, a loaded firearm was found in his pocket.

- Starting in 2008, there is evidence that, in addition to narcotics, Nick began funneling illegal firearms to Thomas, who then sold them to street-level buyers in Baltimore.

- On a recorded phone call between Nick and Paul from March 9, 2008, the following conversation took place:

  o Paul: "How's life in B'more?"

  o Nick: "It's good. Definitely."

  o Paul: "You sellin' both now?"

  o Nick: "Yep, Tommy's handling all of it."

- A storage locker in Philadelphia was located in Nick's name. Inside the locker was a cache of illegal firearms. The locker facility turned over the rental agreement, which was dated October 8, 2007.

For purposes of this exercise, assume that the existence of the conspiracy itself is not in question (i.e., there is a drug distribution ring). Rather, the tasks are focused on the extent of liability for each co-defendant and the evidence that can be used against him or her.

In addition, assume that the federal jurisdiction follows the definition of conspiracy as given in Model Penal Code § 5.03, Criminal Conspiracy.

REQUIRED TASKS

Task One: Conspiracy Charts

Assume the role of the prosecutor. Chart the conspiracy as it relates to the alleged drug trafficking. Draw a graphical depiction of the relationship between the codefendants. Does this conspiracy have aspects of a wheel conspiracy? Of a chain? Both? Assuming your goal is to argue for the most extensive liability possible, which "links" will likely be contested by the defense? You do not need to worry about issues of admissibility of evidence at this time.

ESTIMATED TIME FOR COMPLETION: 30 minutes.

LEVEL OF DIFFICULTY (1 TO 5):

Task Two: Oral Argument; Motion Practice; Evidentiary Problems

Assume the role of counsel for Paul England. The prosecutor alleges that there is one single conspiracy involving all nine codefendants. The prosecutor will seek to introduce the hearsay statements of Thomas and Cyril in its case-in-chief. Prepare for oral argument on your motion to exclude the hearsay statements in the prosecution's case against your client. An example of the substantive law part of a motion on this topic is provided in the online component.

Although you do not need to do independent legal research for this task, you should connect the facts above with the relevant legal principles. Review **Federal Rule of Evidence 801**.

For purposes of this task, consider the following to be a statement of the current law governing your jurisdiction:

For a declaration by one defendant to be admissible against the other defendants under Fed. R. Evid. 801(d)(2)(E), the government must establish by a preponderance of the evidence:

(1) that a conspiracy existed,

(2) that the defendant and the declarant were members of the conspiracy, and

(3) that the statement was made during the course and in furtherance of the conspiracy.

For your oral argument, you should use the law provided to guide you in your argument that the statements of Thomas and Cyril should be excluded.

ESTIMATED TIME FOR COMPLETION: 45 minutes.

LEVEL OF DIFFICULTY (1 TO 5):

Task Three: Fact Patterns

Along with the facts provided above, consider these additional factual scenarios and answer the related questions.

1. On the day Paul was released from prison in 2011, there is evidence that Paul told Robert that he was "going straight" and that he would no longer sell drugs now that he was on parole. Assuming that Paul could meet his burden to prove the affirmative defense of withdrawal, could the prosecution charge Paul with conspiring to sell and distribute *firearms* from October 8, 2007 to today? What will the prosecution argue? How will Paul respond?

2. The prosecution is proceeding with the theory that Cyril is liable for all the drug sales committed in Baltimore, Harrisburg, and Pittsburgh. Cyril is claiming that he is only part of a smaller conspiracy to distribute and sell drugs in Philadelphia. What are the arguments in favor of Cyril's position? Against?

3. Paul England's counsel is contesting the extent of his client's liability. Defense counsel will argue that Paul is not liable for any drug sales in Baltimore. How will the prosecution respond?

4. Imagine into the future. Upon considering the given facts in the text and the additional facts in Question 1, when will the statute of limitations run with respect to prosecuting Paul for conspiring to sell and distribute drugs in Philadelphia?

ESTIMATED TIME FOR COMPLETION: 45 minutes.

LEVEL OF DIFFICULTY (1 TO 5):

PRACTICE SKILLS USED:

Skill 1: Legal Argument; Integrating the Law and the Facts

Skill 2: Motion Writing

Skill 3: Oral Argument; Motion Practice

SKILLS GUIDES

To consider the vast reach of the conspiracy charge and the various contexts in which a defendant may face a conspiracy charge, review the materials provided in the online component.

For examples of cases in which the court analyzes the structure of the alleged conspiracy and the liability of its participants, use an online legal database to read the following:

- *United States v. Borelli*, 336 F.2d 376 (2d Cir. 1964)
- *United States v. Elliott*, 571 F.2d 880 (5th Cir. 1978)

There is a plethora of academic commentary of the charge of conspiracy. For a sample of both pro and con points of view, use an online legal database to review the following articles:

- Neal Kumar Katyal, *Conspiracy Theory*, 112 YALE L. J. 1307 (2003)
- Paul Marcus, *Criminal Conspiracy Law: Time to Turn Back from an Ever Expanding, Ever More Troubling Area*, 1 WM. & MARY BILL RTS. J. 1 (1992)
- Phillip E. Johnson, *The Unnecessary Crime of Conspiracy*, 61 CAL. L. REV. 1137 (1973)

SKILLS GUIDE #1: Legal Argument; Integrating the Law and the Facts

Please refer to Chapter 8, Skills Guide #2.

SKILLS GUIDE #2: Motion Writing

Please refer to Chapter 8, Skills Guide #1.

SKILLS GUIDE #3:Oral Argument; Motion Practice

Please refer to Chapter 8, Skills Guide #3.

ADDITIONAL MATERIALS FOR THE EXERCISE — AVAILABLE IN ON-LINE COMPONENT

MODEL PENAL CODE § 5.03: Criminal Conspiracy

21 U.S.C. § 846: Attempt and Conspiracy

21 U.S.C.A. § 841(a)(1): Unlawful distribution of controlled substances

18 U.S.C. § 3282(a): Statute of Limitations for Non-Capital Offenses

FED. R. EVID. 801: Definitions That Apply to This Article; Exclusions from Hearsay

Chapter 12

ACCOMPLICE LIABILITY

OVERVIEW

"Accomplice liability" is a theory of liability under which a person may be held criminally liable for assisting another individual in the commission of a crime. This type of liability is sometimes called accessory liability or liability as an aider and abettor.

Accomplice liability is considered a form of derivative liability. This means that the accomplice is not guilty of an independent criminal offense (i.e., there is no separate offense for being an accomplice). Rather, he *derives* his liability from the conduct of the principal party. Thus, as a general rule, the accomplice is equally liable for the conduct committed by the principal and can be convicted of the same substantive offense. For example, if the accomplice helps the principal break into a vehicle that the principal then turns on and drives away, they can both be convicted of the crime of stealing a vehicle.

Accomplice liability, like criminal liability of the principal, has both *mens rea* and *actus reus* requirements. Broadly speaking, a person may be held criminally liable under the theory of accomplice liability if he intentionally assisted the principal in the commission of the crime. With respect to the act required, courts generally define "assistance" as aid by physical conduct (e.g., handing the principal a gun or guarding the door) or help via psychological influence (e.g., verbally encouraging the commission of the crime). A person is not an accomplice unless his conduct *in fact* assists the principal in the commission of the offense. In addition, courts often state that "mere presence" is not enough to establish assistance. Nevertheless, the amount of assistance necessary to establish liability is minimal and it is typically a question for the jury whether the defendant was merely present at the scene or was actually assisting in the crime. Small amounts of assistance will usually subject the person to accomplice liability. Furthermore, a person can be held liable as an accomplice even if the principal is not aware of the assistance provided. In cases in which a person has a legal duty to act or provide assistance, the failure to do so also may also provide a basis for accomplice liability.

Accomplice liability is generally thought of as containing two *mens rea* requirements. First, the defendant must have *intentionally* aided the principal in the commission of a criminal offense. Second, many jurisdictions require that the defendant also have the requisite mental state for the substantive criminal offense committed by the principal. For example, if the charged offense of the principal, for instance burglary, requires proof that the principal entered a dwelling with the intent to commit a theft or other felony, the defendant must also have that same *mens rea* (intent to commit a theft or other felony) in order to be held liable as an accomplice. Most jurisdictions require this second *mens rea* for all levels of requisite mental states, including crimes of negligence and recklessness. In practice, the *mens rea* for the charged offense is often inferred from the first *mens rea* requirement — the defendant's intent to assist the principal with the commission of that offense.

In most jurisdictions, in addition to being liable for the assisted criminal conduct of the principal, the accomplice is also liable for all "natural and probable consequences" of the initial criminal offense. Under this doctrine, an accomplice is liable for all crimes committed by the principal that are "reasonably foreseeable." For example, if the principal also takes private property out of the glove box of the stolen car, the accomplice would also be criminally liable for that theft, despite his lack of participation in that particular crime.

Under modern penal law, a person can usually abandon or withdraw his assistance in order to avoid liability as an accomplice. However, in order to demonstrate "abandonment" and escape liability, most jurisdictions require the abandonment or withdrawal to be communicated to the principal and the defendant must have attempted to undo the effect of the assistance previously provided.

There are two specific types of accomplices that are narrower in their factual application: accessory *before* the fact and accessory *after* the fact. A person is considered an "accessory before the fact" when he or she provides assistance to the principal but is not actually or constructively present when the principal commits the substantive offense (e.g., a person who hires someone to murder his spouse or provides a gun that is later used in a robbery). A person is considered an "accessory after the fact" when he helps the principal after the crime is completed — typically this assistance is to avoid capture, arrest, or prosecution — and does so with the knowledge of the principal's criminal conduct. For instance, a person who helps a friend hide the gun used in a robbery the day before would be considered an accessory after the fact.

Historically, the common law distinguished between the principal (then called the principal in the first degree), the accessory (then called the principal in the second degree), the accessory before the fact, and the accessory after the fact. The Model Penal Code and most jurisdictions today have largely abandoned these distinctions. The principal, the accessory, and the accessory before the fact are considered the same for liability purposes and are held equally liable for the conduct of the principal. Accessories after the fact, however, remain a separate type of accomplice liability, which is not equated with the liability of the principal or other accomplices. Accessories after the fact are typically charged with a separate substantive offense and jurisdictions typically punish this type of assistance less harshly.

Although under common law the principal had to be convicted in order to hold the accomplice liable, today's rule is less straightforward. In most jurisdictions, an accomplice may not be convicted unless the guilt of the principal is also demonstrated. However, the prosecution is not required to prove the identity of the principal or charge that individual in court. Consequently, although the existence of a principal and the commission of the criminal offense must be proven in order to establish the accomplice's liability, in many situations it is not required that the actual principal be convicted in order to convict the accomplice.

EXERCISE

Overview

On March 6, Tim Jenkins, Allen Porter, and Karen Abbott were driving in a 2003 blue Honda Accord in the city of Los Angeles. Tim and Karen are dating and Allen is a childhood friend of both. On that date, all were 22 years old. Karen was driving the vehicle, Tim was in the front passenger seat, and Allen was sitting behind Tim in the back passenger seat. The Los Angeles Police Department (LAPD) had previously identified Tim and Allen as members of the criminal street gang, the Boerum Street Boys (BSB). Karen has been identified as an "associate" of the gang. At approximately 4:20 p.m., Tim, Allen, and Karen drove northbound on Morris Avenue alongside Morris Park — a public park with a basketball court. According to the LAPD, Morris Park is in BSB "territory."

On that same day, Victor Cerna and Mitchell Lund, both 15 years old, were playing a pickup game at the Morris Park court. According to Victor's statement to the police, at about 4:25 p.m., two gang members approached him on the basketball court and stole his iPod, which was lying on top of his backpack at the edge of the court. Victor called the police after the two men left the scene. The police spoke with Victor and Mitchell at the park. Both teens gave a physical description of the men, including their clothing, and told the police that they saw them hop into a blue four-door car and drive north. Based on the description of the men and the car, the police located and arrested Tim, Allen, and Karen at the nearby 7-Eleven and took them back to the park to be identified by the two teens. Tim and Allen were identified by both Victor and Mitchell as the two men who approached them at the park. They could not identify Karen. After searching Tim, the police found Victor's iPod in Tim's front pocket. Tim, Allen, and Karen were all placed under arrest for robbery and were taken to the local police station to be booked and processed.

The prosecution charged Tim, Allen, and Karen with the robbery of Victor Cerna. At the preliminary hearing, Victor Cerna testified. Mitchell Lund was uncooperative and did not come to court. Victor made in-court identifications of Tim and Allen. He could not identify Karen as the driver of the vehicle.

Witness Testimony

Victor's testimony was as follows: On March 6, at about 4:20 p.m., he was playing basketball with his friend. He had previously placed his backpack on the ground at the edge of the court. It was approximately four feet away from where he was standing at the time that his iPod was taken. His iPod was laying on top of his backpack because he did not put it away after listening to it on his way to the park. Victor first noticed "a big guy" (later identified in court as Defendant-1, Tim Jenkins) coming toward him. Tim stopped about five feet from where Victor was standing. At that point he was very close to Victor's backpack on the ground. A second guy (later identified in court as Defendant-2, Allen Porter) stopped about 10 feet behind Tim. Victor did not see where these two men had come from. When the two guys stopped approaching, Tim tapped his forearm and said "BSB mother — ers." Tim's sleeves were rolled up and Victor could see what he believed to be a gang tattoo. Tim then leaned down and grabbed the iPod. Victor testified that Allen was standing still while Tim spoke and took the iPod. Victor stated that, in his opinion, Allen seemed as if he was glaring at him. Allen's arms were crossed. Allen did not say anything at any time. After Tim took the iPod, he turned and walked back towards Morris Avenue. Allen walked back with Tim. They were about two feet away from each other as they were walking away. Victor could not tell if they were talking to each other. Victor was not sure where the iPod went after he saw Tim take it from the backpack.

Victor testified that he saw Tim and Allen get into a blue four-door car. The car was parked on a side street by Morris Avenue. It was across the park, he was not sure of the distance but it was at least 50 yards away. Victor could not see the driver and could not tell if the driver was a male or female. He saw Tim get into the front seat and Allen get into the back seat. He could not see anything that happened inside the car. The car then drove away northbound.

At the preliminary hearing, a police officer also testified to the following statements made by Allen after his arrest: Tim, Allen, and Karen were on their way to the 7-Eleven to get a snack. As they drove by the basketball court, Tim saw the two teens playing basketball and said, "Let's go talk to these guys." Allen had never seen the teens before and did not know them personally. Tim told Karen to stop the car. As Tim was getting out of the car, Allen saw Tim pushing up his sleeves. Tim has gang tattoos on both forearms. Allen got out of the car. Allen told the police that he was just going "to hang with Tim." He stated that he did not know that Tim was going to confront the teenager or commit a robbery. Allen denied being a member of BSB but admitted that the letters BSB were tattooed on his upper right arm.

The police officer also testified to Karen's post-arrest statements. Karen told the police that she stopped the car because Tim told her to. She stated that she did not know why Tim wanted to exit the car but she did hear him say, "Let's go talk to these guys." She also admitted that she saw Tim roll up his sleeves and that he has tattoos on his forearms. She denied knowing that Tim was a member of BSB. Karen told the police that after Tim and Allen exited the car, she turned left and drove the car about a half block up on a side street. She had the engine running and the radio on. She stated that she did not watch Tim and Allen and did not know what transpired in the park. Karen said that about two minutes passed, after which Tim and Allen returned to the car. Tim told her "let's go" and she drove off to the 7-Eleven as planned. Karen stated that, as they pulled into the store's parking lot, Tim pulled out the iPod and began talking about the music found on it. She stated that Allen seemed excited about hearing some of the music on the iPod.

Tim, Allen, and Karen were charged as co-defendants and all three were charged with the crime of robbery, a felony. The prosecution's theory is that Tim is the principal in the commission of the robbery. Allen and Karen were charged as accomplices. On March 20, a preliminary hearing was held. After the preliminary hearing testimony, the magistrate found that there was sufficient evidence to proceed with the charges of robbery against all three defendants.

Relevant Law and Procedural Background

The crime of robbery is defined in California Penal Code Section 211. The California Penal Code uses the term "aiders and abettors" as the label for an accomplice.

In California (as in many other jurisdictions), a defendant charged with a felony offense is entitled to a preliminary hearing within a set period following his arraignment on criminal charges. The preliminary hearing functions as a screening tool by a neutral fact-finder and serves as a procedural safeguard against prosecutorial charging power. In some jurisdictions, an indictment by a grand jury serves as a substitute for the preliminary hearing and functions as the procedural check by a neutral third party. A preliminary hearing is an adversarial proceeding — meaning both the prosecution and the defense are entitled to present evidence and to cross-examine the witnesses called by the opposing side. The Supreme Court has recognized the preliminary hearing as a "critical stage" of criminal proceedings and, as such, the defendant is guaranteed the right to have counsel present under the Sixth Amendment.

The essential question at the preliminary hearing is whether there is sufficient evidence to believe that the defendant committed the charge against him. In most jurisdictions, "sufficient evidence" is defined as probable cause to believe that the defendant committed the offense. If the magistrate presiding over the preliminary hearing finds that there is sufficient evidence to support the charges, the defendant is "held over" or "bound over" for trial (also sometimes known as being "held to answer").The case is then sent to the trial court. In practice, the majority of cases pass the preliminary hearing stage, in part due to the lower standard of proof — a standard significantly lower than the evidence required at trial (proof beyond a reasonable doubt). However, the defendant is able to challenge the magistrate's ruling. Once before the trial judge, a defendant is entitled to file a motion to dismiss on the grounds that the prosecution presented insufficient evidence at the preliminary hearing to support the charges against him. In California, this motion is codified in California Penal Code Section 995. Colloquially called a "995 motion," this motion to dismiss asks the trial judge to review the evidence presented at the preliminary hearing (usually through a review of the transcript) and to decide whether the prosecution presented sufficient evidence to proceed against the defendant at trial.

There is one other procedural term you may notice in completing this exercise. The charging document (the document which lists the government's charges against the defendant) is called by a different name depending on the stage in the criminal proceedings and whether the jurisdiction follows the preliminary hearing model or uses a grand jury. In California, the initial charging document in felony cases is called a Complaint. After the preliminary hearing is held, if the defendant is held to answer on the charges, the prosecution files an Information in the trial court (which takes the place of the initial Complaint). As you will see in reviewing the sample 995 motion in the online component materials, a 995 motion seeks the dismissal of the Information filed against your client.

REQUIRED TASKS

Task One: Motion Writing; Motion to Dismiss

You are the defense counsel representing Allen Porter. Using the outline provided in the online component, prepare a written motion to dismiss on the grounds that the prosecution presented insufficient evidence at the preliminary hearing to support the charge of robbery against your client under the theory of accomplice liability. You are not contesting the identification of your client or the grounds for his arrest. You are only arguing that there is insufficient evidence to hold your client liable as an "aider and abettor" under California law. To prepare for this motion, review the relevant statutory provisions and jury instructions provided in the online component. You do not need to do any independent legal research for this task.

You should review the relevant statutes and jury instructions provided in the online component. You should also use the following item, to be found in the online component:

- Fill-In Motion to Dismiss ("995 Motion") for you to complete with your written argument. You are to complete both the Facts Section and the Legal Argument.

ESTIMATED TIME FOR COMPLETION: 90 minutes.

LEVEL OF DIFFICULTY (1 TO 5):

Task Two: Oral Argument; Motion to Dismiss

You are the prosecutor on the case. The defense attorney for Karen Abbott has filed a Motion to Dismiss on the grounds that there is insufficient evidence to support of the charge of robbery against Ms. Abbott (a 995 motion). The judge has asked for oral argument on the motion. Prepare an outline and arguments points for your oral argument in opposition to the defendant's motion to dismiss. As in Task One, you are not required to do any additional legal research. Ms. Abbott is currently charged with robbery as an accomplice. It is likely, however, that defense counsel will make an argument that Karen should rightfully be charged as an accessory after the fact. Under California law, an accessory after the fact is simply called an accessory. The substantive offense for being an accessory after the fact is found in California Penal Code Section 32. The applicable jury instruction explaining the elements of the crime of being an accessory after the fact is CALCRIM 440. A link is provided in the online component. It is also available on Lexis Advance. Use these materials provided to support your argument that there is sufficient evidence to charge Karen as an *accomplice* to robbery.

ESTIMATED TIME FOR COMPLETION: 45 minutes.

LEVEL OF DIFFICULTY (1 TO 5):

Task Three: Cross-Examination

You are the defense counsel representing Allen Porter. The judge has now denied your motion to dismiss and the case will be proceeding to trial. Prepare the questions for your cross-examination of Victor Cerna. You should review Victor's testimony from the preliminary hearing given above.

ESTIMATED TIME FOR COMPLETION: 30 minutes.

LEVEL OF DIFFICULTY (1 TO 5):

Task Four: Small Group Discussion; Ethics; Client Counseling

You again represent Allen Porter. For purposes of this task only, consider the following additional facts: After your client's arrest, in addition to all of the statements given above, he also admitted to the police that he knows that Tim has committed robberies in the past. He also admitted to being in the gang with Tim. You are about to discuss the alleged robbery with your client in order to decide whether or not you will recommend that Allen take the witness stand and testify on his own behalf.

First read the relevant ethical rules listed in the online component and consider the ethical obligation an attorney has to not support or promote false evidence. Then, meet with other students in groups of three or four. Discuss in your small group how you would approach the conversation with your client. How would discuss the topic of what he knew and intended that day when he exited the car. Is that discussion different from a discussion regarding what his testimony would be? Should you simply ask your client, "What happened?" Is it wrong to explain the "mere presence" doctrine and then ask him what happened? Discuss the ethical implications of the questions you ask as defense counsel and the various implications of the answers you receive. Consider both the ethical commitment not to suborn perjury as well as the ethical commitment to be a zealous advocate for your client. How do these two ethical obligations interact in the context of this task? As an alternative or additional assignment, prepare, on your own, the interview questions and talking points for the conversation with your client.

You should consult the following items, which are listed in the online component:

- California Rules of Professional Conduct: Rule 5-200 Trial Conduct
- American Bar Association (ABA) Model Rules of Professional Conduct: Preamble [2]
- ABA Model Rules of Professional Conduct: Rule 3.3 Candor Toward the Tribunal
- ABA Model Rules of Professional Conduct: Rule 4.1 Truthfulness in Statements to Others

ESTIMATED TIME FOR COMPLETION: 45 minutes.

LEVEL OF DIFFICULTY (1 TO 5):

PRACTICE SKILLS USED:

> Skill 1: Motion Writing
>
> Skill 2: Legal Argument; Integrating the Law and the Facts
>
> Skill 3: Oral Argument; Motion Practice
>
> Skill 4: Cross Examination
>
> Skill 5: Ethical Analysis; Client Perjury

SKILLS GUIDES

In the online component, you will find Suggested Video Clips (SVC) that are provided as optional background to aid your familiarity with preliminary hearings generally.

SKILLS GUIDE#1: Motion Writing

Take a moment and read Chapter 8, Skills Guide #1. In addition, review the materials in the online component (listed under Supplemental Materials, Skills Guide 1) specifically addressing a Motion to Dismiss under California Penal Code section 995.

SKILLS GUIDE #2: Legal Argument; Integrating the Law and the Facts

Please refer to Chapter 8, Skills Guide #2.

SKILLS GUIDES#3: Oral Argument; Motion Practice

Please refer to Chapter 8, Skills Guide #3.

SKILLS GUIDE#4: Cross Examination Preparation

Please refer to Chapter 6, Skills Guide #2.

SKILLS GUIDE #5: Ethical Analysis; Client Perjury

As first mentioned in Chapter 9, Skills Guide #5, a lawyer may not engage in any conduct that violates the relevant code of ethics. For defense counsel, one of the most serious potential ethical dilemmas is what to do if you believe your client might be lying, and even more specifically, what to do if your client wants to testify to statements you believe are not true. The lawyer's duty to zealously advocate for his or her client is a bedrock principle of the client-attorney relationship. Furthermore, the duty of confidentiality and the attorney-client privilege prioritize the need for the client to be assured he can say anything in confidence to his lawyer when discussing his case. In addition, the right to testify is a constitutional right of the defendant and one of the few decisions of trial strategy over which the defendant, rather than the lawyer, has the final say.

When a concern regarding client truthfulness arises, these key tenets of client representation and advocacy come into possible conflict with the ethical responsibilities of a lawyer to be truthful to the court. As stated by the American Bar Association's Model Rules of Professional Conduct, a lawyer shall not "knowingly . . . offer evidence that the lawyer knows to be false." This statement, however clear in its words, is less straightforward in its application. Whether a lawyer "knowingly" offers false evidence, or even whether a lawyer "knows" that evidence to be false, is open to much debate and interpretation.

For further reading on the issue of potential client perjury, use an online database to read the following article: Brian Slipakoff & Roshini Thayaparan, *The Criminal Defense Attorney Facing Prospective Client Perjury*, 15 GEO. J. LEGAL ETHICS 935 (2002).

ADDITIONAL MATERIALS FOR THE EXERCISE — AVAILABLE IN ON-LINE COMPONENT

Cal. Penal Code § 211: Robbery

Cal. Penal Code § 995: Grounds; motion to set aside; delay in final ruling

Judicial Council of California Criminal Jury Instruction 1600 (CALCRIM 1600) Robbery (Penal Code § 211) (Relevant Excerpts)

Judicial Council of California Criminal Jury Instruction 1603 (CALCRIM 1603) Robbery: Intent of Aider and Abettor (Relevant Excerpts)

Judicial Council of California Criminal Jury Instruction 401 (CALCRIM 401) Aiding and Abetting: Intended Crimes (Relevant Excerpts)

Chapter 13

SELF-DEFENSE

OVERVIEW

Self-defense is the idea that using force to protect oneself against another's use of force should not be a crime — even though all the elements of that crime are otherwise proven. Self-defense is generally considered an "affirmative defense," not a failure of proof defense. With a "failure of proof defense," the defendant offers evidence from which a jury might have a reasonable doubt about whether the prosecution has proven all the elements of a crime beyond a reasonable doubt. For example, a defendant in a rape case — where the statute requires him to "know" that the woman did not consent — might take the stand and say that, even if the woman did not consent, he honestly believed that she did. Thus he did not "know" of her non-consent. An affirmative defense is different. When a defendant raises an affirmative defense, he is saying, "I am not guilty even if you prove every element of the crime beyond a reasonable doubt because I have an excuse or justification." Self-defense is a "justification," an argument that it was more socially beneficial that I commit the violent acts than that I not commit them. Self-defense is also a "complete defense" resulting in a not guilty verdict rather than a "partial defense," which merely reduces the degree of the crime.

Jurisdictions differ over what burden the defendant faces in a self-defense claim. Some impose on the defendant only the burden of production — the burden of offering *some* evidence of the existence of each of the elements of self-defense. Once this burden is met, the burden shifts to the government to prove that the defendant did not act in self-defense. In contrast, other jurisdictions also place the burden of persuasion on the defendant, that is, the burden of convincing the fact-finder, usually by a preponderance of the evidence, that all the elements of self-defense exist.

Jurisdictions differ widely in how they define self-defense. Generally, there are at least seven elements: (1) the alleged victim threatened the defendant with the *imminent* use of (2) unlawful (3) force (4) that could cause physical injury and (5) which a reasonable person would believe could not be avoided without responding with physical force, and the defendant (6) defends by using only a reasonable amount of force while (7) not being responsible for the situation prompting the need to use it. Some jurisdictions use the term "immediate" rather than "imminent," but the general idea is that the defendant faces the threat or actuality of force now or *very* soon, not at some unspecified or distant time. That the force facing the defendant must have been "unlawful" means, for example, that it not be from an officer entitled to use it to make an arrest.

"Force" is a straightforward, essentially common-sense concept, but the type of force — which is linked to the type of physical injury that could be caused — is not. The key distinction here is between "deadly force" and "non-deadly force." How these terms are defined also varies widely, but the core idea is that deadly force involves a threat of death or serious bodily injury while non-deadly force involves at most a threat of bodily injury. What constitutes mere "bodily" versus "serious bodily" injury is also variously defined, but a common distinction is that bodily injury involves mere physical pain, illness, or impairment of physical condition, while serious bodily injury creates a substantial risk of death or serious, permanent disfigurement or protracted loss or impairment of the function of any bodily member or organ. These distinctions are important because a defendant facing non-deadly force cannot respond with deadly force. This rule is one manifestation of the broader principle that a defendant's use of force to protect himself must be "proportional" to the danger he faced (this is also another way of phrasing element number six above). Accordingly, a defendant cannot respond with a knife if he was threatened with merely a fist (at least not unless the person attached to the fist is a professional boxer and is facing a non-professional fighter as the defendant).

Element number five conveys what is often called the "necessity" requirement. For example, that if someone curses you and wishes eternal damnation for you and all your family members, there are (depending upon what tone of voice and body language the speaker used) likely far more sensible alternatives available to stave off the insults escalating into fisticuffs than you landing the first blow.

The seventh element is often phrased as the requirement that the defendant not be the "initial aggressor." This term's meaning is also subject to debate, but the initial aggressor is usually defined as the person who starts the physical confrontation (as opposed to the one merely speaking insulting words). Thus, a defendant who first brandishes a weapon, combines verbal threats with some physical movement toward assaulting his alleged victim, or actually uses force loses the ability to claim self-defense. However, an initial aggressor who truly quits the fight (for example, announcing his withdrawal and then starting to leave the location of the fight) but faces a "victim" who continues the struggle is no longer the one who started it. Now the former victim becomes the initial aggressor for all subsequent events.

Although not clear from the traditional statement of the seven elements of self-defense, almost all jurisdictions also include one of these two *mens rea* requirements: (1) a purely subjective approach, requiring only that the defendant honestly believed that he was in imminent danger of force (or deadly force) being used upon him, or (2) a more objective approach requiring both the defendant's honestly believing in these things and that the belief was reasonable. Of course, any reasonable person standard refers to the reasonable person "under the circumstances," with what counts as part of the circumstances being a policy question, one sometimes resolved by case law. For example, should we judge a reasonable belief in the case of a battered woman from the perspective of a reasonable "person," "woman," or "battered woman?"

States following the Model Penal Code adopt a third approach: a purely subjective test for crimes requiring proof of purpose or knowledge but a more combined objective approach for crimes involving recklessness or negligence. For the latter two categories, therefore, in addition to the defendant's beliefs being honest, they must respectively not have been recklessly or negligently held. The effect of such provisions is to render an offender holding a negligent belief guilty of negligent homicide but not of knowing or purposeful murder.

Some states also impose a "duty to retreat," though largely in deadly force cases. The idea is that it is better that you run away, if you can do so safely, than stay and fight until someone dies or is seriously injured. This duty is most often imposed in Northeastern states and is generally not imposed in Southern or Western states. Moreover, even where the duty exists, there are often exceptions, notably not being required to retreat from one's own home or place of business.

Finally, it is important to remember that in cases involving a self-defense claim, credibility questions abound, with both sides telling very different stories about what happened or about what they believed happened at the time. Evidentiary issues arise in resolving these disputes. The most important two evidence doctrines in this context are those concerning character evidence and those concerning hearsay. Most state evidence codes bar a party's character (here, character for violence) to prove that another party *acted* consistently with that character in a specific case ("act propensity" evidence). Thus, the prosecutor could not offer evidence that the defendant is a violent man, making it more likely that he was the initial aggressor in this case. But the rules do not bar using character evidence to prove *mental state*. Furthermore, the rules create an exception allowing the defendant to choose to offer act propensity evidence, for example, to show that he is a peaceful person or that his alleged victim was a violent one. But if he does so, the prosecution can now respond with act propensity evidence in rebuttal — evidence it could otherwise not have offered — to show that the defendant in fact has a violent character or the alleged victim in fact has a peaceful character.

The hearsay rule excludes hearsay — an out-of-court statement offered to prove the truth of the matter asserted — unless there is an exception or exemption. Therefore, if a third party told the defendant, "Mr. Victim is a violent man who hates you and is coming here now to kill you with a gun," that would be hearsay if offered to prove the statement's truth (which boils down to using the statement to prove that Mr. Victim was the first aggressor). But if the defendant argues only that he *believed* that the statement was true, regardless of whether it was in fact true, then the statement would not be hearsay. The statement would be relevant to prove the defendant's actual and reasonable beliefs about the first aggressor (and therefore it would not be offered to prove who the initial aggressor actually was).

A word needs to be said about attempt as well. Attempt is covered in detail in Chapter 10. But attempt will prove relevant here in the skills tasks to come, so a brief word on the subject is wise. Attempt is simply the idea that someone who wants to commit a crime but fails to do so is still dangerous and morally culpable. Consequently, though he cannot be convicted of the completed crime, we should convict him for attempting it. Often, however, the attempted crime is punished less severely than if it had been completed. The subject of attempt can be quite complex. What you need to know for now is that even if a defendant completed all acts necessary to the completed crime, but failed to achieve a result the crime required, he is guilty of an attempt if he wanted to (that is, had the purpose to, or, sometimes loosely stated, had the "intent" to, meaning the desire to) achieve the result. Homicide is a result crime, the result being death. Thus, if a defendant caused physical harm to another who did not die, the defendant will be guilty of attempted homicide, but only if the defendant wanted his alleged victim to die. If the defendant was, for example, merely negligent in using force, he could not be convicted of attempted homicide.

EXERCISE

Overview

Robert Johnson and Joseph Ward are co-workers in a machine tool factory in Tucson, Arizona. They work at stations across a room from one another. They have each been working at the factory for 15 years, having been hired at the same time. Robert is a slight, thin African-American man, short in stature. Joseph is a tall, heavy-set, Caucasian, ex-Marine Sergeant. The two have entirely different political views. Robert is an avowed socialist and peace activist, while Joseph (known to his friends and co-workers as "Joe") is a proud conservative "hawk." The two have never liked each other and often get in verbally heated political arguments.

Two months ago, Robert hit Joe in the head with a wrench lying on Robert's workbench. Joe was quickly rushed to a nearby hospital in an ambulance. The hospital records showed that Joe suffered a concussion. Since the event, Joe says that he will unexpectedly get dizzy for hours at a time, occasionally has trouble concentrating, and has some memory lapses. Joe was released from the hospital after an overnight stay, and was scheduled for follow-up treatment. Joe returned to work after one week but says that he has missed a fair amount of work in the past few weeks because of the dizzy spells.

Immediately following the incident, the police arrived at the workplace at the same time as the ambulance. Robert refused to talk to the police. Joe gave a statement to the police when he recovered consciousness at the hospital. The police arrested Robert, who was eventually charged by the Tucson District Attorney's Office with attempted first-degree murder.

The alleged attack occurred during a one-hour lunch break on a Friday. Most of Robert and Joe's colleagues went to a local restaurant and brewery for lunch, as was their custom on Fridays. Robert, Joe, and one other co-worker, George Flynn, however, all decided to eat lunch at their workbenches that day. George is thus the only eyewitness to the attack. George refused to talk about the incident to the police, simply telling them, "Both these guys are my co-workers. I'm not getting involved."

The defendant, Robert, has made clear that his argument will be that he acted in self-defense. Robert is a long-time public critic of the American military, and believes it is a breeding ground for racism.

Given the degree to which the case turns on credibility and the existence of only a single eyewitness, the judge has taken the unusual step of granting defense counsel's request to depose George Flynn. The judge is also hopeful that George's testimony may encourage plea negotiations. The pertinent Arizona law is provided in the online component.

REQUIRED TASKS

Task One: Deposition Planning

You are the defense counsel representing Robert Johnson. Prepare for the deposition of George Flynn. If you are completely unfamiliar with depositions, take a look at the video in the online component, which provides background information on preparing for a deposition.

Federal Rule of Evidence 401 states that "[e]vidence is relevant if: (a) it has any tendency to make a fact more or less probable than it would be without the evidence; and (b) the fact is of consequence in determining the action.

Answer the following questions:

1. What are some general topics of "relevant evidence" in this case?
2. What are the legal matters to be determined in this case?
3. What sources of law might you need to consider before taking this deposition?
4. Given the nature of this deposition, should you ask the deponent questions about the final trial outcome — guilty or not guilty? Should you ask the deponent whether the government has enough evidence to prove its case or whether the defense has a strong enough affirmative defense to exonerate the accused?

ESTIMATED TIME FOR COMPLETION: 30 minutes.

LEVEL OF DIFFICULTY (1 TO 5):

Task Two: Deposition Planning; Direct Examination

You are again Robert's defense counsel. Draft a list of deposition questions for George Flynn. Also draft any additional or follow-up questions that the prosecution might want to ask. Before beginning this task, read Skills Guide 1 and 2, as well the Arizona Rules of Evidence and Criminal Code section provided in the online component. Examples of live depositions are provided in the supplemental materials in the online component.

OPTIONAL DEPOSITION SIMULATION: Your instructor has assigned you a role (as either the prosecutor, the witness, or defense counsel). If your instructor has assigned you the role of Robert's defense counsel, conduct the deposition of the witness, George Flynn. If your instructor has assigned you the role of prosecutor, be ready with proper objections but also ask any follow-up or additional questions after the defense has completed its examination. Take 30 minutes and conduct the deposition of George Flynn. Be sure to take notes on any objections by opposing counsel and the answers provided by the witness.

Be aware: despite appearances or silence, the attorney representing the deponent (in this exercise, the prosecutor) is quite important in a deposition. In fact, an effective lawyer prepares their client or witness prior to the deposition. Why would a deponent need to be prepared? Take a moment and review the video clips located in the online component for this Task.

ESTIMATED TIME FOR COMPLETION: 45 minutes; 90 minutes with deposition simulation.

LEVEL OF DIFFICULTY (1 TO 5):

Task Three: Negotiation

Prior to this task, your professor will assign you the role of either the prosecutor or Robert's defense counsel. In this task you are preparing for a negotiation with opposing counsel, which you will then simulate in class. Read Skills Guides 3, 4, and 5 before beginning this task. In addition, see the supplemental material on negotiation in the online component for this task.

A. Prepare for the negotiation (15 minutes):

a. If you are assigned the role of prosecutor, you will attempt to negotiate an agreement with the defense to talk to Robert in his counsel's presence. Prepare an outline of your talking points. Include an explanation that you want to hear Robert's side of the story and, if you believe Robert acted in self-defense, you, on behalf of the government, will drop the charges against Robert, or, if you believe Robert's act was imperfect self-defense (Robert believed he was in imminent danger but this belief was unreasonable), you may be willing to negotiate a favorable guilty plea. Remember that you will have to convince opposing counsel *why* he or she should agree to the meeting on your terms.

b. If you are assigned the role of defense attorney, be prepared to negotiate the terms of any meeting between the government and your client. Include an explanation of what terms you would agree to if your client spoke with the prosecutor. Remember that you will have to convince opposing counsel *why* he or she should agree to your terms regarding the meeting.

B. Conduct the negotiation (15 minutes): Now partner with a lawyer from the opposing side. Take 10 minutes to negotiate with opposing counsel over the terms of an agreement. If an agreement is reached, document the terms of that agreement in writing.

C. Debrief the negotiation (15 minutes): If this portion is not done via class discussion, your instructor may ask you to turn in a short written summary of the tactics used, results achieved (or not achieved and why), and the legal issues involved in the negotiation.

ESTIMATED TIME FOR COMPLETION: 45 minutes.

LEVEL OF DIFFICULTY (1 TO 5):

Task Four: Closing Argument

You are defense counsel for Robert Johnson. Draft the portion of your closing argument addressing solely the self-defense claim. For purposes of this argument you should use the self-defense law of Arizona as provided in the online component. No additional legal research is necessary.

ESTIMATED TIME FOR COMPLETION: 60 minutes.

LEVEL OF DIFFICULTY (1 TO 5):

PRACTICE SKILLS USED:

Skill 1: Deposition Planning

Skill 2: Direct Examination

Skill 3: Negotiation; Immunity Agreements

Skill 4: Negotiation; Plea Agreements

Skill 5: Negotiation; Ethics

Skill 6: Closing Argument

SKILLS GUIDES

SKILLS GUIDE #1: Deposition Planning

A deposition is an opportunity to question a witness under oath outside of a courtroom. The only persons present are the deponent (the person being deposed), the lawyers, and the court reporter. There are generally two types of depositions: discovery depositions and trial depositions. A discovery deposition is done to: (1) find out what the witness will say at trial; (2) pin down his story so that he can be impeached with his inconsistent words from the deposition should he change his tale at trial; (3) develop other ways to impeach (i.e. argue that the witness is lying, confused, or mistaken) the portions of the witness's story that you do not like; and (4) discover leads to additional evidence. A trial deposition occurs where you fear that the witness will not attend the trial and want to preserve his testimony, thus treating the witness exactly as you would were he a witness at trial. In this exercise, the deposition is done for discovery purposes.

The person who wants to take a deposition sends out a deposition notice notifying the deponent and the opposing attorney of when and where the deposition will be taken. As a matter of courtesy, the deposition's time and place will have been worked out with the attorneys and witness in advance of sending the actual notice. If the witness is not a party, as is true here, the witness will also be sent a subpoena — a court order to appear for the deposition. The lawyer noticing the deposition will have also arranged for a court reporter to attend, and the reporter is paid for his or her services. The point of the court reporter is to have a record of what was said during the deposition. In this exercise, however, no court reporter will be present.

In a criminal case, the defense attorney represents his client, the defendant, who is a party to the action. The prosecutor represents the government, who is the other party to the action. The alleged victim and any eyewitnesses are, therefore, not parties to the action and must be subpoenaed, as is true of Mr. Flynn.

In a few states, such as Florida, depositions are routine in serious criminal cases. In most states, however, depositions rarely occur in criminal cases. If they do occur, there is usually a special need for the deposition and it would require a court order. Nevertheless, depositions do occur periodically, and the skills used in a deposition are valuable in learning how to develop discovery, to question witnesses, to listen carefully, to object, and to think strategically. One example of a deposition from a special criminal case is the deposition of the late rap star, Tupac Shakur, which occurred while he was incarcerated. Take a moment to view part of this deposition in the video provided in the online component. If you have not already done so, you may also view samples of other depositions provided in the online component.

The attorney taking the deposition questions the witness first. Generally, that attorney will proceed as if on direct examination, that is, because he is seeking information, he will usually try to ask open-ended questions rather than leading ones (i.e., questions that suggest an answer). This is because in a discovery deposition, the lawyer does not know what the answers to his questions will be. The opposing attorney might object to questions. There is, however, no judge present to rule on those objections, so they are simply made, and everyone moves on. If the lawyer asking the question thinks that the objection is a valid one, he may rephrase the question. Otherwise, after the objection is made, the questioning lawyer waits for the witness's answer or repeats the question. In general, you need not raise most evidentiary objections that you would at trial. Rather, you need only object to the form of the question. For our purposes here, this means that you should only object if you think that a question will confuse the witness, either because the question is unclear, a compound question (it asks more than one thing), or it assumes facts to which the witness has never testified.

When the noticing attorney has completed her questions, the opposing attorney (here, the prosecution) proceeds with any remaining questions. Because the deponent here is the only eyewitness, he will very likely be called at trial by the prosecution. Therefore, the prosecution will likely ask mostly clarifying questions or ones needed to fill holes in the prosecution's argument. Ordinarily, the prosecutor would have a friendly witness with whom he could talk in private to learn more about the witness's story. Consequently, the prosecutor would not want to ask questions missed by the defense as that would tip the prosecutor's hand. But here, the witness has refused to talk to either side outside the context of the deposition, so the prosecutor must decide whether to flesh out the story more to learn what he does not know, even if that risks getting an answer the prosecutor does not like.

Whether objecting or following up in a deposition, understand your role. Although the attorney taking the deposition may have an impeccably detailed list of questions for the deposed party to answer, the fact is that depositions rarely stick to the script. The deposed party's personality, nervousness, garrulousness, fear, or anger may significantly affect the way in which the deposing attorney conducts the deposition. Follow-up questions will either serve to flesh out an incomplete answer, clarify an unclear one, or give the deposing attorney food for thought, given what the charges are and what is at stake. The deposition is not the time to make an opening statement or closing argument; it also is not the time to argue objections beyond what is necessary to preserve them for the record so that the appropriate judicial decision can be made, in the event the case goes to trial or up on appeal.

In conducting George Flynn's deposition as defense counsel, you will likely be surprised by his answers. There is nothing wrong with that. In fact, this is exactly why you are conducting it! However, when George — or any deposition witness — gives an unexpected, unclear, or surprising response, do not be fearful regarding the integrity and ordering of your script. Make a note where you left off, explore the answer, and then resume your line of questioning once the unexpected, unclear, or surprising response had been thoroughly explored.

Even if the potential deponent seems unimportant because they are not, for instance, an eyewitness or a victim, they may have evidence that helps or hurts your client's (and your opponent's) case. Any deposition preparation begins by a review of all the documents and other information (e.g., recordings, photographs, diagrams, statements, doctor's reports) that triggered the criminal charges. Do not be afraid to ask yourself the "silly" question when examining the evidence in preparation. For example, in the exercise here, "Why were charges not filed against Joseph; wasn't he was also involved?" This question may seem "silly;" but it is not. In fact, asking such a question may help you successfully distinguish between a criminal case's emotional versus legal appeal.

The pertinent Arizona rules of evidence are provided in the online component. The rules are provided to highlight some sorts of questions you might want to ask. You are not expected to understand these rules in detail. Rule 404 is simply Arizona's "act propensity" rule, explained earlier, a rule that matters if a character witness will be offered. Character witnesses can potentially testify about someone's relevant reputation (what others say about him), opinion (what someone who knows him well thinks about him), and specific acts (what things the person did on specific occasions that show the kind of person he is). Remember that act propensity is inadmissible here if first offered by the prosecution but admissible if offered as rebuttal to act propensity evidence already offered by the defense. Rule 405 says that if act propensity is admissible, it can be proven only by testimony about reputation or opinion, not testimony about prior acts. Nevertheless, if you are offering character evidence not to prove what was done but rather to prove the defendant's mental state, it is not barred at all. Therefore, you can ask about reputation, opinion, or prior acts. You need not understand any of this in detail or be able to argue based on the rules for this exercise. The point is to understand that you may want to question the deponent about his own character or that of the accused or the alleged victim, or about each of the latter two's knowledge of the other's character.

You are also given Rule 609. This rule tells you that you can impeach a witness if he has been convicted of certain prior crimes, at least under certain conditions. Felonies can be used to impeach a witness if the trial judge thinks that doing so helps the jury more than prejudicing or misleading it. But crimes involving dishonesty (such as perjury) can be used to impeach, whether unfairly prejudicial or not.

SKILLS GUIDE #2: Direct Examination

Please refer to Chapter 15, Skills Guide #3.

SKILLS GUIDE #3: Negotiation; Immunity Agreements

The skill of negotiation is discussed in the supplemental materials in the online component for Task Three. You should first review that material. Here there are a few additional points of law you need to know relevant to the topic of Immunity Agreements. The Fifth Amendment to the United States Constitution declares that a person may not be compelled to be a witness against himself. This protection is colloquially known as the privilege against self-incrimination. Part of what this privilege means is that a prosecutor may not compel a defendant to talk to the prosecutor. This also means that a prosecutor may not threaten to harm a defendant, for example, by seeking a harsher sentence if the defendant will not talk to the prosecutor. On the other hand, a prosecutor can refuse to negotiate for any reason she likes (so long as it is not for an invidious reason, such as one based on race or gender bias). A refusal to negotiate, for whatever reason is given, is not alone a threat.

On the other hand, if a defendant talks to a prosecutor voluntarily, the defendant waives his Fifth Amendment privilege. Consequently, his statements may be used against him at trial. Most jurisdictions, however, have a rule of evidence that excludes from evidence at trial any discussions between the defendant or his counsel and the prosecutor aimed at reaching a plea agreement. There are some narrow exceptions to this rule that we need not address here. It is important to note that many jurisdictions allow a prosecutor to refuse to negotiate unless the defendant waives that rule. You should assume that that is the law for this exercise.

Sometimes, the prosecutor will want to speak directly to the defendant, in his counsel's presence. This could be because the prosecutor wants to assess the appropriateness of a particular plea bargain or result (e.g., a dismissal), or because the prosecutor wants to get a defendant's cooperation in prosecuting someone else. The prosecutor may want to assess the defendant's credibility and the details of his story face-to-face. A prosecutor also might want to talk to a defendant if the prosecutor thinks that the defendant might be legally innocent, for example, unquestionably acting in self-defense.

There are grave risks for a defendant in speaking with the prosecution. Unless agreed to otherwise, the prosecutor might be able to use the defendant's words against him at trial, and the prosecution will have learned much about the defendant and his case, thus being better able to undermine that case at trial. Defense counsel will ideally seek an "immunity agreement" prior to any conversation with the prosecution.

There are three kinds of immunity: transactional (you cannot be prosecuted for the underlying crime), use immunity (the defendant's statements cannot be used against him) and derivative use immunity (the fruits of his statement cannot be used against him). A prosecutor like the one here will rarely grant transactional immunity, as the defendant is already charged with a serious crime. A defense attorney who cannot get use immunity is taking a very big risk. Ideally, the defense would want to convince the prosecutor to grant use and derivative use immunity. Whether to talk to the prosecutor at all turns on an assessment of whether a plea negotiation is likely to lead to a better result than going to trial.

The goal of the negotiation in Task Three is to set the terms of the immunity agreement. In negotiating the terms, defense counsel might want to talk hypothetically, for instance, to say, "Well, if my client said something like X — and I'm by no means saying that he will — would you be willing to drop the charges? Reduce them? To what? Recommend a lenient sentence? To what?" In this way, defense counsel can feel out the likelihood of reaching a plea agreement and thereby assess whether the risk of talking to the prosecutor is worthwhile at all and, if so, with what type of immunity agreement in place.

If the prosecution's case is strong, they have little incentive to give anything up. If the defense case is strong, they have little incentive to give anything up. But if the case is mixed and credibility matters, or if the prosecution can be convinced that the defendant really can help to catch a much bigger fish, each side has some incentives to make an agreement happen. Sometimes these agreements are in formal writings; equally often they are informal, simply in the form of a letter.

Even if an agreement is reached, once the client is before the prosecutor, defense counsel must ensure that the defendant answers no questions beyond the scope of the agreement. Defense counsel might also want to protect any attorney-client communications as privileged. Additionally, defense counsel might want to clarify with follow-up questions any confusing or arguably misleading answers by the defendant. However, take caution as a too-active role by defense counsel might lead the prosecutor to distrust the credibility of the defendant's statement.

SKILLS GUIDE #4: Negotiation; Plea Agreements

Black's Law Dictionary defines plea-bargaining as "the process whereby the accused and the prosecutor in a criminal case work out a mutually satisfactory disposition of the case subject to court approval. It usually involves the defendant's pleading guilty to a lesser offense or to only one or some of the counts of a multi-count indictment in return for a lighter sentence than that possible for the graver charge."

Plea bargaining involves parties to a criminal lawsuit agreeing upon a way in which to conclude the case without expending the time and costs of trial. In their agreement, the parties negotiate a disposition with which both sides are comfortable (versus happy, although this could also be the case). An offer for a particular plea bargain is usually first made by the prosecutor. The defense must try to assess how strongly the prosecutor believes in her case. (Are there obvious holes in the evidence? Is there a problem with the eyewitness? Is the victim suspicious in his own right?) The defense must also determine how ready and able the prosecutor is to take the case to trial. In contrast, the prosecutor may try to gauge how strongly the defendant believes in his defense (be it one that is an affirmative defense like self-defense, or a failure of proof defense) and whether that defense is likely to be successful(e.g., would the defendant testify before the jury and will he be a credible witness?). Additionally, the defense attorney must determine how willing his client is to go to trial and risk a potentially more adverse resolution than what the government is willing to bargain for prior to trial.

Unlike on television, most plea-bargaining occurs only between the lawyers. Defense counsel must, however, obtain his client's informed consent to any agreement, and lower-level prosecutors, as a matter of common sense, may agree only to matters consistent with office policy or, if not so consistent, to matters approved by superiors. When parties plea bargain, the government offers a plea agreement to the defendant (often, via his attorney) that the defendant is free to accept or reject. Often the plea agreement is made orally, but in many federal cases or where the agreement is complex, the agreement may be written. Either way, the agreement must be stated on the record in open court before a judge, and the defendant must accept or reject the statement of that agreement as complete and accurate.

Plea bargaining may involve three types of negotiation:

- **Charge bargaining**: This involves a negotiation of the specific crimes that the defendant is charged with, and is willing to plead guilty to. Usually in return for a plea of "guilty" to a less serious charge, a prosecutor will dismiss the higher or other charge(s) or counts. For example, in return for dismissing charges for attempted first-degree murder, a prosecutor may accept a "guilty" plea for attempted manslaughter.

- **Sentence bargaining:** This signifies a bargain related to the punishment the defendant will receive as a result of the plea bargain. It necessarily will almost always be a lesser sentence that he would receive if convicted at trial.

- **Fact bargaining:** This involves an admission by the defendant to the truth of specific facts in return for an agreement by the prosecution not to introduce certain other facts into evidence. This type of bargaining may also arise when thinking about consequences of criminal convictions in other areas of the law, for instance in civil proceedings and immigration proceedings.

As you may guess, there is usually a gap between how "high" the defense is willing to go and how "low" the government is willing to go. Traversing or breaching the gap is done through the process of negotiation, often comprised of representations made by each side regarding the strength of, and confidence in, the evidence supporting their theory of the case.

SKILLS GUIDE #5: Negotiation; Ethics

There are several ethical rules that guide a lawyer's negotiation tactics and representations made during the negotiation process. ABA Model Rules of Professional Conduct, Model Rule 4.1 provides that an attorney "shall not knowingly make a false statement of material fact or law to a third person." A Comment to Rule 4.1 further states:

> [w]hether a particular statement should be regarded as one of fact can depend on the circumstances. Under generally accepted conventions in negotiation, certain types of statements ordinarily are not taken as statements of material fact. Estimates of price or value placed on the subject of a transaction and a party's intentions as to an acceptable settlement of a claim are ordinarily in this category. . . .

The comment refers to what is colloquially referred to as "puffery," i.e., when individuals in a negotiation overstate or understate — for strategic purposes — the value of their evidence, the strength of their witnesses, what their client would agree to, and the likelihood of an agreement. Puffery is allowed during negotiation. Misrepresentations — that is, a knowing false statement — of a material fact are now. Although there is certainly not a clear line between mere puffery and a misrepresentation of material fact, lawyers need to be careful when negotiating on behalf of their client or constituency.

All lawyers have an ethical obligation to avoid deceptive or fraudulent conduct. This standard is specified in Model Rule 8.4. Model Rule 3.4 lays out a lawyer's ethical obligations regarding the opposing counsel and party. A lawyer may not block opposing counsel's access to evidence or encourage a witness to testify falsely.

There are ethical obligations unique to criminal prosecutors. Under Model Rule 3.8, prosecutors have an ethical obligation to pursue criminal prosecution against a defendant only where the criminal charge is supported by probable cause. A prosecutor, therefore, cannot bring charges or seek charges greater in number or degree than she can reasonably support with evidence at trial, as prosecutors must assure that guilt is decided upon the basis of sufficient evidence. Furthermore, criminal prosecutors must be careful not to violate a defendant's constitutional rights in pursuit of their professional goals. In short, the prosecutor's duty to seek justice, and not merely to convict, means that the prosecutor has a dual goal: that the guilty not escape or the innocent be convicted.

The defense attorney's role in the criminal justice system — to be a zealous advocate for her client — sometimes carries different ethical obligations than that of the prosecutor. In practical terms, the defense attorney's goal is often to achieve the best possible result for his client. In the context of plea bargaining, defense counsel is obliged to seek a bargain advantageous to the defendant and to support the defendant's choice to accept or reject a bargain offered by the prosecutor. In contrast to the prosecutor, defense counsel is not charged with seeking "justice" or ascertaining "truth." Still, as a member of the bar, defense counsel does have an obligation to represent her client within the bounds of the law and the ethics rules. Defense counsel is obliged to scrupulous candor and truth in representations of any matter before a court, even sometimes to the detriment of the duties of client advocacy and client confidentiality. As discussed above, this obligation prohibits defense counsel from knowingly making false statements of material fact to third parties and also requires them to disclose material facts to third parties when necessary to avoid assisting the defendant in committing fraud.

A link to the ABA Model Rules of Professional Conduct can be found in the online component.

SKILLS GUIDE #6: Closing Argument

The purpose of a closing argument is to bring together the evidence and the law and to craft an argument convincing the jury that your side should prevail. The best closing arguments start with a narrative: simply telling the story that you want the jury to believe. This aspect of the closing is thus not unlike an opening argument. Even before telling that story, however, each side will usually mention the beyond a reasonable doubt standard of proof. The prosecution will state that they have unquestionably proven the elements of the crime beyond a reasonable doubt. The defense version will either tell a tale of what is missing — what has not been proven that is needed to make the case beyond a reasonable doubt — or an affirmative argument that supports a defense, such as mistake of fact, entrapment, self-defense, insanity, involuntariness, or necessity.

Most trials involve credibility determinations: different witnesses telling different stories. After the advocate recites the story of what happened, she must thus often argue about why certain witnesses should be believed, and others not. Poor memory, prior convictions of certain felonies or crimes of dishonesty or false statement, the inability to observe events clearly (e.g., because of darkness), inconsistency with basic principles of physics or with other credible evidence like photographs, bias, motive to lie, the illogic of a witness's story, and a host of similar factors may be mentioned as reasons not to believe a witness. Correspondingly, good memory for details, a clear opportunity to observe (e.g., bright light), consistency with other evidence, lack of bias or motive to lie, a logical story, and other factors may support a witness's truthfulness. One way the argument might be phrased is this: "How do we know that the defendant wanted Joanna dead and did not kill her accidentally? We know it because of the truthful testimony of witnesses A and B and the lying or confused testimony of witnesses C and D." The advocate then explains why the jury should believe the first two witnesses and disbelieve the next two noted. This portion of the closing involves argument and thus clearly differs from an opening argument.

During closing argument, you may want to refer to physical evidence, charts, diagrams, or other visual aids as a way to bring both the overall story and legal argument to life. In addition, such aids may help clarify for the jurors the relationship between the evidence and the legal proof needed for conviction or acquittal.

The last part of the argument is generally a relatively brief request for relief. For example, "You must therefore find defendant guilty of the crime charged" or "The prosecution has not proven this beyond a reasonable doubt."

The argument should not be hyperbolic, but it should be dramatic and capture the jury's interest and attention. It requires variations in volume and tone. It must be expressed in language that jurors of different educational backgrounds can readily understand and integrate the facts and the law in a manner that makes common sense in addition to enabling your side to prevail. This brief outline is not the only way to conduct a closing argument. Different sets of facts require different approaches, and the matter is more one of art than science. But this outline does give you one way to do such a closing and should enable you to complete the assigned task.

ADDITIONAL MATERIALS FOR THE EXERCISE — AVAILABLE IN ON-LINE COMPONENT

ARIZ. REV. STAT. § 13-404: Justification; Self-defense

ARIZ. R. EVID. 404: Character Evidence not Admissible to Prove Conduct; Exceptions; Other Crimes [relevant excerpts]

ARIZ. R. EVID. 405: Methods of Proving Character

ARIZ. R. EVID. 608: Evidence of Character and Conduct of Witness

ARIZ. R. EVID. 609: Impeachment by Evidence of Conviction of Crime

Chapter 14

ENTRAPMENT AND OUTRAGEOUS GOVERNMENT CONDUCT

OVERVIEW

I. ENTRAPMENT

Entrapment is a defense in which the defendant argues that a government agent induced him to commit a crime he otherwise would not have. Entrapment is grounded in the notion that the government, and more specifically the police, should not unfairly persuade innocent people to commit crime. The Supreme Court first recognized the defense in *Sorrells v. United States*, 287 U.S. 435 (1932). The defense of entrapment has developed through caselaw and today, nearly all jurisdictions have adopted the defense.

The claim of entrapment arises from undercover operations involving law enforcement or third parties who act as agents of the government. The defense is generally viewed as a means of discouraging government misconduct and overreach during undercover operations. Thus, the defense does not apply to inducements made by a private party. Entrapment is a complete defense. If the jury or judge finds that the defendant was entrapped by the police or their agents, the defendant is entitled to an acquittal.

There are two formulations of the entrapment defense. Most state jurisdictions and the federal courts employ a "subjective" test. Subjective entrapment focuses on the character of the defendant and is comprised of two elements. In order to prevail, the defendant must first demonstrate that he was overcome by excessive government inducements, and second, that he lacked the predisposition to commit the crime. Under this framework, even if the government inducements were severe, the defendant is not entitled to prevail unless he was not predisposed to commit the crime. In contrast, the Model Penal Code and a minority of states use an "objective" test, which does not include an examination of a defendant's predisposition. Rather, the objective test asks whether the government actions were sufficient to induce an average, law-abiding person to commit the crime.

An inducement can be defined as persuasion that overcomes a defendant's reluctance to commit the crime. Inducements include verbal threats, coercion, below market rate prices for contraband, and extraordinary temptations more favorable than similar real-world criminal opportunities. The offering of the mere opportunity to commit a crime is generally considered insufficient to demonstrate entrapment.

Predisposition, as considered by the subjective entrapment test, is typically understood as a trait of character — a dispositional willingness to commit this sort of crime even before being approached by the police. An analysis of the defendant's predisposition differentiates the "unwary innocent" who was induced by the government to commit the crime from the suspect who was ready and willing to commit the crime even without the various inducements. In assessing whether a defendant was predisposed to commit the crime, courts consider several factors, including the defendant's responses to the inducements offered, his conduct both before and after the criminal transaction, his prior criminal history and involvement with similar crimes as the one charged, and his state of mind at the time of the criminal transaction.

Subjective entrapment is considered an affirmative defense and is typically a question of fact argued before the jury. Before the defendant may argue entrapment to the jury, however, the defendant first bears the burden of production and must present the judge with some evidence that he was improperly induced by the government. If the defendant presents sufficient evidence of entrapment, the judge will then instruct the jury on the requirements of the defense. If the judge decides, as a matter of law, that no reasonable juror could find that the defendant was entrapped, the court has the power to deny the defendant's request to present an entrapment defense.

Once before the jury, the parties' evidentiary burdens vary by jurisdiction. The defendant commonly has the burden of production; that is, he must present some evidence of improper government inducements. With respect to the element of predisposition, in some jurisdictions, the defendant retains the evidentiary burden (the burden of persuasion) and must demonstrate by a preponderance of the evidence that he lacked the predisposition to commit the charged offense. The prosecution is then given the opportunity to rebut either element of the defense. In other jurisdictions, after the defendant has met his burden of production with respect to the presence of inducements, the burden shifts to the prosecution to prove beyond a reasonable doubt that the defendant was predisposed to commit the crime.

Objective entrapment is typically a question for the judge. Objective entrapment focuses primarily on the actions of the police and is designed to deter police wrongdoing. Decisions concerning whether deterrence is necessary — as it would be if the police conduct would have entrapped an objectively reasonable and innocent person — are left to the court. In contrast, subjective entrapment focuses on whether a specific individual has had his otherwise innocent nature overcome by the government (and thus is not truly a "criminal"). This is essentially a question of moral culpability and therefore the decision rests with the community's moral voice: the jury.

II. OUTRAGEOUS GOVERNMENT CONDUCT

"Outrageous government conduct" is a second claim that centers on allegations of improper conduct by the police or their agents. In *United States v. Russell*, 411 U.S. 423 (1973), the Supreme Court suggested that there may be times when government conduct is so extreme and outrageous that a conviction of the defendant would be barred by the principles of the due process clause of the United States Constitution. In contrast to the entrapment defense, which is usually presented at trial, the claim of outrageous government conduct is raised by pretrial motion. The judge decides, as a matter of law, whether the conduct of the government violated the defendant's due process rights. If the defense motion is granted, the criminal prosecution is dismissed.

The existence, scope, and precise meaning of the outrageous government conduct claim is a matter of some dispute in the lower courts and has not yet been clarified by the Supreme Court. What is clear is that the standard of "outrageous government conduct" is extremely high. As the Court stated in *Russell*, the government conduct must be "so grossly shocking and so outrageous as to violate the universal sense of justice." As a result, very few courts have ever found the facts before it to justify the dismissal of the criminal complaint.

The outrageous government conduct claim focuses solely on the conduct by law enforcement. It does not include a consideration of the defendant's predisposition. It is, therefore, akin to objective entrapment but rooted in the Constitution instead of state or federal statutory law. In jurisdictions that follow a subjective approach to entrapment, presenting an outrageous government conduct claim may enable the defendant to bring the arguably troubling police conduct to the judge's attention without the consideration of the background of the defendant. A defendant with a significant prior record might prefer this objective constitutional claim rather than the subjective entrapment defense, under which his criminal history would be admissible evidence against him. On the other hand, as mentioned above, the requisite standard of "misconduct" in an outrageous government conduct claim is extremely high and typically this claim is viewed as requiring more egregious government conduct than that required by the entrapment defense.

EXERCISE

Overview

Ward Parker is a 56-year-old African-American male and the head of a large federal agency in the District of Columbia. The FBI suspects Mr. Parker of being a methamphetamine user and is investigating him on charges of drug possession with the intent to distribute. In March of last year, the FBI, with the approval of the local U.S. Attorney's Office, decided to set up a sting investigation targeting Mr. Parker. The Metropolitan Police Department of the District of Columbia generally lacks the resources to conduct undercover operations of government officials. For this operation, the FBI enlisted the help of Dorothy Matthew, an acquaintance of Mr. Parker's and someone whom he had dated a few times more than 20 years ago. Ms. Matthew is currently facing federal drug possession charges in Maryland and so agreed to participate in the sting operation in order to gain the favor of the government in her own criminal case.

At the FBI's direction, Ms. Matthew reestablished contact with Mr. Parker in April of last year. Mr. Parker is recently divorced and was happy to hear from Ms. Matthew. Over several phone conversations last April and May (taped by the FBI), Mr. Parker told Ms. Matthew that he was lonely and depressed. Twice he expressed his interest in seeing her again romantically. At the instructions of the FBI, Ms. Matthew rejected his advances in these two phone conversations.

In June of last year, again at the behest of the FBI, Ms. Matthew called Mr. Parker (the conversation was recorded) and told him she would be in D.C. for work and that she was staying at a local hotel for one night. She invited him to meet her for drinks at the end of the work day. Mr. Parker suggested meeting in the bar in the hotel lobby. Ms. Matthew stated that the bar would be too noisy and it would be better to meet in her room. Mr. Parker agreed. They made a plan for that Tuesday at 7:00 p.m.

On that Tuesday afternoon, the FBI installed audio and visual recording equipment in Ms. Matthew's hotel room. FBI agents were also stationed in the adjoining hotel room. Ms. Matthew was not wearing a wire. Unfortunately, a few minutes before 7:00 p.m., the recording equipment stopped working. The FBI decided to proceed with the operation anyway and instructed Ms. Matthew on how to signal to the agents in the adjoining room when they should enter if an arrest was justified or she needed to stop the operation.

Mr. Parker arrived at the hotel room door at 7:00 p.m. Ms. Matthew and Mr. Parker happily greeted each other in the hotel room. The hotel room was a single room, containing a queen-sized bed and a small table with two chairs. A bottle of red wine and two glasses (approved by the FBI) were set on the table. After having a glass of wine and making small talk, Mr. Parker left the table where he had been sitting and sat down on the edge of the bed. He then propositioned Ms. Matthew and asked to have sexual intercourse. Ms. Matthew responded that she would, but that she wanted to use methamphetamine first.

As stated above, there was a malfunction in the taping and therefore there are neither audio nor video recordings of what occurred in the room. Not surprisingly, the accounts of Mr. Parker and Ms. Matthew differ with regard to what occurred after Ms. Matthew raised the topic of methamphetamine. Mr. Parker stated that he at first refused but Ms. Matthew vehemently and repeatedly insisted on taking the drug. Finally, given his strong desire to have sex, he relented and said that they could use methamphetamine together. In contrast, Ms. Matthews stated that when she first proposed using methamphetamine, Mr. Parker immediately agreed and did not appear reluctant at all.

Once he agreed, Ms. Matthew took the methamphetamine out of her purse. (Approximately 5½ grams of methamphetamine were provided to her by the FBI). Mr. Parker later told the police that he had asked Ms. Matthew to show him how to use methamphetamine as he had never used it before. Ms. Matthew denied that he made such a statement. After Mr. Parker accepted the methamphetamine, Ms. Matthew prepared the methamphetamine for use. She then stood up, excused herself to the bathroom, and knocked on the wall to alert the FBI agents in the adjoining room. Hearing the pre-arranged signal, the agents entered the room and placed Mr. Parker under arrest for the possession of methamphetamine.

Ward Parker is now charged in federal district court in Washington, D.C., with possession of methamphetamine. Several other witnesses have now come forward. Two witnesses are willing to testify that Mr. Parker has the reputation of having a current drug problem and that he has struggled with methamphetamine use in the past. Both of these witnesses have personal drug histories of their own. Mr. Parker has also brought forth three women that he has casually dated since his divorce. All will testify that he has been very lonely and almost desperate to date. The defense has also located prior statements made by Ms. Matthew suggesting that she knew that Mr. Parker liked her romantically and that, several years prior, he hinted that had a "sex addiction."

In addition, there is some evidence that a long-time Caucasian head of a smaller federal agency has had a serious drug problem for years. That evidence, however, is all from at least five years ago. As of this date, there has been no investigation by the FBI or the local U.S. Attorney's Office into that administrator's drug use. Until this sting operation, there is no evidence that there had ever been a sting operation of this sort related to a person serving in the administration. There are also no similar operations currently pending.

REQUIRED TASKS

Task One: Legal Research

You are the defense counsel representing Ward Parker. You are now preparing for trial in the federal district court of Washington, D.C.

    A.   Research the case law in the D.C. Circuit on entrapment and outrageous government conduct. Keep a research trail of your work. For this task, also complete the "Reflections on Research Questions" found in the online component.

B.   Provide a brief written summary of the Circuit's position on both defense claims.

ESTIMATED TIME FOR COMPLETION: 90 minutes.

LEVEL OF DIFFICULTY (1 TO 5):

Task Two: Motion Writing; Entrapment Defense

You are the defense counsel representing Ward Parker. Draft the Legal Argument that will accompany your motion requesting the entrapment defense jury instruction. If you previously completed Task One, draft your argument applying the facts of this case with respect to the law that you've researched. If you did not complete Task One, use the federal entrapment defense as presented in the jury instruction below. Draft the argument addressing the facts of this case and how they do or do not satisfy the federal entrapment defense.

In order to warrant a jury instruction on the defense of entrapment, you must persuade the judge that there is sufficient evidence to support an entrapment defense.

As an alternative assignment, envision you are the Assistant United States Attorney (AUSA) prosecuting Mr. Parker. Draft the memorandum of law that will accompany your motion to preclude an entrapment defense.

Links to sample motions and legal arguments on the subjects of entrapment and outrageous government conduct claims can be found in the online component. These samples should not be taken as the "correct" or only way for you to approach your legal argument. Rather, they are simply guides for a sample structure of legal arguments in the context of a motion.

ESTIMATED TIME FOR COMPLETION: 90 minutes.

LEVEL OF DIFFICULTY (1 TO 5):

Task Three: Professional Responsibility; Ethics

You are the AUSA prosecuting Ward Parker. Defense council has filed an ethics complaint with the D.C. Board of Professional Responsibility that you have violated Rule 3.8(a) of the Rules of Professional Conduct. This Rule reads as follows:

"The prosecutor in a criminal case shall not:

> **(a)** In exercising discretion to investigate or to prosecute, improperly favor or invidiously discriminate against any person."

Prepare your oral statement that you will make during the hearing before the D.C. Board of Professional Responsibility on whether you acted ethically in endorsing this undercover operation and charging Mr. Parker. Include a discussion of the defense allegation of "selective prosecution" as well as a response to allegations of entrapment and outrageous government conduct. The claim of selective prosecution is discussed further in the Skills Guide below.

For purposes of this task, you can assume that you and your office followed the ABA Standards for Criminal Justice for Prosecutorial Investigations. The relevant portion of these standards should be read before you begin this task. A link is provided in the online component.

You should also review these professional conduct standards found in the online component:

- Rules of Prof. Conduct, Rule 3.8 Special Responsibilities of a Prosecutor
- ABA Standard for the Prosecution Function 3-3.1: Investigative Function of Prosecutor

For optional background information on the process of investigations of ethics complaints against federal prosecutors, review the procedures of the United States Department of Justice, Office of Professional Responsibility and the D.C. Bar, Disciplinary Process. Links to this information are provided in the online component.

ESTIMATED TIME FOR COMPLETION: 60 minutes.

LEVEL OF DIFFICULTY (1 TO 5):

Task Four: Client Counseling

You are defense counsel for Ward Parker. Imagine that you are about to have a conversation with your client regarding the defense claims of entrapment and outrageous government conduct.

A. Prepare a list of talking points that you will use in your client meeting. Prepare your presentation of the law as you will explain it to your client and explain the facts of the case or how the relevant law would apply to his case. Also be prepared to explain to your client the government's likely arguments in opposition. If you have already completed Task One, use this research as the basis for your discussion. If you have not, use the background provided in the text as well as the federal jury instruction and rule of evidence listed in the online component.

B. Break up into teams of two. Choose one student to play the role of defense counsel and the other will play the client, Ward Parker. Have a 10- to 15-minute attorney-client meeting in role. Defense counsel should deliver the prepared talking points as well as answer any questions the client may have regarding the information presented. Defense counsel should also be sure to alert Mr. Parker to the risks of making these two defense claims and the evidence that could be used against him by the prosecution. The client should feel free to react and interact with the lawyer in a manner you feel is realistic for a person who honestly believes he was entrapped and unfairly targeted by the government.

ESTIMATED TIME FOR COMPLETION: 30 minutes.

LEVEL OF DIFFICULTY (1 TO 5):

PRACTICE SKILLS USED:

Skill 1: Legal Research; Keeping a Research Trail

Skill 2: Motion Writing

Skill 3: Legal Argument; Integrating the Law and the Facts

Skill 4: Ethical Analysis; Prosecutorial Discretion and Selective Prosecution

Skill 5: Counseling a Client

SKILLS GUIDES

For examples of cases in which the defense has argued the entrapment defense or has requested a dismissal due to outrageous government conduct, review the supplemental material provided in the online component.

For sample arguments of the government in response to such claims, review the sample motions linked in the online component for Task 2.

As mentioned above, the entrapment defense is presented to the jury via an instruction read to the jury by the judge. For contextual information on the giving of jury instructions, review the optional SVCs provided in the online component.

SKILLS GUIDE #1: Legal Research; Keeping a Research Trail

Take a moment to read Chapter 6, Skills Guide 3: Legal Research and Analogical Reasoning. In addition, consider the following information on preparing a research trail:

A research trail is a document that tracks the legal research steps you undertake to answer a particular question or inquiry. In order to have this document be as complete as possible, you should keep track of your research as you are doing it. This means noting every search and the results of that search in an abbreviated or note-taking manner. The method by which you keep track of your research is up to you. For searches in online databases, it is most helpful to keep track of both your search terms and the databases in which you searched. It is also important to keep track of any additional research you conducted after the initial database search (for example, checking citing references or subsequent history of a particular case, reviewing secondary sources).

The research trail has two primary purposes. First, it helps organize your research in order to remember what aspects of the legal research you have already completed. Second, upon completion of your research, the research trail should be reviewed and assessed in order to help improve your research skills for future tasks. As asked in the "Reflections on Research Questions" provided in the online component, analyzing your research trail enables you to reflect on which searches were most helpful and to learn more about how to best structure successful searches in the future. These skills will enable your research to become more time efficient as well as increase accuracy and completeness.

SKILLS GUIDE #2: Motion Writing

Please refer to Chapter 8, Skills Guide #1. Links to sample motions related to the topics of this Chapter are provided in the online component under the Supplemental Materials for Task Two.

SKILLS GUIDE #3: Legal Argument; Integrating the Law and the Facts

Please refer to Chapter 8, Skills Guide #2.

SKILLS GUIDE #4: Ethical Analysis; Prosecutorial Discretion and Selective Prosecution

Discretion in charging decisions is an essential feature of the prosecutorial function. The power to review the evidence and to decide whether, and what, criminal charges apply is at the heart of the prosecutor's duties. Correspondingly, there are few limits on prosecutorial discretion in charging and courts are generally reluctant to review — much less to question — prosecutors' charging decisions. The United States Constitution does, however, prohibit the charging decision from being made on the basis of race, religion, or other "arbitrary classification."

The claim of "selective prosecution" is one in which the defendant argues that the prosecutor made the decision to prosecute him based on one of these prohibited grounds. A selective prosecution claim is a difficult one for the defendant and carries a high burden of proof. To prevail, the defendant must first demonstrate with "clear evidence" that the prosecutorial decision was discriminatory in its *effect*. For claims based on race, the defendant must demonstrate that similarly situated individuals of a different race were not prosecuted. A defendant must also prove that the prosecutor's decision was discriminatory in its *purpose*.

Regardless of the strength of any defense claim, a prosecutor should always exercise his or her discretion in a manner consistent with the Constitution and the societal values the prosecutor's office strives to uphold. It is the responsibility of all prosecutors to make charging decisions on the basis of evidence of criminal wrongdoing, as well as decisions that are in the interests of justice.

Examples of a selective prosecution motion and an opposition to such a motion can be found in the online component. Also in the online component are SVCs that provide additional background information on ethics hearings regarding issues of prosecutorial conduct.

SKILLS GUIDE #5: Counseling a Client

Please refer to Chapter 9, Skills Guide #4.

ADDITIONAL MATERIALS FOR THE EXERCISE — AVAILABLE IN ONLINE COMPONENT

FED. R. EVID. 405: Methods of Proving Character

S1-8 Modern Federal Jury Instructions-Criminal 8.05

Chapter 15

INTOXICATION, INSANITY, AND COMPETENCY

OVERVIEW

The legal concepts of intoxication, insanity, and competency combine issues of mental capability and understanding with questions of criminal guilt and liability. Although all three terms have common everyday meanings, in the criminal law context, these terms have specific legal definitions and function in particular ways when raised in a defendant's case.

I. INTOXICATION

In most jurisdictions today, intoxication is an accepted defense though it is limited in its application and effect. The Model Penal Code defines intoxication as "a disturbance of mental or physical capacities resulting from the introduction of substances into the body." Courts most often face questions of a defendant's "voluntary intoxication" — that is, the defendant voluntarily chose to ingest a substance he knew or should have known would cause his intoxication. Voluntary intoxication is usually due to the ingestion of alcohol, illegal drugs, or prescription medication. Voluntary intoxication is rarely a complete defense, meaning the law seldom views intoxication as fully "excusing" the alleged crime. On the other hand, only a few jurisdictions prohibit the consideration of intoxication completely. Most jurisdictions permit voluntary intoxication to be a partial defense or a defense to a limited set of crimes. It is typically a question for the jury whether or not the defendant has sufficiently proven his defense of intoxication.

Many jurisdictions allow evidence of intoxication to negate the requisite *mens rea* of the charged crime. A few states allow intoxication to negate any level of *mens rea*. The more common approach, however, is to allow intoxication as a defense to *specific intent* crimes only. In jurisdictions following this approach, evidence of intoxication may be admissible to negate the specific intent required to prove a particular crime. Intoxication would not, however, be a defense to a general intent crime. Thus, in these jurisdictions, a defendant may be acquitted of a specific intent crime due to his voluntary intoxication, but still be convicted of a lesser-included general intent crime. For example, a conviction for sexual battery requires proof that the defendant committed a touching for the specific purpose of sexual arousal or abuse. In a jurisdiction that allowed intoxication as a defense to specific intent crimes, the defendant could argue that his intoxication rendered him unable to form such a specific purpose. This defendant, however, may still be convicted of the lesser-included general intent crime of battery, which only requires proof that the defendant willfully touched the victim.

There are several other variations on courts' approaches to the use of intoxication evidence. A few jurisdictions permit the defendant to argue that his intoxication negated the required *actus reus*. In other words, a defendant could argue that he was so intoxicated that he did not commit a voluntary act. This argument, however, is not often accepted by the courts in practice. Intoxication also sometimes provides the basis for an insanity defense. Courts commonly reject the argument that a defendant's voluntary intoxication rendered him temporarily "insane," but often allow a defendant to present an insanity defense based on the argument that, due to long-term intoxication, he now suffers from a more permanent mental disease or defect. Finally, some jurisdictions allow the consideration of intoxication as a factor in sentencing.

The term "involuntary intoxication" describes the circumstances in which a person becomes intoxicated not of their own knowledge or free will, typically due to duress, force, or from taking a medicine without knowing its intoxicating effect. If a court finds the intoxication to be involuntary, such intoxication may negate an element of the crime or act as the basis for an insanity defense, even if the defendant argues that his "insanity" was only temporary. Some states also recognize involuntary intoxication as a separate complete defense, distinct from insanity.

II. INSANITY AND COMPETENCY

The defendant's mental health and mental capacity may be raised in two distinct phases of the trial: as a question of competency to stand trial and as a defense to the charged crime. Questions as to the defendant's mental health *at the time of the proceedings* will be raised as a question of the defendant's competence to stand trial. Questions as to the defendant's mental health *at the time of the alleged offense* may be raised in the form of an insanity defense. Both competency and insanity combine legal standards and tests with medical concepts and diagnoses, raising important questions as to how issues of mental health should intersect with criminal liability and punishment.

The first context in which issues of mental health may be raised is in the question of whether a defendant is competent to stand trial. It is a violation of the Due Process Clause of the United States Constitution for the government to try an incompetent defendant. Broadly speaking, a defendant is not competent to stand trial if he lacks the ability to understand the proceedings or assist his lawyer in his own defense. Doubts as to the defendant's competency may be brought to the court's attention by the defense attorney, the prosecutor, or by the court itself. Whether the defendant is competent to stand trial is a question for the judge to decide, most often with the assistance of mental health evaluations ordered by the court. If the defendant is found incompetent, he is typically committed to a mental health treatment facility. There, he is subject to civil commitment checks regarding his competency and treatment. If the defendant regains competency, he would have to stand trial at that time. If it appears that the defendant will never be competent to stand trial, he will still be subject to civil commitment laws and will likely remain hospitalized or under mental health care.

The second context in which issues of mental health arise is with the insanity defense. Insanity is an oft-criticized and much debated legal term of art. "Insanity" is an affirmative defense. The defendant argues in essence that, although he committed the crime charged, he was legally insane at the time of the offense and therefore should not be criminally punished for the offense. The defendant must give notice to the government that he intends to present such a defense at trial. The defendant would then be evaluated by mental health professionals, potentially by both government and defense-hired experts. The nature of the burden of proof and which party carries that burden varies by jurisdiction. At the end of a jury trial in which the defendant presents an insanity defense, the jury will have its choice of three verdicts: guilty, not guilty, or not guilty by reason of insanity. If the jury finds the defendant not guilty by reason of insanity, the defendant is usually committed to a mental health hospital until he is no longer mentally ill or no longer poses a danger to himself or others. In many states, a trial in which the defendant raises an insanity defense is bifurcated. First there is a trial on the question of the defendant's guilt (guilty versus not guilty). If the jury finds the defendant guilty, there would then be a second trial solely on the question whether the defendant was legally insane at the time of the crime (guilty versus not guilty by reason of insanity).

There are two main definitions of "insanity" in use today. The first, known as the *M'Naghten* test, has its roots in a case of that name from the English House of Lords in 1843. Under the *M'Naghten* test, a defendant is deemed legally "insane" if, due to a mental disease or defect, the defendant: (1) did not know the nature and quality of the act he was doing, or (2) did not know at the time that what he was doing was wrong. With respect to the second prong, jurisdictions differ on what it means to not know one's actions are wrong. Some courts state that it is sufficient if the defendant did not have the mental capacity to know that his actions were against the law, whereas other jurisdictions require evidence that the defendant did not know that his act was morally wrong. In addition, some courts choose not to define the second prong any further, leaving it for the jury to decide whether the defendant met his evidentiary burden.

The second definition of "insanity" used by many jurisdictions today is the test proposed by the American Law Institute in the Model Penal Code. Under the Model Penal Code (also sometimes called the A.L.I. test), the defendant must demonstrate that, as a result of mental disease or defect, he lacked the substantial capacity to appreciate the wrongfulness of his conduct or to conform his conduct to the requirements of the law. The Model Penal Code test is viewed as broader than the traditional *M'Naghten* test in part because it does not require complete mental impairment ("did not know" versus did not "appreciate" and "lacked substantial capacity").

As is evident from the definitions given above, it is a prerequisite of both tests that the defendant suffer from a "mental disease or defect." Rarely defined by the courts, it is usually a question left up to expert witnesses in the field of mental health to give their opinion to the jury about the state of the defendant's mental health and his psychiatric diagnoses. Expert witnesses may not give their opinion on the ultimate question, however — whether the defendant was legally insane at the time of the offense. This is a question solely in the province of the jury.

Most state jurisdictions, as well as the federal courts, have adopted variations of the Model Penal Code or the *M'Nagten* test. Some states have abolished the insanity defense completely. Nevertheless, a defendant's mental health is usually an accepted consideration at sentencing. In addition, several states have created an additional verdict: guilty but mentally ill. This verdict applies to individuals who may be mentally ill, but the jury decides that they should still be held criminally liable for the committed offenses. Punishment as a result of this verdict varies by jurisdiction.

EXERCISE

Overview

In November of last year, Richard Smith was living in a halfway house in Harbor, Tennessee. He had served 4½ years of a five-year prison sentence for burglary. He was sent to the Region IV Halfway House to serve the remaining six months of his sentence prior to being released on parole. On the night of November 5, he fatally stabbed his roommate, Paul Moore. Richard was charged with willful and premeditated murder in the first degree.

You are the assigned public defender representing Richard Smith. When you met your client, you had immediate concerns as to his mental health. Richard spoke to you about a "conspiracy" and that Moore was an "agent" of the government. You saw from his criminal rap sheet that he appears to have a history of mental illness and drug abuse. In addition, he is alleged to have been high on PCP on the night of the murder. In a pretrial appearance, you raised the issue of Richard's competency to stand trial and asked the court to order a competency evaluation. The court granted the defense funds to hire an expert, Dr. Philip Carter, to conduct this evaluation on behalf of the defense. The court also ordered the Tennessee Mental Health Institute, Forensics Services Program, to perform a competency evaluation on behalf of the government.

In the online component, you will find the psychiatric evaluations of Richard Smith by the defense expert, Phillip Carter, and the prosecution's expert, Leonard Mullins. Take a moment and read both competency reports now. The facts contained in these two expert reports comprise the facts of this exercise.

REQUIRED TASKS

Task One: Advising the Client's Family

Richard Smith's mother and brother would like to speak to you about Richard's case. Specifically, they would like to know how the fact that he was high on PCP and that he suffers from schizophrenia might help him in his defense.

Plan your meeting and conversation with Richard's family. Outline your explanation of the charges against Richard and plan your discussion of how evidence of intoxication and mental illness may be introduced on Richard's behalf. Include in this discussion answers to the following questions from Richard's family:

1. *Richard was high that night. He didn't know what he was doing. Doesn't that matter?*

2. *Richard has taken PCP and many other drugs since he was 16. How does that affect his case?*

3. *Richard is mentally ill. He needs to be in a hospital, not in prison. Can you make sure that happens? What are you going to say to the judge?*

As a supplemental exercise, pick a partner to play the role of Richard's mother or brother. Take 10 minutes and have the conversation as planned. The actor playing the family member should respond and ask follow-up questions in a manner that is appropriate and relevant.

Before beginning this task, you should review the statutes and jury instructions listed in the online component.

ESTIMATED TIME FOR COMPLETION: 30 minutes.

LEVEL OF DIFFICULTY (1 TO 5):

Task Two: Direct Examination

The judge will now hold a competency hearing in order to determine whether Richard is competent to stand trial. You will be conducting the direct examination of Dr. Philip Carter. For purposes of this task you can assume that the State expert, Dr. Mullins, will also be testifying and that the prosecution is asking that the Court find Richard competent to stand trial.

Before beginning this task, review the supplemental materials in the online component. These materials discuss the relevant standards of a competency hearing.

Prepare your direct examination of Dr. Carter for purposes of the competency hearing. List the topics that you want Dr. Carter to cover in his testimony and the facts that you want to elicit. In addition, list the specific questions you will ask to elicit the desired expert testimony. For purposes of this task, you do not need to include questions that go to his professional training and expertise.

ESTIMATED TIME FOR COMPLETION: 60 minutes.

LEVEL OF DIFFICULTY (1 TO 5):

Task Three: Working with Expert Witnesses

After receiving several months of steady medication and mental health treatment, Richard has now been found competent to stand trial. You have provided notice to the State that you are raising an insanity defense at trial. In the online component you will find an example of a Notice of Insanity Defense.

You are now preparing for trial on the charge of first degree murder. Specifically, you are preparing for a meeting with Dr. Phillip Carter, your psychiatric expert. Although he initially gave his opinion as to your client's competency, you would now like him to testify at trial regarding his opinion as to whether your client was legally insane at the time of the murder.

Prepare for your conversation with Dr. Carter. Create an outline, notes, or written document that you will use to guide you in your meeting. Please expand on the following topics:

- Explain the relevant test of legal insanity to Dr. Carter.

- Explain your ideas regarding the evidence of intoxication and mental illness. How are you going to address the intoxication evidence? Are you arguing an insanity defense based on his drug use, or does it not factor into your defense?

- Brainstorm questions you will ask him regarding your client's sanity.

- Other topics of discussion?

Before completing this task, you should review the relevant statutes and jury instructions listed in the online component.

ESTIMATED TIME FOR COMPLETION: 45 minutes.

LEVEL OF DIFFICULTY (1 TO 5):

PRACTICE SKILLS USED:

Skill 1: Counseling; Working with a Client's Family

Skill 2: Legal Argument, Integrating the Law and the Facts

Skill 3: Direct Examination

Skill 4: Working with Expert Witnesses

SKILLS GUIDES

For general background about the issues of insanity and competency in today's criminal justice system and in recent cases, see the supplemental materials provided in the online component.

SKILLS GUIDE #1: Counseling; Working with the Client's Family

Before beginning this task, take a moment to read Skills Guide #4 in Chapter 9 (Counseling a Client). Speaking with a client's family involves many of the same skills as advising and counseling a client. There are, however, important additional considerations when working with a client's family. First, client confidentiality and the attorney-client privilege are of primary importance. You should never disclose — unless you have the client's permission — information that you have learned from your client or because of your position as the attorney of record. In fact, you may want to explicitly inform the family that you are not allowed to disclose all aspects of their loved one's case. Second, before you begin any conversation, take a moment to reflect on the nature of a criminal case and the impact such a case has on a family. A criminal case is potentially a traumatic and extremely serious event in that family's life. It is important to approach every conversation with empathy and an awareness of the impact the case may be having on the family. Third, as is true with almost all lawyering tasks, the language and content of your speech should take into account your audience. Consider the family's background and experiences. Will they understand legal terminology? Have they had experiences with the criminal justice system before? Were they positive or negative experiences? Finally, although it certainly depends on the case and the context, in general, try to remember the saying, "don't make a promise you can't keep." As the attorney (whether defense or prosecution), you are not in complete control of the outcome of the defendant's case. You are not in a position to promise a conviction, an acquittal, or any outcome that relies on a decision made by the judge or jury. Family members may not immediately understand that the outcomes in criminal cases depend on many factors other than simply the strength of one side's position, such as the admissibility of evidence and the application of sentencing laws. Although it can be difficult to remember when facing family members who understandably want to hear a particular answer, it is important to remember to not make promises that you may not be able to fulfill.

The development of a good relationship with a client's family is important for several reasons. Not only is it a component of being a professional lawyer, it is potentially to your client's benefit as well — that is, it often contributes to your ability to be a zealous advocate for your client. Family members may provide important facts related to the offense or give information relevant to sentencing or plea bargaining. Family may also play a role when discussing a possible plea with a client. In short, developing a rapport with the client's family benefits the client, the family, and your ability to fully represent your client and his interests.

SKILLS GUIDE #2: Legal Argument; Integrating the Law and the Facts

Please refer to Chapter 8, Skills Guide #2.

SKILLS GUIDES #3 and #4: Direct Examination; Working with Expert Witnesses

Direct examination is the process by which a party introduces the testimony of a witness for "their side" of the case. In criminal cases, the prosecution will usually conduct the direct examination of a police officer. Defense counsel may prepare the direct examination of the defendant. Direct examination is an opportunity to present the facts of your case to the jury and to advance your theory of the case. In contrast to cross-examination (when the focus is primarily on the attorney asking the questions), in direct examination, the focus should be on the witness. The witness should present his or her testimony in a clear, concise, and organized manner. The goal of direct examination is to have the jury (or judge) understand the witness's testimony itself and how that testimony fits in to the overall theory of the case.

A successful direct examination involves preparation with the witness beforehand. You are not coaching the witness in his or her answers. Rather, you should work with your witness so that when you ask a particular question in direct examination, you will know how your witness will respond. In addition, preparation with the witness ensures that your witness will understand what information you are seeking when asking a particular question. Direct examination is typically conducted by the asking of open-ended questions such as "What happened next?" "What did you see?" and "What did the Defendant say?"

The direct examination often begins with the witness introducing him- or herself and explaining his or her connection with the events at hand. With an expert witness, the direct examination will usually begin with the expert explaining his or her background, training, and experience. Although the rules vary by jurisdiction, generally a lawyer must establish the witness as an "expert" before the witness can state his or her opinion about matters requiring a particular expertise.

While clarity and the organization of testimony are always of concern in a direct examination, it is particularly important in the elicitation of expert testimony. Experts may speak in a language that is not relatable or familiar to the jury. An important part of working with an expert witness prior to testifying is to ensure that the expert is able to put his or her statements in layman's terms.

Additional optional materials on conducting the direct examination of an expert witness are provided in the online component.

ADDITIONAL MATERIALS FOR THE EXERCISE — AVAILABLE IN ON-LINE COMPONENT

Tenn. Code § 39-11-501/Insanity

Tenn. Code § 39-11-503/Intoxication

Tenn. Code § 39-13-202 (Relevant Excerpts)/First Degree Murder

Tenn. Code § 39-13-210 (Relevant Excerpts)/Second Degree Murder

Tennessee Pattern Jury Instructions — Criminal 7.01(b)/FIRST DEGREE MURDER (PREMEDITATED KILLING) (Relevant Excerpts)

Tennessee Pattern Jury Instructions — Criminal 40.02/DEFENSE: INTOXICATION (Relevant Excerpts)

Tennessee Pattern Instructions — Criminal 40.16(b)/AFFIRMATIVE DEFENSE: INSANITY (Relevant Excerpts)

Chapter 16

THE DEATH PENALTY

OVERVIEW

The death penalty, also called capital punishment, is one of the most controversial aspects of our criminal justice system. As of the printing of this text, 32 states and the federal government authorize the death penalty. Proponents argue that death is an appropriate punishment for those crimes that are considered "the worst of the worst." Critiques of capital punishment range from the principle that the government should not kill to the argument that the death penalty is arbitrarily applied and intertwined with complex issues of socioeconomic status and race.

Jurisprudence surrounding the death penalty is varied in scope and topic. Over the last 30 years, the United States Supreme Court has issued many important opinions regarding who may be sentenced to death and under what circumstances. It is now unconstitutional to execute the legally insane or mentally incompetent, defendants who are mentally retarded, and individuals who were under the age of 18 at the time of their offense. There have also been significant developments surrounding the method of execution and the standards of appellate review of capital trials. In addition to Supreme Court precedent, there is a large body of federal caselaw developed through *habeas corpus* review of state court decisions in capital trials.

Offenses that are subject to the death penalty are set by statute. "Capital murder" commonly includes murders that occur during the commission of a specified felony, for instance, during a kidnapping or robbery. Other examples of capital murder include a murder of a victim younger than 14, a murder committed by someone who has been convicted of murder before, and a murder for hire. Although as of this printing there was no defendant on death row for a non-homicide crime, a few jurisdictions do authorize the death penalty for crimes other than murder, such as for treason, aggravated kidnapping, or drug trafficking.

If the defendant's alleged offense qualifies as capital murder, the government must then decide whether to seek the death penalty against the defendant. Prosecutors' offices typically have internal procedures to decide whether or not the death penalty would be an appropriate punishment in any particular case. Once the prosecution announces its intention to request the death penalty, the defendant's case is immediately impacted. A capital trial has its own unique rules, procedures, and protections.

Jury selection for a capital trial centers on an explicit discussion of the potential for a death sentence. In a non-capital trial, a jury would not know the punishment a defendant might receive if found guilty. Sentencing is generally considered a matter for the judge and not within the province of the jury. In contrast, in a capital case, the potential jurors are told from the outset that it is a case in which the government will ask the jury to sentence the defendant to death. Potential jurors will be told during jury selection that, if the defendant is convicted of capital murder, they will then have to decide whether to impose a death sentence or a lesser sentence of life imprisonment. Currently, all jurisdictions authorizing the death penalty also provide a sentence of life in prison without the possibility of parole as an alternative sentence. Jury selection for a capital trial, therefore, includes specific questions as to whether a potential juror could sentence a convicted defendant to death (a "death qualified" juror) or could impose life in prison even if they believed the defendant was guilty of capital murder (a "life qualified" juror).

A capital trial is a bifurcated trial. It consists of two phases: the guilt phase and (if the defendant is convicted) the penalty phase. In the guilt phase, like in a non-capital trial, the jury hears evidence of the charged offense and must decide whether the defendant is guilty or not guilty. If the jury finds the defendant guilty of capital murder, then the trial proceeds to the penalty phase. In this phase, the jury decides whether the appropriate sentence is death or life in prison. The Supreme Court has held that the death penalty cannot be mandatory. In other words, there must be some discretion for the jury or judge to not impose the death penalty and instead sentence the defendant to a lesser sentence such as life in prison without the possibility of parole.

The central focus of the penalty phase is the consideration of aggravating and mitigating factors that weigh, respectively, for or against the imposition of the death penalty. Aggravating and mitigating factors are defined by statute and vary by jurisdiction. Aggravating circumstances include factors such as a "heinous, atrocious, cruel or depraved" murder, murder while the defendant was in custody, and murder of a young or elderly victim. Mitigating circumstances include the defendant's age, history of mental illness, and whether the defendant acted under extreme duress or had minor participation in the crime. In addition, most death penalty statutes provide that any relevant aspect of the defendant's background or character may be introduced in support of his argument against death. Thus, a defendant's family history, his behavior while incarcerated, and his upbringing could all be mitigating evidence that would be introduced during the penalty phase.

In *Ring v. Arizona*, 536 U.S. 584 (2002), the Supreme Court held that a defendant has the right to have a jury decide the existence of an aggravating factor. Although there is some variation among jurisdictions, typically the prosecution has the burden of proving at least one aggravating factor beyond a reasonable doubt. Then, the jury undertakes a weighing process of the various aggravating and mitigating factors presented. In most jurisdictions, the defendant may not be sentenced to death unless the jury finds that the aggravating circumstances outweigh the mitigating circumstances. Of those jurisdictions with the death penalty, all except for Alabama and Florida require that the jury be unanimous in its sentence of death. If the jury is split between death and life, the defendant will be sentenced to life in prison. In all jurisdictions with the death penalty except for Alabama, Delaware, and Florida, the jury issues the ultimate verdict of life or death. Alabama, Delaware, and Florida permit a "judicial override," a mechanism by which the judge can impose a death sentence despite the jury's recommendation for life, or vice versa.

Although the guilt phase of a capital trial requires an immense amount of work, capital litigation also requires a particular focus on preparations for a possible penalty phase. Defense penalty phase preparation often includes the use of mitigation experts and mental health experts, and requires factual investigation into the defendant's personal and family history.

EXERCISE

Overview

Barry Simons is a 19-year-old African-American male. On March 24 at 11:00 a.m., Simons, armed with a handgun, entered the convenience store of a local gas station. Simons pointed his gun at the cashier, Robin Moreland, and demanded he empty the cash register. When Moreland hesitated, Simons fired his gun at Moreland, killing him instantly. Simons was arrested and charged with capital murder, on the grounds that it was a murder that occurred during the course of a robbery. The State has announced its intention to seek the death penalty.

You are now part of the defense team representing Barry Simons. An investigator with your office has given you the following preliminary information on your client:

Defense Investigation

Barry Simons is the youngest child of four. Barry lives with his three siblings and mother. When Barry was three years old, his father was convicted of murder and sentenced to 25 years to life in prison. His father remains incarcerated today. His mother has struggled with drug use and extreme poverty. The family currently lives in a dilapidated trailer in a rural area of town. Barry's siblings have been in and out of jail. From the age of five to the age of seven, an uncle lived with the family. The family is unsure of the uncle's current whereabouts, but they believe he may be in prison in another state on sexual abuse charges.

Barry has a relatively minor criminal history, with arrests and misdemeanor convictions for vandalism, theft, assault, and marijuana possession. He has not served time in prison before. He has served three short jail sentences, each of one to three months. When he was 16 years old, he spent six months in juvenile hall for the offense of assault with a deadly weapon. Two of his misdemeanor convictions for vandalism were with the same two co-defendants.

Barry dropped out of high school at the age of 15. He attended the local public schools. When speaking with his mother about Barry, she referred to him as "slow" and repeatedly mentioned that he was a "quiet boy" when he was young. She said it was a hard birth. His mother stated that Barry did not have a job right now but that he sometimes helped the man who owned the local liquor store.

REQUIRED TASKS

Task One: Client Interviewing

Assume for purposes of this task that you are meeting Barry Simons for the first time. The only information you have at this time is the brief case background as provided above. You do not yet know any of the information provided by the investigator. Take a moment and read Skills Guide #1 (Interviewing; Initial Client Interview) and the following document provided in the online component:

- Equal Justice Initiative of Alabama, *"Getting Started: Building a Relationship of Trust with the Client,"* in ALABAMA CAPITAL DEFENSE TRIAL MANUAL 44–49 (4th ed. 2005) (reprinted with permission of author).

Next, form a small group of three or four students. Plan as a group the initial client meeting, addressing all of components discussed in assigned reading. In addition, discuss as a group the following questions:

- What sorts of questions will you ask to begin learning about the client and the case?

- Consider the potential differences between you (the lawyer) and your client. Differences may include personal background, socio-economic status, gender, and race. In what way will these differences affect, or not affect, the attorney-client relationship?

- How will you work to develop a rapport and trust between your client and the defense team?

ESTIMATED TIME FOR COMPLETION: 30 minutes.

LEVEL OF DIFFICULTY (1 TO 5):

Task Two: Mitigation Planning

You have now received the preliminary investigation report as provided above. Conduct your initial assessment of the necessary penalty phase investigation plan. Assume for purposes of this task that your jurisdiction allows any relevant evidence of mitigation to be introduced at the penalty phase. Brainstorm all possible avenues of potential mitigating evidence. List witness interviews to conduct, record requests, and potential areas of investigation.

Before beginning this task, take a moment to review the American Bar Association (ABA) Guidelines on mitigation investigation. A link is provided in the online component.

ESTIMATED TIME FOR COMPLETION: 20 minutes.

LEVEL OF DIFFICULTY (1 TO 5):

Task Three: Professional Writing; Client Advocacy

This task is based on the facts presented in *Wood v. Allen*, 542 F.3d 1281 (11th Cir. 2008). Use an online database to read the case. The facts presented in the opinion and the dissent comprise the facts for this task. The relevant law for this task is provided in the online component. After reading the case and the relevant law, complete *one* of the following two tasks:

1. You are defense counsel for Mr. Wood. Write a one- to three-page letter to the prosecution, arguing why the State should not seek the death penalty against your client. This letter should be in the format of a professional letter. For purposes of this task, assume that all the evidence is able to be shared with opposing counsel and you are not violating attorney-client privilege by disclosing this evidence. You may use any of the facts in the *Wood* opinion and dissent, and are not limited by when the facts were disclosed or discovered in that case.

2. You are the state prosecutor in the case against Mr. Wood. In addition to the facts provided in *Wood v. Allen*, you may also use the facts provided in the Respondent's Brief excerpted in the online component. Write a one- to three-page memo to your supervisor explaining your reasoning in support of seeking the death penalty against Mr. Wood. Assume the mitigating evidence has been provided to you by defense counsel. Your supervisor has asked for your opinion in light of the material provided to you by the defense. This letter should be in the format of a professional intra-office memo.

ESTIMATED TIME FOR COMPLETION: 90 minutes.

LEVEL OF DIFFICULTY (1-5):

PRACTICE SKILLS USED:

Skill 1: Interviewing; Initial Client Interview

Skill 2: Planning and Brainstorming

Skill 3: Professional Writing

SKILLS GUIDES

For additional information and resources on the death penalty, see the supplemental materials provided in the online component.

SKILLS GUIDE #1: Interviewing; Initial Client Interview

The materials provided in the online component for Task One provide a good overview of the goals of the initial client interview for all types of cases, not simply capital cases. Establishing a relationship of trust is a critical step in the attorney-client relationship. If your client does not trust you or your work, your efforts to be an advocate on his behalf and to be effective and successful in that role will be severely hampered.

The structure of an initial client interview can be viewed in the following segments:

- *Introductions and Parameter-Setting* establish the agenda for the interview, lay down the groundwork for the collaboration between lawyer and client, and identify the rules of the road for the balance of the interview;

- *Solicitations of Narratives* invite the client's story and create space for the client to present the story without premature categorizations by the lawyer;

- *Client Narratives* challenge the lawyer to listen to the client's story with rapt attention and minimal interruption;

- *Elaborative Dialogue* revisits the client's story, probes the client's thoughts and emotions, clarifies ambiguous statements, and begins to focus on the client's goals;

- *Issue Definition and Synthesis* shape the issues the client has presented and propose a strategy, or at the very least, the initial steps for addressing them; and

- *The Session Coda* memorializes the agreements between the lawyer and client about both the nature of the matter to be addressed and the role each person will play in addressing it.

Excerpted from Anthony G. Amsterdam, Peggy Cooper Davis & Aderson Bellegarde Francois, *Lawyering* 148–49 (NYU School of Law, Lawyering Program 2012) (reprinted with permission of author).

These six segments should guide you in your planning for the initial client meeting. The key to an effective client interview is both preparation and flexibility. When planning the initial meeting, you should determine what topics you want to cover, in what order, what questions you want to ask the client, what questions you expect the client to ask you, and how you are going to approach potentially tricky personal and legal issues. Flexibility, however, is also a critical aspect of a successful interview. You need flexibility in order to respond to your client and assess the dynamics of the meeting as it unfolds. The ability to maintain structure, cover the necessary ground, and respond to your client in the moment is a skill that you will continue to develop and strengthen over the length of your professional career.

SKILLS GUIDE #2: Planning and Brainstorming

Please refer to Chapter 1, Skills Guide #3.

SKILLS GUIDE #3: Professional Writing

When writing a professional letter or memorandum, you must always consider your audience. Are you writing to a judge? Opposing counsel? A supervisor? The reader of your written document impacts many aspects of your writing, including the content, formality, tone, and language. With respect to the content, think of what information will be most useful or convincing to the reader. One goal of your writing is to present the information in a clear and concise way and, if required, in a way that will be persuasive to your reader. Have you backed up your opinion with authority? Have you cited to material (i.e., cases, documents, witness statements) that explains and justifies your opinion? A professional writing should demonstrate that your opinion — that is, the exercise of your lawyerly judgment — is credible and justified based on the relevant law and facts.

There are many resources available that can assist you in professional legal writing. As is true in other contexts, proper grammar, spelling, and citations are required for a professional letter or memo. Errors and sloppiness reflect badly on you as a professional, and may ultimately hurt your client's case if the errors and sloppiness undermine the credibility or persuasiveness of your content.

ADDITIONAL MATERIALS FOR THE EXERCISE — AVAILABLE IN ON-LINE COMPONENT

AMERICAN BAR ASSOCIATION GUIDELINES FOR THE APPOINTMENT AND PERFORMANCE OF DE-
FENSE COUNSEL IN DEATH PENALTY CASES

GUIDELINE 10.11 — THE DEFENSE CASE CONCERNING PENALTY (Relevant Excerpts)

ABA SUPPLEMENTARY GUIDELINES FOR THE MITIGATION FUNCTION OF DEFENSE TEAMS IN
DEATH PENALTY CASES

GUIDELINE 10.11 — THE DEFENSE CASE: REQUISITE MITIGATION FUNCTIONS OF THE DE-
FENSE TEAM